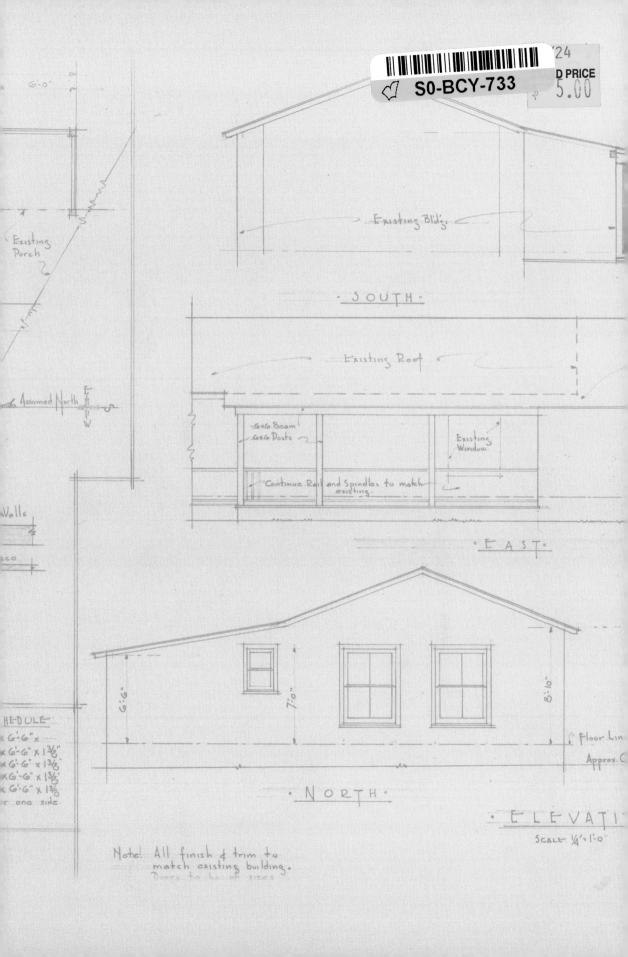

6'-0"

Existing
Porch

Assumed North

Walls

Existing Bld'g

· S O U T H ·

Existing Roof

6x6 Beam
6x6 Posts

Existing
Window

Continue Rail and Spindles to match
existing.

· E A S T ·

6'-6"

7'-0"

8'-10"

· N O R T H ·

· E L E V A T I

SCALE ¼" = 1'-0

HEDULE
6'-6" x
6'-6" x 1⅜"
6'-6" x 1⅜"
6'-6" x 1⅜"
6'-6" x 1⅜"
r one side

Floor Lin

Approx C

Note! All finish & trim to
match existing building.
Doors to be of sizes

Diane Y. Welch

The Life and Times of
Lilian J. Rice
Master Architect

Foreword by Audrey Geisel

Schiffer Publishing Ltd

4880 Lower Valley Road • Atglen, PA 19310

Library of Congress Control Number: 2015951873

Designed by Danielle D. Farmer
Cover Design by RoS
Type set in Adobe Caslon Pro/Brisa

ISBN: 978-0-7643-4958-4
Printed in China

Published by Schiffer Publishing, Ltd.
4880 Lower Valley Road
Atglen, PA 19310
Phone: (610) 593-1777; Fax: (610) 593-2002
E-mail: Info@schifferbooks.com

For our complete selection of fine books on this and related subjects, please visit our website at www.schifferbooks.com. You may also write for a free catalog.

This book may be purchased from the publisher. Please try your bookstore first.

We are always looking for people to write books on new and related subjects. If you have an idea for a book, please contact us at proposals@schifferbooks.com.

Schiffer Publishing's titles are available at special discounts for bulk purchases for sales promotions or premiums. Special editions, including personalized covers, corporate imprints, and excerpts can be created in large quantities for special needs. For more information, contact the publisher.

Another Schiffer Book by Diane Y. Welch

Lilian J. Rice: Architect of Rancho Santa Fe, California. ISBN: 978-0-7643-3456-6

Other Schiffer Books on Related Subjects:

California Colonial: The Spanish & Rancho Revival Styles. Elizabeth McMillian. ISBN: 978-0-7643-1460-5

California Bungalows: The 1911 Ye Planry Catalog. ISBN: 978-0-7643-4454-1

California Mission Architecture: A Survey and Sourcebook. Jock M. Sewall, A.I.A. ISBN: 978-0-7643-4200-4

With deepest love for Joan, Louisette, and Liese
And for Lilian J. Rice

Praise for
The Life and Times of
Lilian J. Rice, Master Architect

"Diane Welch has taken fragments of information and woven them together to re-create the life and times of a forgotten figure in women's history. Lilian Rice is now tangible, her story inspirational, and like so many influential women, she is finally being written into the history books where she is so deserving of a place."

—Dame Zandra Rhodes
Haute couture fashion designer
London, England

"Through her unique genre of repertoire, Diane Welch takes the reader back in time to experience the world of master architect Lilian Rice. By referencing reported news, and conducting her own interviews of those connected to Rice's life, a complete picture has emerged. This is so much more than a portrait of a forgotten woman, this is an incredible story well-told."

—Leslie Hoffman
Award-winning photographer
Del Mar, California

"As the biographer of the architect who built our family's ranch home in 1935, it is Diane Welch's goal to share, with a national audience, the life story of Lilian Rice. By including the history of San Diego County in her book, Diane is paying a great tribute to our region, its local legends, and its treasured landmarks."

—Paul Ecke III
Former owner of Paul Ecke Ranch
Encinitas, California

"Diane Welch has presented an impeccably researched historical account of Lilian J. Rice and the era in which she lived and worked. A female entrepreneur, decades ahead of her times, this largely unknown powerhouse—who vaulted the gender hurdle of the business of architecture—is finally getting her due recognition. California should be proud to call Lilian J. Rice one of its most historically significant architects and businesswomen."

—Jenny Craig
Cofounder of Jenny Craig, Inc.
Del Mar, California

CONTENTS

CONTRIBUTORS

Heartfelt thanks go to the following photographers for their contributions to this book:

Darren Edwards
www.darrenedwards.com

Half Full Photography, April and Joe Bertocchini
www.wearehalffull.com

Paul Body Photography
www.paulbodyphoto.com

Leslie Hoffman
www.lesliehoffmanphotography.com

This work has been enhanced greatly through the talents of the following people:

Audrey Geisel, for her generous foreword
Christopher Real, for his drafting
Monique Parsons, for her drafting
Carol Beth Rodriguez, for her sketches www.carolbethart.com
Sara Motamedi, for her architectural renderings
Juliana Welch, for her creative design work http://julianawelch.weebly.com

Editors:

B. Paul Welch, John Paul Welch

PREFACE

This is a story about an architect. It is also a story that includes my journey of discovery in my efforts to retell it. For the architect, little written documentation remains from her forty-nine years on this earth. In fact, her personal story has literally been taken to the grave as practically all of her private effects were disposed of after her death in 1938. What has been salvaged from her life, her buildings, are in danger of being razed and lost to history forever. There are no documents that reveal her inner world: her relationships, her loves, her self-pride and her disappointments. For the author, however, a fountainhead of information on the architect's outer world has been gathered and documented from disparate points during almost ten years of focused research. This book is a companion publication to *Lilian J. Rice, Architect of Rancho Santa Fe, California* (Schiffer, 2010) and is also a work of non-fiction. I portray the subject honestly, and do not take artistic license by the invention of events and dialogue. My own dialogue, along with that of the people I have interviewed, who provided invaluable first-hand accounts that have enhanced this book, is faithfully recounted from many hours of digital recordings. These interviews have been transcribed and archived over the past decade and are now part of my Lilian J. Rice archive. Each chapter stands alone as its own story, and local people hold just as an important place in these pages as the international movie stars who entered Lilian's sphere.

I didn't expect this project to be such a challenge on that fateful day on June 12, 2005, when I made a self-imposed assignment to devote my time—what would turn out to be part of my life—to the research of this little-known master architect and to write a book about her life and work. Despite the fact that several of Lilian Rice's buildings are listed on the National Register of Historic Places and many are listed as California State Historic Landmarks, these combined accolades did nothing to reveal any insights into Lilian Rice as a human being.

With no Lilian J. Rice archive to pull information from, no diaries, no letters, few business documents, and no central source that contained accurate, verifiable documentation about her life, it became clear that I had to find alternative sources. And so I turned to those closely linked to Lilian's life in some way. This project then took a surprising turn as it became a wonderful partnership of trust and of sharing personal memories. A deep respect grew from these shared recollections and there was mutual agreement that it was paramount to retell Lilian Rice's story as accurately, and as honestly, as possible. This book aims to do just that and in so doing it weaves in this remarkable journey of discovery as my curiosity deepened with each clue along the way. It is as much Lilian's story as it is mine, and is as much about the people who joined me along this path as it is about the memories that they shared.

When I read a statement that was published on the Internet in 2005, on the website of a local historical organization, my curiosity was heightened further, as these words, in effect, painted a picture of Lilian Rice that did not reflect what I felt I knew about her from my research and from my conversations with others. It claimed that Lilian Rice was deceptive and seduced many of her clients into believing that she was the architect of record for the community of Rancho Santa Fe, when this was patently untrue, according to the statement. In effect, she lied to and cheated her clients in order to win over their trust and receive their lucrative residential commissions. While this may have been an acceptable business practice for male architects in the 1920s who competed for the same local commissions, for Lilian Rice it was deemed unethical by me. However, again I was curious, and the words naturally led me to ask two basic questions: Was Lilian a liar and, if so, was she following the lead of some of her professional peers during a time when the national economy was on its knees and hungry architects struggled to survive? Or was Lilian being unfairly labeled in an attempt to bar her rightful place in history? By any measure it was a mystery that I wanted to unravel, and notwithstanding which side of the argument the truth would ultimately lie, I was determined to get to the root of it. And so the project went to another level: it would either confirm the accusation or exonerate Lilian Rice. These pages bring you, the reader, along on my journey of discovery to decide for yourself. No matter what the outcome, the book pays sincere homage to Lilian's achievements and those within her sphere, and retells of the zeitgeist of the era in which she lived, a time when most women were content to be homemakers.

 As a child, Lilian was often photographed with her pet dog Nono. Even in her adult life, Lilian had a dog for a companion. *Author's collection*

1.
A Bright-Faced Baby Girl

My drive down Interstate 5 was unremarkable except for the anticipation that I felt with the hope of finding buried treasure in the archives of the history room in National City Library. Cruising the twenty miles from my home-base of Solana Beach, south to the port town now famed for its strip of automobile dealerships known as the Mile of Cars and the biggest naval base in the nation, my mind pondered the possibilities of what I would find in the recently relocated archives. On the top floor of a new library facility these archives were tucked away in a very modern, neatly decorated room with beech-wood furnishings that contrasted with sepia photographs. I would soon find myself spending many hours sequestered in that room. As I exited the freeway and coursed west toward the bay, I could see how industry now dominates here. Steel and concrete, power lines and cranes, and nondescript functional buildings fill the horizon blocking the view to the ocean. The footprint of the US Navy, an overpowering neighbor who moved in during World War II, looms large along these three miles of port area and swallows up any possibility of a return to what was once a quaint seaside port nestled in a pretty bay.

As I steered the cloverleaf bend and traveled inland toward the residential sector, my mind snapped back to the present. Streets, lined with neglected homes and front yards filled with discarded automobiles and long-abandoned junk, told their story. This was a neighborhood for decades in decline, home to those without the economic means or the motivation to rally 'round and rescue it, to take it back to its former pristine condition during the turn of the twentieth century.

In a swift change of plan, I chose to drive toward A Avenue to Heritage Square and discover for myself how the architecture of the late 1800s had once looked and compare it with modern-day National City.

In efforts to rescue important fragments of the former nobility of National City, some of its historic stately homes have been rescued and replanted in Heritage Square, close to the city's modern civic center. This parkland setting is now the location of the former home of Elizur Steele—Rice's great uncle—a Queen Anne Revival Victorian, today painted in vivid hues of purple and lavender; the Rice-Proctor home, that once housed the office of Julius Rice; the Kimball House once owned by National City's founder; and Brick Row, like its name hints, rowhouses constructed from red brick, originally built for visiting railroad VIPs. The square is an architectural oasis in the industrial urban surroundings and speaks volumes about the pride of local citizens who remember, and wish to preserve, what little is left of the former genteel era of National City during its late nineteenth century gilded years.

Today, the latest data from the US Census Bureau informs us that National City has a population of about 60,000 and is diverse in its demographics with sixty-three percent of its population Hispanic or Latino, and twenty-three percent of its residents receiving incomes below the national poverty level. In the 1980s and 1990s, National City had significant gang and drug activity. But in 2008, it was homicide-free for the first time since 1963, and today, parts of the city are experiencing a noticeable Renaissance. But the coastal community is still a far cry from its glory years when National City was founded over 120 years ago.

Buoyed by my visit to Heritage Square, I nevertheless needed to head back toward the civic center where the library had recently opened. A community-wide celebration had marked its ribbon-cutting ceremony, with mariachi bands and Mexican dancers heralding its inauguration and dedication. Mary Allely, the library archivist, unlocked the door to the Kile Morgan Local History Room to give me access to its collections. I was curious about the person the history room was named for and I soon found out. From a scrapbook newspaper clipping, I read that in 1973 Kile Morgan led a grass-roots movement to rescue the almost derelict home of the National City founder Frank Kimball. A grand Victorian, with fifteen rooms that had once entertained

Lilian, about two years old, circa 1891.
Author's collection

prominent officials, including at least one president, it was then about to be demolished to make way for a parking lot. Kile facilitated the sale of the house to the city, had it moved to Heritage Square, and oversaw a total refurbishment that re-created the house to represent that of a Victorian-era residence. He was my kind of man, I thought.

In the archive room, I thumbed through more scrapbooks with stacks of clippings, read out-of-print books, and studied monochromatic images on yellowed pages. I was shifted back in time to the last year of the nineteenth century and found myself absorbed in a place where salty coastal breezes mingled with the unforgettable tangy scent of orange and peach blossom, a place acclaimed proudly as the Bay Region of Southern California. A meticulously organized photo album, though, as is so often the case, without dates and names, brought the Rice family to life for me. In its pages appeared a pretty child, Lilian Rice, who would develop into a determined young woman who would outshine others and belong ultimately to an era when women stepped out of their restrictive Victorian corsets and into the freedom of loose fitting, knee-length dresses, bobbed their hair to look like males, and demanded, and received, the privilege to vote. This woman, throughout her too-brief lifetime, would not only be witness to a daring fashion revolution, but also to some of the world's most significant technological achievements, and she would find herself in the inner orbit of some of the nation's most famed stars of the silver screen.

The monotony of poring over reels of scratchy microfilm that recorded the comings and goings in National City was occasionally broken as hidden gems—small but important details about the Rice family revealed themselves to me. On one such occasion in the society pages of the June 13 *National City Record* newspaper a single sentence stood out as it published notice of Lilian Jeannette Rice's healthy delivery into the world, the day before. The factual date of Lilian's birth year has been up for debate for decades. It is often noted in the historic record as 1888. The error was perhaps perpetuated by Henry F. Withey, who included Lilian in his directory of deceased architects, stating her birth year erroneously as a year earlier. But the microfilm of the 1889 newspaper did not lie: "A bright-faced baby girl brightens the home of Mr. and Mrs. J. A.

Rice" read the announcement that published proof of the Rice's third child's safe birth at their home at 740 East Second Street, on June 12, 1889. The occasion must have been bittersweet, I imagined. Relief at the happy outcome to the healthy pregnancy of Lilian's mother, Laura, but also a sad reminder of their darling Walter, "the little pet of the family," who had died unexpectedly of a childhood disease, the year before Lilian's birth. The death of their second son had been a tragic blow to the family. At just five years old, Walter, with his angelic face, buoyant curls, and wide eyes, had been cruelly wrenched from them. It is said that parents never completely recover from the death of their child, and in the stoic, stiff upper-lipped society of life in the Victorian era, the pushed-down pain must have taken an emotional toll on both Laura and Julius Rice.

Few images have been found of Julius Rice, but of those photographs that remain, it is apparent that his most notable and instantly recognizable feature is the shape of his eyes. The eyelids slope down slightly at their outer corners and give him a distinctive appearance that is both warm and stern. If this is an indicator of the inner personality of the man, it would be an accurate one. Julius was a man of firm principles and determination. Although he appeared to have a soft side, his quickness to temper would on occasion rock the stability of the Rice household and result in him working away for periods of time. His other son, Jack, born in 1880, did not inherit the gene that gave the Rices the distinctive eyes, and had more of the facial handsomeness from Laura's side of the family, the Steeles. Jack was good looking and athletic. His grades from his senior year at San Diego High School indicate that he was passionate about football and failing at math and literature. At almost nine years Lilian's senior, he would be less like a brother and more like an alternate father, as Julius Rice spent months at a time working away from the family home.

Census data from the 1860s informed me that Julius Augusta Rice was raised on his father's farm in Stockbridge, Vermont. His father, Azro Aritis Allen Rice, fought gallantly in the Civil War, and was a casualty of the battle of Gettysburg in 1863. Of valiant descent, Julius was one of four children, the third son, with a younger sister, and as he came of age, he evidently married very well. Laura Steele was a stunning beauty, with a pale complexion and noble, classical features. The handsome couple moved to the burgeoning farming community of National City in the late 1870s to join Laura's well-to-do aunts and uncles who had already rooted themselves comfortably in the nascent, coastal development. Laura and Julius had both been trained as teachers in Randolph, Vermont. Their work as educators there would be relegated to memory along with the brutal winters that drove many easterners to the westward migration as California opened up to settlers in the mid 1800s when it became a state. The warm climate of the Southern California location tempered by the coastal breezes must have felt like heaven on earth for the Steeles and the Rices. Abundant sun and frostless seasons created ideal conditions for farming—the Southern California way. Avocados, peaches, walnuts, grapes, citrus, and olives flourished with little effort. And Julius tended his orchards and vineyards judiciously like every other neighbor in the dusty port town, which hugged the coastline fifteen miles north of the Mexican border.

When the local newspapers reported on Eiffel's controversial tower, which caused a sensation at the famed 1889 world fair—the French Exposition Universelle—it coincided with a landmark event closer to home that would dramatically change the course of National City's future and be cause for much news coverage. This was not only the year of Lilian's birth, it also marked the merger of the California Southern and the California Central Railway creating the Southern California Railway. Although the merger seems innocuous today, at the time of the event it shifted National City's aspirations for a prosperous future into a fierce struggle for survival and the city was plunged into a severe economic depression. Just nine years earlier the economic health of the township was on a boom trend, and the proud community had staged its own exposition, the San Diego County Fair, one destined to be the precursor to the annual fair that exists today at the permanent site of the Del Mar Fairgrounds in San Diego County. Hardly comparable to the grandeur of the Parisian exposition that showcased Europe's advances in engineering and technology, this humble celebration by National City's citizens, however, was no less impressive as it proudly showcased its bounty of home cooking, crafts, and harvested produce that had sprung from its roots as a former

Lilian, about six years old, circa 1895. *Author's collection*

Spanish land grant ranch transformed into a prosperous community by Frank Kimball.

A New Hampshire native, with thick sable hair, deep set intelligent eyes and symmetrical face, Frank Kimball was perfectly suited to the role of founding father right down to his last whisker, which was waxed into shape to form a magnificent moustache. He had come to California for health reasons and, with his brothers, Warren, George, and Levi, had bought the Mexican land grant acreage of El Rancho de la Nacion in 1859. When the Rices first came to National City, Laura's uncle, Elizur Steele, had helped shape the architectural growth of the fledgling town. As a land developer and builder, he held a social and economic position in National City that equaled that of the founding Kimballs. Elizur had first contracted with the Kimballs in 1868, along with Elijah Valentine, to sell land on the "National Ranch" as it was then known. The agreement between the partnership of Steele and Valentine with the Kimballs was unique as rather than take payment of a cash bonus for exceeding their sales, they instead received tracts of land. Steele was land rich.

After the Kimball brothers had purchased El Rancho de la Nacion and had subdivided the northwest corner into the townsite, they then subscribed over 10,000 acres to secure the backing of the railroad into making National City its Pacific Coast Terminus. The California Southern Railroad had been organized in 1880 to build from the National City terminus northward to connect with the Atlantic and Pacific Railroad, which would open up the west through Arizona. Plans were swiftly set in motion and materials, shipped to National City by boat, began arriving at the port. Rails, track fittings, and most of the steam locomotives and cars had traveled in sailing vessels around Cape Horn, the sole route for cargo freight prior to the completion of the Panama Canal in 1915. Ties were brought down from the north and 225 acres had been set aside for terminal purposes: for shops, a roundhouse, wharves, yards, and warehouses. A creosoting plant was established to treat bridge timbers, piling, and ties. Work on the railroad, aided by the dogged labor of teams of Chinamen, clipped along at a blistering pace and, by 1885, the last spike had been driven, and through-service between Kansas City and National City had been established. For a few glorious years, National City basked in its position as the Pacific Coast Terminus of the great intercontinental route.

But what transpired next must have unfolded like a waking nightmare compared to the optimistic scenario held in the hopes and dreams of the Kimballs, the Steeles, the Valentines, and other civic-minded individuals who had willingly given money, and land, to secure the development of the terminus in their town. In a heartless change of mind, with not an iota of sympathetic thought given to the citizens of National City, the California Southern and the California Central Railway were merged to form the Southern California Railway, a local branch of the national Atchison, Topeka and Santa Fe Railway Company and with the merger came executives with a hidden agenda. This change of plan brought National City to the brink of collapse as a relocation of the railway's terminus was ordered by those in charge. As efficiently as supplies had rolled in, they were rolled out. The machine shops were transferred north to San Bernardino, the company's headquarters were moved to Los Angeles, and the local plant was shut down.

Following this fateful double-crossing, and displaying a constitution as strong as his name implies, Elizur Steele took a bold business risk. He opted to capitalize on the cheap cost of land, a backlash of the railroad's executive decision that caused an exodus of residents and the death knell of businesses. Steele decided to revitalize the downtown area of National City. With a dwindling population, the signs did not portend well for the prosperous outcome of Steele's real estate venture and one wonders if the man was ill-advised or stubborn. Cutting a figure that would have compared favorably with a presidential candidate, Elizur Steele's outward appearance evinced his social status and possibly contributed to this speculative move. Bearded with thick, raven hair and the mandatory hat, Steele looked every bit the gentleman of success. The same could not be said for this business decision. Steele's real estate venture took courage and cash to pull off, but it would require economically sound people to make it succeed, and this was the lacking piece of the equation.

When Steele opened his business strip, which stood along National Avenue and Eighth Street, it was lauded as the most prestigious commercial structure in National City. The imposing three-story edifice gave further celebrity to the Steele clan. Constructed on three sides with bricks fired in the kilns of the Kimball's brick-making company, in an apparent show of optimism, the fourth side of the structure was fashioned in timber to allow for expansion. Microfilmed pages of the local newspaper carried the derisive headline, "Elizur Steele's monster business block is completed." It was 1887 and just a year after Steele had purchased the prime quarter block of land for a knockdown bargain price of $600, and that included a house. The bold undertakings of Steele's commercial venture were nevertheless welcomed as a sign of economic recovery. Reporters in an apparent change of tack then seemed to support Steele's highly visible development and were quick to publish that a massive $100,000 would be spent on improving the commercial district, which included the acclaimed Hotel Royal with no expense spared in its furnishings. "Let the boom and Elizur continue," rallied the *National City Record*.

Railroad tracks had been laid directly in front of the Steele Block. A plank walkway spanned from the hotel's entrance directly to the rails, and

Lilian at sixteen years of age, circa 1905.
Author's collection

style home Steele had built for himself, or the elegant home built for his newly wedded niece, and numerous other residences designed by him.

But even Steele's touch could not reinvigorate a depressed populous. In less than two years, the celebration turned into commiseration. By February 1889, the news reported the closure of the hotel and recounting the manager's statement published, "We have lost nothing by you who came, but by those who didn't come. We have kept open the last six months for the name of it. Now must close for the gain of it and on account of improper sewage and insufficient 'boom.'" It would be just a few months to the much anticipated birth of Lilian, and Julius Rice must have agonized over the future of his growing family and wondered how in God's name he was going to support them. With the loss of jobs and a drastic decline in the town's population, Julius continued to stubbornly attempt to carve out a living in real estate until the depth of the housing collapse had him turn his efforts toward

for a year, at least, it seemed that Steele had struck gold. The Hotel Royal rivaled the popularity of the Hotel Del Coronado across from National City's port. Tourists enjoyed the entertainment of the railroad's popular daily excursions. For a fare of one dollar, day trippers could partake in a sixty-mile sojourn over the railroad's entire system, heading south through the aptly named Paradise and Sweetwater Valleys and across the Mexican border into Tijuana.

The first official trip of the new motor road excursion was cause for press coverage. June 15, 1887 witnessed a group that read like a "Who's Who" of the town's elite enjoying a "jolly excursion": the Kimballs, the Copelands, the Dickensons, the Burgesses, and Elizur Steele and "all the new business men of the town." Dressed to be noticed, the local paper reported how the day trippers, with their derby hats and silk parasols, could enjoy marine view dining at the Royal, a ride by rail, then a steam boat trip across the bay to Coronado. The hotel seemed destined for greatness. It would be another Steele monument erected for posterity that represented the respectable ambiance of the port town of National City, like the St. Matthews Episcopalian Church, which he had designed and funded, like the classic stately Victorian-

Laura S. Rice, Lilian Rice's mother, was a New York native. Raised in Randolph, Vermont, she came to National City as a newlywed in 1880. Laura was a former teacher, a fine artist who crafted delicate landscape scenes in oils, and an interior designer. *Author's collection*

In 1887, Frank Kimball, founder of National Ranch, contracted with architect R. C. Ball to build ten rowhouses. It cost $30,000 to build all ten units, which initially served as accommodation for out-of-town railroad officials. The rowhouses are now located at A Avenue in National City's Heritage Square, between Ninth Street and Plaza Boulevard. *Photo by Diane Y. Welch*

Lilian Rice's great-uncle, architect and developer Elizur Steele helped shape the architectural growth of National City. This Victorian-style residence, known as the Elizur Steele, Crandell-Ennis House, typifies his design aesthetic. It was donated to the city of National City in 1977 by George Matheson, when it was moved to Heritage Square. *Photo by Diane Y. Welch*

education. He would be revisiting a former career path begun shortly after his arrival in National City. It had been almost a decade since Julius had first joined the ranks of civic-minded educators.

On August 9, 1880, Julius entered into his teaching career in National City. The small school where he spent his first two years as an educator had been built by the Kimball family and was located along National Avenue at Twelfth Street in the town's bustling civic center. By the following year, Julius had been appointed to the County Board of Education. Then, when a state-of-the-art, new eight-room, two-story school—the Russ School—was built in nearby San Diego in 1882, Julius opted for a promotion when he accepted the position as the school's inaugural principal. The school was named for local lumberman Joseph Russ, who donated $5,136.55 worth of lumber to build the school, one which was remarkable not only for its sound construction, but for its magnificent panoramic views. "There is not a school building in the continent that has a more beautiful site," boasted the local paper. As its principal, Julius received $120 a month, a munificent salary for the day. But after just one year, Julius handed in his resignation.

While accounts as to why Julius once again changed schools have been lost to time, of note is the role that Kate Sessions (a San Diego horticulturist, who would later make her own mark in local history) played following Julius's departure. As there were no qualified contenders for the principal's post in San Diego County, Kate Sessions, who at the time was a teacher in Oakland, Northern California, heard of the open position and applied for it. The vote of the school board was unanimous and Kate was hired to start employment in January 1884 to complete the school year. When students entered school, however, on the morning of April 7 of that same year, their former principal had returned, just as abruptly as he had left, and Kate Sessions was demoted to assistant principal. By July, Julius's salary was raised to $125 a month, for the following school year, and his assistant received a mere $80 a month, a fact that was sufficient cause for Kate to mention it in her memoirs.

At that time, the San Diego School District was wracked with financial difficulties and several elections were held to raise funds from local taxes to keep the schools open. Teachers' salaries were cut and partially paid in scrip and Julius once again changed jobs when he accepted the position of principal, this time at the National City School where he also did double duty and taught students in the ninth through eleventh grades. Despite his strict, firm hand, Julius had real concerns about the economic survival of his school in National City and used creative solutions to meet his students' basic needs. Five dollars of his own money was slated to head a campaign to raise funds for tennis courts for the girls and a rugby ball for the boys. News reports stated that students opted to collectively service the school themselves, and rather than have the district spend money on a janitor, they all pitched in keeping the classrooms picked up and the bathrooms clean. The money saved went toward the students' athletic programs.

A newly appointed school board trustee, Mr. T. R. Palmer, a lawyer, objected to Julius Rice's unorthodox program of student extra curricular activity and made a formal complaint, which was reported openly in the local newspaper. Facing up to Palmer's vocal complaints, and perhaps fueled by his own temper, Julius Rice once again resigned. With a local depression still entrenched in San Diego County, with cuts in teaching salaries, and few open teaching vacancies, Julius looked outside the county for employment. Despite his tendency to change schools, Julius was awarded a life diploma from the State Board of Education, the year before his daughter was born. During Lilian's early childhood years, Julius was separated from the family as his employment as a teacher in Hemet and later in Corona in Riverside County, took him several hours journey north from National City. During school vacations he would be reunited with his family, who remained in the grand home on East Second Street.

Along with her neighborhood friends, which included the children from the Valentines, the Reeds, and the Boals, Lilian attended grade school just a few blocks from her home. The little girl with the tightly woven braids, the neatly laced leather boots, and the buttoned-up tailored suits, was the picture of perfection. And it wasn't just her outward appearance that was agreeable. The inner child was delightful. When not at school she was always close to her pet dog, Nono, an endearing trait that she would carry with her all her life as her pets inevitably aged and died and a new pet dog would replace her former companion. Her childhood friendships also lasted well into her adulthood telling of the veracity of her comradeship and charm. Lilian was evidently a much-loved friend. With Lilian's early childhood innocence must have come a blissfully ignorant awareness of the economic hardship that blighted her town. Being shielded from the adult worries that concerned her family, Lilian had an upbringing typical of a privileged young lady in society, with many parties to attend, fine clothes to wear, piano lessons, and a lasting appreciation for the arts and the classics.

As Lilian approached her graduation from National City High School in 1906, she was already primed for her chosen career as an architect. A sharp, quick mind resulted in a skipped grade during her high school years. Her intelligence and creative sensibilities provided the perfect combination of academic mastery and artistic skill necessary for the intense path of architecture. Her home environment also nurtured the artist within.

Throughout Lilian's childhood years she had seen and been influenced by her mother's own artistic proclivities. Laura, the daughter of John B. Steele, Elizur Steele's brother, had transformed one of the upstairs rooms in the Rice family home into a painting studio. Large bay windows encircling the room's exterior provided the necessary natural light to illuminate the space. There, small but detailed oil paintings depicting landscapes and flowers, were skillfully brought to life. Neighborhood children were invited to explore the studio; they would be cautioned to be respectful and polite and reminded not to touch, except for Lilian, who must have relished in the fact that she could not only touch but most probably had created her own mini-masterpieces in this room.

Laura also had shown a creative sensitivity to the built environment, which was expressed in her personal make-over of the family home. Several stories have retold how Laura, before her daughter was born, directed the contractors who carried out the exterior changes and interior remodel. Her project must have been the topic of animated conversation as, years later, Lilian mulled over her possible choices

of university courses. Laura's aesthetic efforts to improve the home that became the talk of the town and known locally as the red wood house of Mr. and Mrs. Rice, would no doubt have informed her daughter's ultimate career path.

By her teen years, outwardly blossoming, but displaying more character than classic beauty, Lilian nevertheless carried herself with dignity and grace. Her blonde hair, neatly coifed in a french braid and embellished with a grosgrain silk bow at the nape of her neck, gave no hint at the two braids that had once been her preferred style. The high school head-shot may have suggested a delicate society debutante, but it belied Lilian's internal fortitude that had developed from a determined spirit far stronger than this portrait suggested. When she was formerly presented at her high school graduation in 1906, having just turned seventeen, she had already resolved to make her mark in society by the acceptance of her place at the University of California.

The Pythian Hall in the Granger block, located at the southeast corner of Eighth Street and National Avenue, provided a dignified setting for Lilian's high school graduation and the launch of her future years into academia. No matter the small detail that Lilian was only one of two seniors to be graduating from the National City High School in the summer of that year of 1906. Rather than embarrassment at the oddity, there was pride. The planned program of events was as thoroughly organized as though a hundred students were to receive their diplomas that day. Fellow student Halpert Johnson, who would later become a civil engineer, shared the limelight with Lilian. Essays were written, speeches conducted, well-wishes poured, and songs heartily sung. So noteworthy was the event that the *National City News* published the story in the following week's edition. It was a marvelous tribute to National City's darling. The reporters would be carefully following Lilian's journey into the world of university life, tracking her comings and goings as she returned to National City during vacation time. They would not be disappointed. The news would later satisfactorily report the success of the Rice couple's precious daughter who would return in May of 1910 wiser, more mature, and with her degree from the University of California.

2.
1906: A Landmark Year

My four children, followed by the driver, my husband, bundled out of our minivan; we stretched our legs, and breathed in the crisp, breezy summer air of Berkeley. The city reminded me of England with its green hills and cool climate. Berkeley was one of our scheduled stops on the family trip and this particular year we had taken a drive north up California's coast. The journey took us from San Diego through the central county of San Luis Obispo, then up to San Simeon, where we took a memorable tour of Hearst Castle, north to San Francisco, across to Sacramento and east to Reno. It was the summer of 2006 and the visit to Berkeley was a welcome break from hours of driving and naturally of great interest to me. Together we strolled through the University of California campus, snapped photographs of the classic architecture of the Campanile and Sather Gate and some of the remaining historic buildings. We also walked through the side streets that crisscrossed the perimeter of the campus and we traced the tree-lined avenues where I knew Lilian had lived. We found the boarding house on Hillegass Avenue—still perfectly solid, and no doubt still housing undergraduates—where Lilian had roomed as a student with her sisters from her sorority, Alpha Omicron Pi. In that moment when I snapped the shutter of my camera to capture the sagging white-painted house with its simple wood siding, my mind was taken back 100 years. I imagined the scene that met Lilian on her first day in Berkeley as one that would have brought forth mixed emotions for the freshman student. On the one hand, it represented a future full of excitement and promise, and on the other hand, it represented a duty to aid the city's crippled neighbor, San Francisco.

On Wednesday, April 18 at 5:13 a.m., the worst earthquake of the twentieth century hit the city of San Francisco barreling like a hellish Titan into the city's still-sleepy neighborhoods. Though the quake lasted only one minute, it would be known historically as the nation's worst natural disaster. Its destruction caused buildings to jolt sideways, then buckle and fall like a pack of cards spewing plaster, cement, brick, and stone, terrifying those who happened to be up during those early dawning moments. "Big buildings were crumbling as one might crush a biscuit in one's hand," said one eyewitness.

Bystanders had to dodge the debris, and news accounts told of one man who was crushed to death when a cornice from the highly-ornamented city hall fell on him. It was a building that was twenty-six years in the making, cost six millions dollars to create, with its showy domed-topped tower and rich ornamentation, but it was almost completely demolished in that one-minute quake, the fortune having been spent on adornment rather than structural integrity. It was a fact that would not be lost on the young architects who were studying to hone their craft in degree programs at the University of California, and who would soon become licensed architects.

The Daily News, San Francisco, was the only newspaper to publish the initial devastation caused by the earthquake on the actual day it occurred. Its dramatic headline in huge capitals simply stated, "HUNDREDS DEAD!" But the greatest catastrophe came from the fires that followed as severed gas lines created unstoppable flames that raged through 490 city blocks and rendered the city a mass of smoldering ruins with 25,000 buildings destroyed. The destruction caused by the blaze, which raged for four days, and the necessary dynamiting of city blocks in an effort to tame the out-of-control conflagration, found 250,000 homeless and between 450 and 700 mortally wounded. Damage estimates topped $350,000,000.

However, one building did not relinquish to the quake: the recently and solidly built James Flood Building, which was a state-of-the-art flat-iron structure. Boasted by its architect as a fire-proof creation, the modern building unfortunately caught fire on the inside as flames jumped Market Street and engulfed its interior. On seeing the fire's fury, a smartly-dressed young

The campanile, *Sather Tower*, designed by architect John Galen Howard, provides an impressive focal point for UC Berkeley's university campus.
Photo by Diane Y. Welch

man would have been prevented from going to work that day. Leone Sinnard, the disciplined overachiever, and the promotional brains behind the Southern Pacific Railroad's publicity for its colonization, would have been unable to even enter the company offices in the Flood Building. The fierce blaze barred his conscientious day at work on that fateful morning, and he was likely irritated.

Despite the utter devastation, San Francisco quickly recovered from the great earthquake of 1906. And during the next four years, the city arose from its ashes. Its destruction actually paved the way for city planners to create a new and improved San Francisco. Formerly the stereotypical western boomtown, the city had built-up in a haphazard manner since 1849 when the gold rush brought hundreds of thousands of fortune seekers to the area. Working with a fresh canvas, San Franciscans were able to rebuild their city with a more logical and elegant approach.

On the title page of a special edition of the *San Francisco Examiner*, published on October 21, 1906, six months after the earthquake, a woman, dressed in an haute couture suit with hat and gloves, wielding a saw in one hand and a hammer in the other, steps confidently onto an iron girder while men in the background take part in the city's reconstruction. The symbolic image would not be far removed from a role that Lilian would find herself undertaking almost twenty years later when she became the architectural designer, with Leone Sinnard, on the development of the community of Rancho Santa Fe in San Diego County.

The razing, then rebuilding of San Francisco, was the prelude to Lilian's arrival into the noble halls of academia at the University of California and, in that fateful year of 1906, as she took her first steps on the threshold into adulthood, she could not have imagined that sixteen years later she would be designing a community styled for movie stars and Hollywood's elite. She would also have been unaware that Leone Sinnard was then living with his second wife, Hazel, just blocks away from the university campus, and that years later she would work side-by-side with him on a master-planned garden city. Intelligently designed with single-story buildings, in contrast to San Francisco, this San Diego County development would withstand the beating of any future earthquakes. But all this was in the future for

The title page of the *San Francisco Examiner*, October 21, 1906, depicts a high-society woman with tools, as a symbol of the city's reconstruction. *Author's collection*

Lilian, who was not only embarking on a life-changing journey that would take her from a seventeen-year-old girl to a woman, but who would soon prove that she could hold her own with the male graduates from her architectural classes.

Along with hundreds of other freshmen that fateful year, Lilian was mandated to aid San Francisco's displaced citizens who were set up in a temporary tent city across the bay in Berkeley, while the city of San Francisco was being rebuilt. This start of academia was unusual to say the least, but it is easy to imagine that the "volunteerism" was done with appropriate enthusiasm from this young and energetic group, one that would give the homeless a much-needed sense of connection to the larger community. And in this sense it would symbolize Lilian's lifelong path of good citizenry and service to others.

On board the paddle steamer the *State of California* that chugged its way out of National City port, Lilian, a first-class passenger, had arrived in Berkeley in early fall. In coincidence with her life-changing journey, the newspapers reported a spectacular comet, *15P/Finlay*, that hurtled through the sky during August and September. Also by coincidence, another celestial body, Halley's Comet, would create a national fever-pitch sensation as it streaked through the atmosphere in 1910, creating a spectacular heavenly show and dominating newspaper headlines as Lilian graduated. And so these two rare otherworldly phenomena symbolized the bookends of Lilian's undergraduate years at Cal.

The City of Berkeley, on the east shore of San Francisco Bay, couldn't have been more different from the arid coastal desert of Lilian's hometown in Southern California. Here woodsy lots and hilly, narrow streets, with tightly packed buildings characterized the bustling university town where Lilian would be spending most of the next five years of her life. The Berkeley campus, the oldest of the University of California system, had opened up to students in 1873. Five years earlier, on March 23, 1868, the state governor had signed into law the Organic Act, "To Create and Organize the University of California." Ten faculty members and nearly forty students made up the new University of California when it opened in Oakland in 1869.

The university had a student body that had swelled to almost 200 students within four years. And with UC President Henry Durant at the helm in September 1873, they moved en masse to the new campus in Berkeley on an elevated site that adjoined the picturesque Strawberry Creek.

When the university was being developed, groves of ancient live oak, fir, and acacia trees covered the sloping site on the eastern side of Berkeley. It resembled a park rather than a campus. It is said that President Durant gazed from the high ground overlooking this picturesque 250-acre spot and realized that the search for the new campus was at an end. It was later reported, "On the hills before him he [imagined] the stately edifice opening wide its gate to all—the rich and the poor, the woman and the man." The university

was fully endowed and entrance to any of the courses were free to California residents; so Lilian's parents would not have been burdened with the cost of her education. In 1910, the endowments amounted to thirteen million dollars, which yielded a million dollars in interest each year, massive amounts of money for the day. Major benefactors included Phoebe Apperson Hearst, widow of George Hearst mining magnate and US senator, her son William Randolph Hearst, and Charles F. Doe, "a first rank San Francisco capitalist" who made his fortune in the lumber business.

Phoebe Apperson Hearst underwrote a contest to create an ambitious architectural plan to design buildings for the university's still-emerging campus. Bernard Maybeck, then a mechanical drawing instructor in the engineering department, had proposed the competition to transform the campus into a "City of Learning." The winner was Parisian Émile Bénard, who presented a showy, elaborate plan using the formal Beaux Arts neoclassical style. However, when he traveled to Berkeley, he insulted virtually everyone he met, and was deemed unsuitable to carry out his own work. The task then was passed on to John Galen Howard, who had placed fourth in the contest. Howard modified Bénard's plan and, although for over a hundred years the plan was attributed to Bénard, a recent book by Sally Woodbridge explains that this is a myth. In truth, Howard thought the plan "utterly impractical," she wrote, and consequently the constructed campus should rightly be credited to him wrote Woodbridge. By toning down the austere formality of the buildings' classical lines, Howard created a campus more fitting for the California environment and the hilly park-like site. "Beaux-Arts artistry meeting Bay Area informality to produce an early expression of environmental design," to quote *Sunset* magazine. This approach would later influence Lilian's own design style as she followed Howard's environmentally sympathetic lead in her future building projects.

John Galen Howard was born in Chelmsford, Massachusetts, and studied architecture at the Massachusetts Institute of Technology and the École des Beaux-Arts in Paris. It was after working in Los Angeles, that he entered Phoebe Hearst's competition.

Professor Bernard Maybeck as he appeared in the 1904 *Blue and Gold Yearbook. Author's collection*

classes, the female students took active roles in the Architectural Association that formed the following year. These architecture students would have been given an unprecedented opportunity of literally seeing their campus being designed and built around them and no doubt were engaged in its construction. Nearly twenty buildings, including some of the campus's most elegant and stately structures, were built under Howard's direction. Among them the Hearst Memorial Mining Building, the Hearst Greek Theatre, California Hall, Doe Library, Wheeler Hall, and Sather Tower. The new campus had a pedigree of respectability and prestige and today, many of John Galen Howard's designs are recognized as California Historical Landmarks and listed on the National Register of Historic Places. In that regard, Lilian is Howard's rightful peer.

Fate played a hand, not only in his stature as an important figure in architecture, but as he took over the campus project in 1901, two years later, he became the founder and dean of its architectural department. Coinciding with the university's construction Howard also opened his own private practice in San Francisco in 1906 to aid the rebuilding of the city.

Prior to the department's development, undergraduates of architecture had been admitted into the school of engineering. California architect Julia Morgan was one of its alumna, a graduate in the class of 1894. She would go on to be the preeminent lady architect of her era with the jewel in her crown, Hearst Castle in San Simeon, built for Phoebe Apperson Hearst's son, William Randolph Hearst. Some of her work also complemented Howard's campus design plan as she was the lead designer for the university's Greek Theatre and provided the decorative elements for the Hearst Mining Building. In the inaugural graduating class of architecture in 1904, out of the ten students enrolled, half were women and no doubt they were influenced by Julia Morgan's example. Considered on an equal footing in their

University of California patron Phoebe Apperson Hearst as she appeared in the 1910 *Blue and Gold Yearbook. Author's collection*

Overlooking the temporary tent city that had sprung up by necessity on the east shore of San Francisco Bay in 1906, were the homes in Berkeley's hillside neighborhoods. While the plans for a new and improved San Francisco were being discussed, several neighbors on the north side of the hill were coming together to make plans of their own to hire esteemed architect Bernard Maybeck to design and build a clubhouse that would serve as a communal meeting place for their organization, the Hillside Club. Founded by a group of Berkeley women who wished to protect the Berkeley hillsides through their promotion of community development that was environmentally sensitive, the club took wing in 1898. Spurring the idea to craft homes that blended with the surrounding hills was the result of Bernard Maybeck's first residential commission in Berkeley. Built three years earlier, the notable project was an unpainted redwood house for author Charles Keeler, a keen advocate and follower of the literary work and idealism of the Victorian art critic John Ruskin.

Delighted with Maybeck's efforts, Keeler voiced his concerns that the simple rustic nature of his home would be "completely ruined when others come and build stupid white-painted boxes all about us." In response, Maybeck simply advised Keeler that he should see to it that "all the houses about you are in keeping with your own." The concept resonated with Keeler who began recruiting his own friends to buy land and build artistic houses next to his own. As more homes were constructed on the hillside, the ladies of the residences organized themselves as a club, with Keeler's encouragement, to disseminate Maybeck's architectural principles in a more formal fashion and to protect the neighborhood against the construction of any undesirable homes. Their stated mission was "to protect the hills of Berkeley from unsightly grading and the building of unsuitable and disfiguring houses; to do all in our power to beautify these hills and above all to create and encourage a decided public opinion on these subjects."

In *The Simple Home*, a self-published manifesto for the club that laid down the basic principles rooted in the combined design philosophies of John Ruskin, William Morris, and Bernard Maybeck, Keeler wrote:

> Hillside Architecture is landscape gardening around a few rooms for use in case of rain—a dining porch on the southeast, a sleeping porch on the northeast, a play ground court on the east and an observation porch on the west, but room to move and to breathe.

Homes should hug the hill and be sited parallel to the slope. Roofs should be low-pitched, windows must be large to let sunlight flood in, and the exterior should be crafted in such a way that the natural plantings cast shadows that create patterns of light and shade, the only exterior ornamentation. Observable from a distance there would be no need for paint or artificial covering. Keeler concluded:

> This with the help of the hill buyer, the Hillside Club can lay out on Berkeley Hills a perfect landscape, connecting green canyons with piling green forests, making of the barren places a park with only here and there a tower, a glimpse of roof to tell of the city underneath.

While it is not known if Lilian was a member of the club, or if she attended meetings, she would certainly have been informed of its work and philosophy, which evidently had a marked effect on her later design ideals. Those in Lilian's sphere were members of the club, however. Through Charles Keeler's invitation, John Galen Howard had joined as did the university president Benjamin Ide Wheeler, along with Berkeley architect Lilian Bridgman. The club's ideology strongly influenced Lilian's later architectural design ideology in her work in San Diego, and she did not hesitate to apply Arts and Crafts principles to the interiors of her Mediterranean-type homes using master craftsmen in all aspects of the construction phase. In 1928, she later wrote of her work on the Rancho Santa Fe project:

Evelyn Morrill   Olive Cutter   Grace Weeks   Rose Gardner   Rose Schmidt   Jennett Miller   Lillian Rice   Mary de Witt
Blanche Ahlers   Gladys Courtian   Emma Black   Evelyn Bancroft   Florence Weeks   Mildred Hunter   Irene Flanagan
Lucile Kistler   Myrtle Anderson   Elaine Standish   Wynne Meridith   Ethel Porter   Marion Crosett   Carrie Bright

Lilian with her Alpha Omicron Pi sorority sisters. Note how Lilian, spotlighted, is the shortest of her group. At age eighteen, when the photograph was taken, she would also have been the youngest.
1910 *Blue and Gold Yearbook. Author's collection*

With the thought early implanted in my mind that true beauty lies in simplicity rather than ornateness, I found real joy at Rancho Santa Fe. Every environment there calls for simplicity and beauty—the gorgeous natural landscapes, the gently broken topography, the nearby mountains. No one with a sense of fitness, it seems to me, could violate these natural factors by creating anything that lacked simplicity in line, in form, and color.

As Lilian began her freshman life at Cal, in San Diego county, representatives of a subsidiary of the Atchison, Topeka, Santa Fe Railway Company were signing a real estate contract that sealed the purchase of two square leagues of Southern California back water ranch lands, almost 9,000 acres, that had cost them $100,000. With the closing of the sale of the once-vibrant ranch owned by the Osunas, its past was in danger of being lost in the shadows of time as, acre by acre, its historic holdings were chipped away. In 1906, when the Santa Fe Land Improvement Company (SFLIC)

purchased the majority of the Osuna acreage that was remaining, the Osunas' fate was sealed.

As officially recorded on October 22, 1906, the SFLIC, headed up by Walter E. Hodges, the company president, now owned most of the acres within the original boundaries of the former Spanish land grant of Rancho San Dieguito. Unknown to Lilian and Leone Sinnard in 1906, this remote transaction, some 500 miles away, would fatefully bring the two together sixteen years later in an unprecedented partnership between promoter and designer that would simultaneously launch Lilian into the solar system of Hollywood stars, yet historically prove to be the final curtain for Leone Sinnard. With no possible hint at what was destined ahead for either of them, for Lilian her immediate future was predetermined and meant four years to not only prove herself among her male peers in the department of architecture, but to also excel in her studies. However, college life would be so much more than that as Lilian grew into womanhood, accepted leadership roles enthusiastically, and in so doing paved the way for her future career path. The seventeen-year-old likely never looked back at her former life growing up in the picturesque port town of National City.

3.

College Life

The start of the inaugural college semester meant introductions to Lilian's academic professors and classmates, and with lower-level courses, this first year would have been a breeze for the intelligent seventeen-year-old, who was the youngest in her class. In that first month there was also a flurry of social activities with welcoming banquets and freshman dances; consequently, Lilian's social calendar was extremely active. It would not have taken her long to gravitate toward one of her fellow students, Grace E. Morin, who was also taking classes in architectural design. The two became as close as sisters and clearly had a deep affection for each other. Throughout Lilian's adult life, it is evident from numerous newspaper reports, and Grace's own biographical data archived at Cornell University, that the ladies stayed in touch long after their years together at Cal. After receiving their respective degrees, Grace stayed on in the Bay Area as a teacher who worked part-time in the office of Julia Morgan. But the two reconnected as Lilian later became the architectural designer for Rancho Santa Fe in 1923, and Grace came to San Diego County to work as a part-time draftsman in the Requa firm, while also teaching at the Sweetwater High School. It must have been a wonderful reunion for the two women who shared a common passion for the built environment and the related talent to interpret it. It is likely that Grace was replacing Lilian at the Requa firm, who must have left a void as she took over the planning and design of Rancho Santa Fe. The two women were bonded friends and had Lilian lived to see it, she would have no doubt served as maid-of-honor for Grace when she married later in life and became Mrs. Conant Van Blarcom.

At university, Lilian was enrolled in the School of Social Sciences and embarked on a bachelor of letters degree program, with a double major in architecture and drawing. I was able to get copies of Lilian's university transcripts from Berkeley, which showed that her freshman classes included Latin, English, history, math, anthropology, drawing, and other lower-division subjects. Lilian fully embraced college-life and participated in activities both on and off campus, putting her organizational and artistic talents to full use. Along with Grace, during her freshman year, Lilian pledged to join Alpha Omicron Pi sorority, which was founded in 1897 at Barnard College in New York City, New York, by four progressive women: Stella George Stern Perry, Jessie Wallace Hughan, Helen St. Clair Mullan, and Elizabeth Heywood Wyman. Their collective founding principles included character, dignity, scholarship, and college loyalty and are still relevant today for the 178 collegiate chapters spread across the nation. The sisterhood was based on a firm foundation of friendship and Stella George Stern Perry wrote in 1936: "We wanted a fraternity that should carry on the delightful fellowships and cooperation of college days into the workaday years ahead and to do so magnanimously. Above all, we wanted a high and active special purpose to justify existence and a simple devotion to some worthy end." A principle exemplified by Lilian's later life and career.

There were no university-operated dormitories, with the exception of College Hall, a private dormitory experiment for women students that became available in August 1909, under the unofficial sponsorship of the dean of women. However, throughout her four-year graduate course, Lilian lived off campus, residing in different all-female boarding houses, located within pleasant walking distances from the university campus.

While firsthand accounts of Lilian's time in college are forever lost, her scrapbook—one of a pair held in the Kile Morgan Local History Room in the National City Library—gave me valuable clues to her social activities and her popularity as a teenager about to blossom into womanhood. The scrapbook had been donated by Luella Mordhorst in 1959, which had my mind in a spin wondering who this person was and why she was able to donate Lilian's property, a mystery that would take me five years to solve. In this first year at college, Lilian attended parties, dances (her dance cards were filled to capacity), plays, and athletic pursuits. Mementos from each social event were meticulously pasted into her scrapbooks, a practice that students were encouraged to undertake to document their years at school. In Lilian's case, as there is no extant record of these years, the scrapbook is a priceless form of documentation and gave me an insight into the excitement of her new world. It must have been a wonderland of new experiences and with no parental watchful eye overlooking her shoulder, Lilian's social life took wing.

The yellowed pages of the scrapbook, with a spine twisted, decayed, and pulling away from these fragile leaves, spoke loudly to me of the social aspect of college life for a young woman in the first decade of the twentieth century residing in a progressive city like Berkeley. The first few pages tell of Lilian's arrival there: a note of concern from her "papa" instructed her to "stay on board until morning." Lilian had arrived by steam boat, traveling first class; her ticket issued from the Pacific Coast Steamship, Co., was carefully preserved and placed in the page next to her father's loving note. Her certificate of admission, showing that she was registered as a regular student in the school of social sciences, also named her adviser, Professor Hart. And her ticket for membership into the Association of Students indicated that she had diligently paid her one dollar annual dues. By page two, invitations to dances are included and the dance cards are full of eager male dance partners requesting Lilian's hand for turns in quick step and waltzes. In subsequent pages, Lilian has savored and saved friends' invitations to dinner, theater, and private soirees. By page nine, Lilian is in her sophomore year of 1907, and there is quite a collection of calling cards of friends who she obviously considered of great value. Lilian was evidently extremely popular with her college friends, both male and female. The calling card of Mr. Max Thelan, who was an emerging lawyer of some note from National City, was included. He later would be assigned to the State Commissioner for Railroads and play an important role in the expansion of the

rail system throughout the nation. His mother, Fannie Thelan, had the foresight to meticulously handwrite her firsthand recollections of the fledgling years of National City as it grew from its former Spanish land grant era to a bustling port town, an account that is invaluable today.

This freshman year also served to test a student's academic caliber with an emphasis on the challenging course of descriptive geometry. While some of her classmates failed this course, Lilian passed it without difficulty. It was the benchmark that determined whether a student was capable of the mathematical aspects of their career choice. Lilian was clearly well-suited to architecture with a father who was an educator, and no doubt mentored his daughter in high-level math, and a mother who was an artist and designer. This blend of left-brained logic and right-brained creativity was the perfect balance of cerebral dexterity for the role of architect and it served Lilian well. Her artistic skills would be in demand as she later volunteered on the art staff for school publications and created posters that advertised upcoming events.

Oddly, in 1906, there was no art department located on the campus of Cal, but there was an art college in San Francisco—the Mark Hopkins School of Art—that was affiliated with the university. However, several of the students of architecture with their artistic proclivities, and no doubt Lilian was one of them, clamored for art classes on their own campus. When these students planned to arrange to do life study classes using nude models, it caused a scandalous debate that was written up that year in the *Oakland Tribune* with the headline, "Plan to study the nude shocks the modest."

Professor Seawell offered to teach the classes twice a week and presented his side of the debate to the reporter that the class will be offered as an aid in architectural and shade drawing. The sentiments of the day were mixed. "The staid matrons and the modest-minded maids of Berkeley are shocked. No...they are horrified," noted the *Tribune* writer. Mrs. Oliver Carlisle, a member of the Hillside Club, was strongly opinioned that the aesthetics of the nude was a fit study for the university students. "There cannot be achievement in art without the study of the nude," she stressed. While Mrs. Miller, wife of Admiral Miller, held an opposing view stating that university buildings should not be used for these classes, as President Wheeler had dictated. "The perspective should always be that the university authorities know what is best for its students." It is interesting to see the architectural students' determination in this isolated matter and how they dug in their heels to get their figure-drawing class. Perhaps this head-strong nature was the precursor to the later Berkeley students' campus demonstrations during the civil rights era of the 1960s.

It's not known if Lilian was one of the students taking Professor Seawell's figure-drawing class, but it's easy to imagine, given her headstrong nature, that she was. However, it is documented that in the fall of 1907, Lilian's name, among others, was proposed for membership into the mostly male Architectural Association. During a special meeting held two weeks later, on September 8, 1907, she was officially voted in. The association had been founded in November 1905, a year after John Galen Howard had opened the department of architecture. Among the eleven male charter members was the name of Charles H. Cheney whose path would cross with Lilian's twelve years later in Rancho Santa Fe, California. Lilian, Grace, and Gertrude Comfort were the only females who "according to their qualifications" were accepted into membership at that time.

Lilian's extra-curricular roles extended beyond the Architectural Association and like many of her female peers she was instrumental in the organization of social events in other areas. She was responsible for providing refreshment arrangements and decorations for the Charter Day luncheon, held in Hearst Hall on March 23, 1908, which served over 200 people. The local news published a lengthy column that described the lovely affair in detail. Tables were decorated in the class colors of crimson and white, with red geraniums as centerpieces, and the women wore white gowns with red ribbon sashes, as reported in the *Daily Californian* with the headline, "Sophomore Women Give Enjoyable Luncheon." But Lilian's studies did not suffer and, by 1908, she had completed sixty-four units of lower-division work and earned her Junior Certificate with honorable mention.

During her summer break in 1908, Lilian was able to put to use her newly developed skills in architectural design in the construction of a "*little gray* [*sic*] *home*" for her father. A newsworthy event

the local paper published notice of the intent to build. It is also likely that Lilian could have had a direct hand in the design of several more speculative domestic buildings commissioned by her father and brother Jack during that period, although there is no written record of her involvement with such projects. The design and construction of Lilian's cottage in National City is thankfully well-documented because Irene Phillips, a National City feature writer, who wrote mostly local history-based articles in the 1950s, published a story about it. By happenstance, her grandmother had purchased the home from Julius Rice in the late 1920s. The article with several others was pasted into a scrapbook that is held at the National City Library archives. "Mr. Rice...told me the story of the house and why he had valued it," wrote Irene. "His daughter, Lillian [*sic*], coming home from her first year at the University of California, where she was studying architecture, wished to put some of her new ideas to work and during the summer, had designed and watched the construction of the house." Built from wood frame and cement, it was the first of its kind in National City. "The cement is so hard on the outside that it will turn a twenty penny nail," wrote Irene. Lilian brought the inside plaster flush with the window and door casings. At the time, it was typical for doors to be grooved "enough to be dust catchers," but Lilian used a plain panel door. The oak flooring she installed was one-inch thick and the kitchen cupboard doors were also solid-inch-thick panels. An innovation that must have created interest in 1908 was the built-in hood over the kitchen stove. And the landscaping was enhanced with colorful Plumosa Palms, which were the first to be brought to National City from the Kate Session Gardens near Pacific Beach.

The *National City News* on July 18, 1908, reported the plans to build the cottage:

> The Mission-style cottage which Mr. J. A. Rice is having erected on the corner of Seventh and A Street will be a distinct improvement to this part of town. It will be 34.6 x 24 feet on an ornamental foundation of concrete and cobblestones. The house will contain five rooms, besides a screened porch, closets etc. It will have all the modern improvements and conveniences.

Irene lived in this home as a child and remembered it fondly, but over the years it was expanded and modernized, yet it still stands in National City. Converted into apartments, however, it is unrecognizable today, with no hint of its former Mission-inspired design, and the nascent aptitude of an architect-in-training that so pleased a proud father.

The closing scene of the stage play *Eclipse of the Moon*. Lilian Rice played the leading role of Ruth Norton. *Author's collection*

Lilian's talents went beyond the design of the built environment. In so many ways she typified the modern, educated woman of her era: she was athletic, could ride horses, played tennis and golf, was an eloquent writer, and had acting skills that earned her lead roles in stage plays. It is possible that Lilian could have been a stage actress of some talent had she not chosen a career path in architecture; but during her era, the profession of acting was not considered suitable for a lady of society. However, true to Lilian's strength of character, and undaunted by public opinion, she seemed to embrace the stage, and during her junior year, she had the opportunity to take part in the Junior Farce Curtain Raiser play staged at Ye Liberty Theater in Oakland. The annual Junior Day event celebrated in November broadened students' public performance skills and was great fun for all involved. Two plays were written and staged by junior students. Lilian auditioned—one of more than 125 vying for sixty parts—and was given the lead role of Ruth Norton in the play *Eclipse of the Moon*. The play opened to rave reviews on November 27, 1908. "Rollicking Farce Keeps Audience

in Roars of Laughter Throughout" noted a reporter for the *Daily Californian* the day after the event. The review included particular mention of Lilian, "Mr. McClellan, as the husband, and Miss Rice, as the young bride, made the most of their parts."

In the preservation of these clippings in her scrapbook, and the congratulatory notes with their withered remnants of flowers that she had received after her stage debut, show the importance Lilian placed on this treasured memory. White carnations came with "world's of love," conveyed by Lilian's stage "husband" John James McClellan. And we also learn of Lilian's nickname through a card of congratulations from "the girls": *love to our Pinkie*, they wrote endearingly.

Lilian's junior year was also highlighted by what must have been a spectacular and fun ball in January of 1909 that marked the completion of "*the Ark*" (a playful contraction of the word, "architecture") which referred to a major addition to the architectural department's building.

The dedication of the building was celebrated with an exhibition and elaborate costume parade. Again we find Lilian in a leadership role as she helped organize this prodigious affair staged on January 20 though 22. The theme was playfully based on Noah and his Ark, with John Galen Howard and his wife taking on the role of "Mr. and Mrs. Noah." The January 15 *Daily Californian* in its preview commentary included a photo of Lilian and L. H. Hibbard, captioned with, *Architecture to form Exhibition*:

> The reception is an annual affair with about 400 guests expected...students clad in jungle attire representing the beasts of the field and the birds of the air will file past in procession. The exhibition will include clay modeling, charcoal renderings, pen and ink and water colors by the students.

This was the association's third such event, with Lilian registering some of her work to be exhibited.

Fast on the heels of this celebration, it appears that Lilian had become seriously ill. Included in her scrapbook are pages devoted to get-well wishes from several of her friends. While it is unknown what ailed her, it could be that her illness was directly related to exhaustion, as Lilian had clearly taken on many extracurricular responsibilities above the rigors of her academic classes. The shriveled fragments of violets with a short note written by Ralph E. Robson on February 25, 1909: "Dear Miss Rice, heard you were having a little visit at the infirmary," indicate that Lilian was confined in the college hospital for the duration of her ailment. A group sent "get well" card was signed by "the animals of the ark," her fellow students, and illustrates their concern and affection for Lilian.

But by the spring semester, Lilian had bounced back and, typical of her natural conscientious nature, was ready for more extracurricular work. The Architectural Association minutes record a regular meeting held on April 23, 1909, and note that nominations made for new officers include Lilian as Massier. The minutes show that she was unanimously elected to this position. The Massier's responsibilities included the assignment of academic papers on architectural matters to members, the organization of exhibitions, and, surprisingly, the safekeeping of the tea set. Three days later, the minutes from another regular meeting note that Lilian is part of a committee appointed to look into the matter of making the Architectural Department into the College of Architecture, a fact that would be realized in later decades.

About the same time, Lilian was also elected into membership of the English Club and served on the art staff for its monthly publication, the *California Occident*, a position that she would hold until her 1911 post-graduate year. In a copy of Volume LVII, number 1, published September 10, 1909—Lilian and Grace are credited as art staff. The delicately rendered illustrations in this issue depict Spanish-style archways, a mission bell tower, and eucalyptus trees that foreshadowed Lilian's later architectural design work. A news story published in the *National City News*, April 8, 1910, noted with pride that Lilian had been elected as art editor for a special edition of the *Occident* that celebrated "Women's Day," a then newly established annual tradition. This was the first time that the publication had been printed in color and Lilian was praised for her cover design of an Indian head rendered in red and gold, and for the frontispiece, a poppy girl wearing a white gown decorated with golden poppies.

Aside from her extracurricular activities, Lilian kept abreast of her academic work. Some of her coursework included Professor Howard's lectures on the history of architecture and his instruction on planning, Mr. Seawell's instruction on watercolor and pen and ink renderings, Mr. Cummings' workshops on modeling of architectural ornament, and Assistant Professor Hay's instruction in the theory of architecture, along with instruction in drawing of the classic orders and their application. Lilian's transcripts show that most of her classes were in architecture during her junior year, with English, Greek, and drawing classes rounding out the instruction. During her senior year, Spanish, drawing, and general science augmented her major.

One of Lilian's most notable achievements, in 1910 before she graduated, was her successful efforts to design a hall to be used solely by the senior women. The men had one—designed by John Galen Howard—so why not the women? All that was needed was the design ability of a budding architect and the necessary funding so that the hall could be built. Both it seemed were attainable. On February 23, 1910, the *San Francisco Call* published that nearly $600 had been collected by the senior women for the hall fund. When news of the project was first announced, the ladies of the fundraising committee started a campaign during the winter break to collect coins as seed money, which evidently had been successful. More money had been promised, the reporter noted, and upon President Wheeler's return from an out-of-state trip, the women expected that they would be able to go ahead with the planning of the building. The design had already been produced and accepted; that budding architect was Lilian.

The article also included an illustration of Lilian's expertly crafted rendering of the front elevation of the hall, a single-story structure with an open veranda, rustic exterior, low sloping eaves and narrow, multipane windows. It would have looked right at home in the Berkeley Hills and would have been approved of by members of the Hillside Club, such was its natural simplicity. Photographs of the three women who were spearheading the campaign for the hall, Leila McKibben, Grace Hunter, and Pearl Kenyon, were published with the story. There was an additional $2,000 needed to complete the hall and, from the tone of the article, that was almost assured. However, it did not happen and Lilian's design was not realized before she graduated. It is a mystery why the women's hall campaign stalled, but there are two likely explanations: that the remaining monies were out

A copy of Lilian's sketch for the Senior Women's House, a concept that was later adapted, then built, by architect Julia Morgan. *Author's collection*

of reach for the students or perhaps the monies were available, but President Wheeler was not taken with Lilian's design. It's unknown what steps led to the next decision, but in 1911, the senior women did finally get their own dedicated hall, but the architect was not budding, she was the well-established Julia Morgan. Girtin Hall as it was named—a nod to the women's college in Cambridge, England—was a single-story, rough-finished room with a central fireplace with cooking facilities at one end and a porch at the other. Julia evidently had taken Lilian's same concepts and adapted them for a slightly larger structure likely due to a greater construction budget. It does sadden me to think that the commission for the project would have been tremendously meaningful for a talented young student of architecture on the verge of her career and would have been an impressive addition to her resumé. If the hall had been built with her name as designer, it would have helped immortalize Lilian's standing with the university that she loved so much, along with an increased awareness of her achievement.

There was a fever pitch to the coming of the comet. The month was May, the year was 1910, and Halley's comet, named for the young Englishman who first documented it in 1682, symbolized light, speed, and a promise of progress into an optimistic future. Many though considered the comet a foreboding harbinger of destruction, which resulted in tales of hysteria and fear that the earth would be plunged into a hot mass of glowing gas as reported in the press. The ignorant and the superstitious

believed that the world would be set on fire, and their paranoia spread as fast as the comet tracked its course.

To quell their fears, New York reporter Mary Procter wrote:

There is absolutely no reason why any alarm should be felt on its account. Let us enjoy the approach of the comet as the experience of a lifetime, giving us practical illustration of the marvelous law of gravitation and spectacular display of cometary glory on a magnificent scale.

Enjoying this experience was a large group of buoyant, spirited seniors about to graduate from the University of California at Berkeley. The comet's coming coincided with their senior week preparations and the latter held just as much prominence and reason for high jinx as Edmund Halley's namesake. More importantly for students at Cal, May 14–May 18, 1910, coincided with the celebration of the university's Golden Jubilee. Pages of the university's news publication, *The Daily Californian*, had no mention of the comet, but were instead devoted to various events that not only included the usual annual rites of passage for seniors—dances, banquets, and the Degree Commencement—but also included the big buildup to a fantastic Jubilee Extravaganza, the sight of which must have been a jaw-dropping spectacle that eclipsed the comet as far as the participants were concerned.

"Week's Program Promises Spectacular and Impressive Entertainment" noted the headline from the *Californian Newspaper* with more than a hint that the event would not to be outshone by the comet. Its most notable highlight was a May 17 parade of 8,000 students and graduates, each adorned in thematic costume. Students from the schools of mining and engineering were dressed as miners and carried the tools of their trades; those in agriculture wore traditional farmer's attire and led domestic animals along the parade walk; the different stages of college life were depicted from "awkward freshman to wise senior." A dragon was created by the Chinese students and a throne was crafted by Hindu students. Students from prior classes showcased their college customs with the class of '07 reviving the pajama and ax rallies; the class of '04 recreating their customary circus parade; and '06 holding a carnival. In addition, the cast of the senior extravaganza wore their costumes as did participants of the past year's Greek plays. Four hundred women students, dressed in white tunics, carried olive branches and swung lanterns to light the way along the parade that started at 7:15 p.m. in front of South Hall, then wended its way through the campus and the surrounding neighborhood streets. When revelers reached California Field, a long line of men dressed in a rainbow of colored suits weaved "about a gigantic bonfire like fire worshippers." The preparations for the parade must have been monumental, and even more impressive was the fact that the parade was just one highlight of an entire week devoted to "gaiety and merriment."

Jubilee Week had opened with a concert by the New York Symphony orchestra; a Greek play, *Oedipus and the King,* was staged in the Greek Theater on May 14 and senior men and senior women held their respective farewell banquets on Saturday evening that same day. Lilian was praised as one of several women who were on the organizing committee for the women's banquet that was held in Hearst Hall and featured an eight-course dinner with such delights as oyster patties, consomme with crackers, roast chicken, tomato and shrimp salad, topped off with fancy cakes, ice cream, and coffee. She was congratulated for creating the winning design for the poster that advertized the senior extravaganza play *The Chasers* with a design that represented a

For the 1910 graduation extravaganza, Lilian played the role of a Dutch girl. *Author's collection*

college man being pursued by four women characters, French, Spanish, German and Chinese, for which she was awarded five dollars. Lilian was also singled out as being "prominent in the chorus" of the play staged in the Greek Theater on the evening of Monday, May 16. Dressed in traditional clothing with an apron, a white bonnet with winged corners, and wooden clogs, Lilian looked her part as a member of the cast portraying a Dutch girl. She posed for the paper with her counterpart Mildred Ahif flanking a photograph of the play's leading lady, Mildred Martin, and the accompanying article was published with the headline, "Clever College Women Will Help Celebrate Birthday of University." Tryouts had been held just a week earlier with Lilian being one of sixteen women selected for main parts out of many scores of "aspirants." The women "will trip the light fantastic toe" continued the news story, their dance being a feature of one of the acts of the play written by Nathaniel Schmulowitz, with original musical score by John Doane Hartigan, and stage direction by Frederick Carlyle. It was the last spectacular event before the more serious events of the graduating exercises.

That final week of university life for the energetic student of architecture must have outshone any reports of comet histeria that may have been reported elsewhere in the local news. For Lilian Jeannette Rice, Halley's comet passing through the western skies was merely tangential to the start of her own slow but steady meteoric rise in the ranks of that modern phenomenon, the career woman. The rise, however, would not be as smooth and as fast as what she hoped and dreamed for, a fact that she could not have predicted as she accepted her bachelor of letters degree on May 18, 1910.

4.
Postgraduate Life

*A*fter the jubilant graduation celebrations, Lilian would have gathered up her belongings from the boarding house on Hillegass Avenue, said tearful good-byes to fellow students and professors, and made arrangements to transport her trunk to the steamboat that would leisurely take her back to the South Bay area of San Diego. Whether there was a plan already in Lilian's agenda to return to Cal in the fall for a teaching course or whether this was something decided upon during the summer break, is impossible to say. But Lilian's chosen career path was that of a high school teacher of drawing and descriptive geometry, which today may be considered the lesser use of her talent, but in the early twentieth century, it was the appropriate road to follow for a young woman of society. Without any primary source documentation, it's not known exactly why Lilian opted to become a teacher after she was awarded her degree, and it is a mystery that is not likely to be solved. University transcripts show that Lilian received a bachelor of letters in social sciences with a major in architecture in 1910, followed by postgraduate studies in education. Lilian received her teaching certificate from Cal in 1911.

A newspaper report in the *San Diego Union* makes mention that Lilian was also one of a large group of graduates from the State Normal School in 1911, which suggests that she needed a separate credential to teach in San Diego County. And it was essential that Lilian returned to San Diego as there was urgent need for her to assist her mother, Laura, who was ill for several months. The National City papers published regular updates on her health reporting that Laura took several trips with Lilian into the desert regions to immerse herself in the therapeutic hot springs of San Jacinto and Warner Springs seeking relief from her rheumatic malady. It's interesting to speculate how Lilian's future may have played out had her mother not been ill at that exact period when family obligations over-ruled any possible plans that she may have had to work in Julia

In 1912, Lilian could be found driving a new Cole 30-40 open-top speedster. *Author's collection*

Morgan's office like her friend Grace. But fate brought Lilian back to her native National City and lost are the reasons why. Whether it was parental pressure that moved her in the direction of education, or the social conventions of the day—with the belief that women were more suited for a career in teaching—

Lilian would be spending the next twelve years as an instructor of mechanical drafting and drawing.

Despite Laura's chronic illness, the year 1910 appeared to be a prosperous one for the Rice family. Julius Rice had returned to the business of real estate and sold a half block of land on the south side of Seventh Street to a Mr. D. E. Lozier. And Lilian was able to return to university and complete her one-year course in art education. The following summer, the *National City News* reported on June 17, 1911:

Miss Lillian [*sic*] Rice has finished the necessary practice teaching and received her high school teaching diploma Thursday evening.

It is not wholly clear what happened next in Lilian's professional time line. However, from Lilian's sorority publication, *To Dragma*, there is a notable mention of her work. It states the following:

Lilian Rice '10 teaches mathematics in National City. She continues her work along artistic lines for her own enjoyment and has sent the girls of the chapter name cards and similar favors.

There was another mention in *To Dragma* that retold how Lilian had designed a home, "that was in the English Tudor style" for a client. Clearly,

Lilian was also keeping busy with her outside architectural design pursuits apart from teaching, but with an unfortunate lack of written documentation on these projects, we will never know their details.

While Mrs. Rice continued her recuperation, Lilian found distraction and social companionship with her large group of friends. A love of nature and a gregarious character meant Lilian could often be found spending weekends and holidays at a back-country retreat owned by her friends, the Boal family. Named Idler's Camp, the idyllic getaway in Ramona was a favorite spot for the Boals, which provided relief from daily life during an era when radio was not yet widely available and motor cars were just replacing the horse and wagon as the daily mode of transportation. One page, of what must have been an entire notebook of entries, has survived that retells Lilian's post university years. Like her scrapbooks carefully maintained while at school, Lilian continued this practice of documentation with her daily life while at home. Three fading sepia photographs have captured the twenty-two year old as a carefree, spirited young woman, with her skirt hitched up above her knees wading in a stream in the back woods of Ramona. "If Bryn Mawr could see her now," was her playful caption. These carefree excursions traversing unpaved, dusty roads into former Spanish land grant territory, would not only serve as inspiration for Lilian, but offer ample opportunity to practice her developing skill: driving.

During the first decade of the twentieth century, the automobile was already changing American life and more women were getting behind the steering wheel. In 1910, there were about 500,000 motor vehicles in the US and while women couldn't vote, they did have the right to drive; five percent of all drivers in the US were women and Lilian was one of them.

In volume 22 of the 1911 publication *Automobile Topics* an announcement was published by The Cole Motor Car Company of Indianapolis that its 1912 Cole 30 automobile would be improved and have a higher price tag and would be known as the Cole 30-40 due to its increase in engine horsepower and an aesthetic change that used an elegant Queen Anne style of body paneling and doors that was specifically designed to appeal to wealthy women. These changes were made after company owner

Mr. Joseph Jarrett Cole held what we know today as focus groups. He met with workers, carriage builders, and his friends and asked their opinion on his new design. They were "firmly convinced that Mr. Cole has arrived at what the aristocratic public will require." The new line would have nickel trimmings, all metal parts would be nickel-plated or black-enameled, giving the car a distinctive, dignified appearance. These classic vehicles manufactured for the Cole company in 1912, would elevate the prestige of their models to rival that of the comparable Cadillac®. It was successful, Cole became acclaimed for its high standards in quality and craftsmanship, and the Cole 30-40 had an $1,800 price tag to match its status.

Lilian is photographed in 1912 posing in her new, open-top Cole 30-40 roadster, with its two auxiliary seats and her pet bulldog riding shotgun. The car must have been special ordered as the factory color was navy blue and, even though this photograph on page 28 and 29 is monochrome, it appears that Lilian's car is white. Whether Lilian was aware of the technical specifications and recent upgrades to her new acquisition of automobile, is not known. But she no doubt considered the car very elegant and fitting for a young lady of her social standing.

It took some patience and time to discover the make and year of the car when I first saw this photographic image, which was taken outside Lilian's home in National City. My question initially even stumped some members of the Society of Automotive Historians, but eventually the answer came back via e-mail, ironically from Leroy Cole (no relation, he assured me), that correctly identified the car. Cole was a very popular upscale car competing in the Cadillac-Packard field, he wrote. Leroy sent me a photograph of the same model of car owned by Vera Michalena, a famed stage actress in early twentieth-century entertainment. The shot was taken during a wintry morning in Boston and she was captured placing her trunk in the rear luggage compartment behind the cylindrical gas tank. Miss Michalena looks every bit the stage celebrity, tall and elegant, and chic in her winter fur coat and impressive hat with ostrich feathers. She was clearly a lady of means.

Leroy added to the image:

Note the following similarities: hood line, fenders and doors are same shape; trunk is identical; round gas tank behind seat; bail handle cowl lights. Both cars are white, which was an unusual color. Running board brackets and the wheels and number of spokes are the same. Also note side the view of the radiator shows the emblem with a white center which can be seen on the emblem insert.

There was no question, this was the exact same make and model as Lilian's car. Leroy included in his e-mail to me a photograph of Barney Oldfield and Bob Burman, "the two greatest American automobile speed kings, first time photographed together in new 1912 Cole Speedster."

It was a classic image of a bygone age, two men, shoulder to shoulder, in an open-topped car in the chill of winter, enjoying that modern contraption, the motor car.

But I wondered why Lilian was driving such an expensive and relatively rare car. Mim Sellgren, my sole living link to the Rice family, suggested that perhaps it was a result of the friendship between Lilian's brother, Jack, and the speed marvel Barney Oldfield, who is reputed as being the first man to drive a car at sixty-miles-per-hour on an oval track. A fearless race car driver, Barney shattered numerous speed records during his racing career. The two men shared a keen interest in cars so perhaps there could be some truth to Mim's suggestion. Barney raced often in Indianapolis, so it is highly likely that he would have seen the new Cole cars rolling out of the Cole's facility. And from Leroy Cole's e-mail, we know that Barney was photographed driving a Cole 30-40 speedster with his friend Bob Burman. However, in 1912 it was a novelty to see a woman driving such a fine vehicle and it caught the eye of a reporter at the National City newspaper who wrote, "Miss Lillian [*sic*] Rice is driving a brand new Cole 30, it is the handsomeest [*sic*] car yet seen in National City."

By the year 1918, concerns for the world conflict cast a shadow over the entire country and Lilian did what any young, headstrong, single career-minded woman would have done in that era: she enlisted to

Lilian was drawn to nature; she is captured relaxed and carefree at Idler's Camp in Ramona, circa 1914. *Author's collection*

join the Naval Reserves. The University of California had announced courses in Marine Engineering and Naval Architecture on January 15, 1918, opening with twenty-one students enrolled. The students admitted were either graduates from, or seniors in "technical schools or colleges of recognized standing." To quote the *San Francisco Chronicle*:

> The work in Naval Architecture has been arranged in conformity with directions issued by the United States Civil Service Commission for ship draftsmen. The items included in this course relate to ship design and construction.

Members of the class were allowed to operate certain machinery of the Key Route Ferry system, thereby demonstrating the actual working of a completed design. The work was given under the direction of Professor David W. Dickie, lecturer in

Marine Engineering and Naval Architecture and was a short course of twelve weeks, designed by the United States Civil Service Commission at Washington. By September, Lilian had signed up to take this course, following the lead of her friend Grace Morin. "Three University of California Girls Busily Engaged at Unusual Tasks" reported the *Oakland Tribune*, April 7, 1918, as the course came open for women's enrollment. The "three attractive co-eds"—Beulah Woods, Jeanette Ralph Dyer, and Jennie Kramer—were learning to design battleships for the government as "their share toward helping the war." The women would visit shipbuilding plants to learn about the industry, along with the designing of boilers, a "supplementary feature of the work." The *Oakland Tribune* says that Miss Woods is quoted as saying:

> We will be ready for service if our government needs us and are only too anxious to do something toward winning the war.

When Grace and Lilian took the course in September, Jeanette Ralph Dyer had been promoted to instructor under David Dickie's leadership, and the two women were assigned to Mare Island Naval Shipyard. It's likely that Lilian echoed Beulah Wood's words, but unlike her fellow naval reserves before her, Lilian was not able to help the war effort for very long as the war was over within a few weeks of her passing the course.

But Lilian's postgraduate years continued to be full, professionally and socially. It was a carefree period when she had a very active social life with "the younger set of ladies" as the newspapers labeled them, the young adult children of San Diego high society. Lilian attended tea parties, was active in ladies social clubs, and as in her Berkeley days, was drawn to the stage. A member of the College Women's Club, and serving as its recording secretary, in October 1914, Lilian participated in a one-act farce, *Standing Room Only*, written by Miss Willowdean Chatterson and staged in the Wednesday Club on Ivy Lane in San Diego. Lilian was cast as Uncle William, an eccentric character who refused to take off his heavy coat and muffler "because of the detestable climate of California." The *San Diego Union* published photographs of the all-woman cast, with half of them taking male roles, along with the article that promoted the play. The women were graduates of Mills College, Stanford, and Berkeley, and three of them rowed at the ZLAC rowing club, where a year later Lilian again would find herself in a leadership role as she accepted the position of club president.

Opposite \ One surviving page, of what must have been several, from Lilian's journal, circa 1910. *Author's collection*

The Generalissimo, by name Morris,
started the cavalcade. Here we have
the commissary wagon about to take
its departure.

At the ruins of the Samuel
ranch house, we took
our morning on the
first day

No names being mentioned,
no offence can be "took"
but some of the party
went in wading around
the corner under the bridge.
If only Bryn Mawr could
see her now!

5.
ZLAC *Rowing Club*

I had arranged to meet with Mary Maddox Grandell at 10 a.m. in the grounds of the ZLAC rowing club, located down a side street in Pacific Beach, almost hidden among neat bayside homes and upscale condominiums. We had talked a few days earlier by phone when I'd learned that Mary's mother, Marian Boal Maddox, had rowed on Crew IV with Lilian Rice. I was eager to talk to Mary and I suggested that we meet in person, and she agreed.

Mary's sunny personality had shone through the line as we chatted by phone, and she seemed genuinely pleased to meet with me and facilitate my entry into the private clubhouse. When we met, it came as no surprise that my impression was accurate: Mary was a bright lady who giggled as she spoke. Tanned from years of San Diego sunshine, Mary, then in her seventies, was still rowing on the bay. I was introduced to the club manager, Polly, and they both gave me a private guided tour of the clubhouse. Not only did we look at the architecture—its interior and exterior—and the attractive grounds colored by hydrangea plantings, bird of paradise, and hibiscus, but we also explored the trophy room that was formerly the boat launch that had been remodeled along with the addition of a new boat house by Sim Bruce Richards in 1962. Mary pointed out one particular cup, handed it to me, and I read the long list of award-winning sportswomen inscribed into the silver Lilian J. Rice Trophy cup that was created to memorialize Lilian in 1939, the size of the lettering gradually getting smaller and smaller over the decades as the trophy cup had been passed on to the next year's recipient.

Above the brick fireplace, patinaed with decades of smoke residue, hung a portrait in oils of Commodore Lena Polhamous Crouse whose appearance resembled a military officer. Captured by artist Barbara Roy, Lena appears strong-jawed, straight-backed, and dressed like a naval captain, striking a formal and formidable pose with her characteristic no-nonsense glint in her eye. Lena was inarguably the guiding force behind the start of the club and, as I gazed at her portrait, it appeared that she was still keeping a watchful eye over her club members.

On the day that Mary and I met, the heavy blue sateen drapes were tied at the base and lifted a few feet up from the floor as the oak paneling had been recently varnished, a regular and necessary renovation due to surface damage done by the fine particles of sand tracked in from the bay. Together we rummaged through a heavy wood trunk that was brimming with yellowed newspaper clippings and flipped through the ZLAC's archived club records and crew logs that date back to the turn of the century. The club is the longest running women's sports club in the nation, and members are intensely proud of its history. We found what I was looking for: the actual dates that connected Lilian to the club. The record books showed that she joined Crew IV in 1910; two of her closest friends were her crew mates: Marian Boal and Helen Waterman. Lilian was elected as president in 1915, which would have been a rapid rise in the ranks, and was commodore the following year. I lifted some of the fragile newspaper broadsheets from the trunk and one dated Sunday, August 3, 1895, grabbed my attention.

The fragile newspaper published a lengthy article headlined by the "aquatic event of the season." This nautical event drew over a thousand onlookers when the population of San Diego was only 18,000 and was appropriately marked by a terrific bang from a naval gun—a salute by eighteen naval reserves. The occasion wasn't a formal military event but the civil

A whimsical treatment for the gates at the ZLAC
Rowing Club, restored from Lilian's original 1932
design. *Photo by PaulBodyPhoto.com*

launch of the ZLAC's eight-oared barge that was ceremoniously hauled onto the launch jetty and pushed off into San Diego Bay by refined society ladies who provided the muscle with style.

The *San Diego Union* newspaper recorded the event with a full-page article and a panoramic photograph that showed the wood-hulled rowing barge—designed by Fred Carter, architect and designer of the famous Herreschoff yachts—draped in the Stars and Stripes flag, flanked by eight women attired in ankle-length black skirts, black middy-blouses with their rank embroidered in yellow on the back, and black dinner-plate hats topping off their uniforms, which were edged in yellow. They were the first eight members of ZLAC Rowing Club's Crew I. Half of them the founding quartet whose initials served as the club's name: **Z**ulette Lamb, with sisters **L**ena, **A**gnes, and **C**aroline Polhamus.

The cool morning mist soon gave way to a sunlit afternoon on Saturday August 3, 1895, and by 5 p.m. it was a pristine San Diego day with a cloudless sky. The launch was a formal affair, attended by club supporters, reporters and photographers from the local daily papers, the City Guard band, and naval reserves. The launch took place at H Street—now Market Street—in downtown San Diego. The crowds of friends gathered on the launching float, the public packed the wharves, and ships floated in midstream with officers and guests at the rail and sailors in the rigging. The bay was spilling over with small craft, and everyone shouted and cheered and wished the crew good luck. Flags flew from the wharf and a variety of watercraft from other rowing clubs cheered on the ZLACs: the Nereids dressed in blue and white, the Water Babies in white, the Gondoliers in brown, and La Feluca sporting red and white, "all young women stout of arm and ruddy-cheeked ready to honor to the ZLAC," noted the *San Diego Union*. The crowds that witnessed the launch of the barge that day marveled at the local women who had labored so hard to fund the construction of the barge by raising money through garden parties and the sale of bonds from close friends and relatives. And there was no hint that the day's earlier panic had set in as the barge was not quite ready for its maiden voyage.

With just two days before the ceremonial launch, the finish of the boat was yet to be completed and, as the painters had agreed on an ill-timed strike, there was no hope that it would be ready in time. But these were unstoppable women of great determination, and with 500 invitations sent out, and expectations high, a strike would absolutely not interfere with their well-choreographed plans—a fact that would later inspire Lilian when she had to deal with striking truck drivers during a critical phase of construction of a project that she was supervising. Lena made sure that the launch would go on as arranged and gathered her crew together on the Thursday evening and told them to be ready the next morning at 6 a.m. and to "dress in your brother's worst work clothes" to report for varnishing duty. The girls spent all day Friday shellacking the boat's interior and the job was completed on schedule, all-be-it cutting it a bit fine. When the news leaked out that the women had taken matters into their own hands, during these early years they were known affectionately by their nickname, "The Shellacs."

At the turn of the century, women's rowing clubs and collegiate teams became very popular and the ZLACs were the epitome of these determined *fin de siècle* young women of society getting healthy outdoor exercise and creating a tight bond of camaraderie with their Victorian zeal. The ZLACs rowed around the wharves, would find a shaded spot to tie up, and Lena would read poems to them. One day the boat was crushed between a tug and a lighter, so they borrowed the butcher boat that belonged to Mr. Charles Hardy, who owned a meat packing factory nearby. The butcher boat needed four oarsmen, so Zulette was put at the stern. The women were so enamored with their rowing jaunts that they felt others would love it just as well and so they agreed to start a club naming it with the initials of each of their first names.

Lilian joined the club in the summer after she graduated from university. Two of the uncompromising conditions were that firstly, members had to be strong swimmers. Tests for strength and endurance were carried out in the calm waters of San Diego Bay. And secondly, members also had to be unmarried. Within five years of joining, Lilian, who remained single, unlike some of her crew members, was selected as president, which was a considerable rapid rising in the ranks. During these years, rowing was done from the ZLAC's first clubhouse. Built in 1902, the building was a variation on a Polynesian fishing hut

Caught in action, Lilian rowing with ZLAC Crew IV, circa 1910. *Author's collection*

to quote one article in the *San Diego Union* newspaper, written in 1986, that traced the history of the club. When the club was thirty years old, in 1922, it became clear that what Lena Crouse termed as its squatters' rights on San Diego Bay were fast running out and, as membership had grown considerably, the facility was no longer adequate for all the members. So the search for waterfront property was begun, and some four years later, the club settled on property in Mission Bay. "We intended to take all the time we needed to find a good place to live for the rest of our days," said Lena in an oral history when she recalled these early decades. But it would take several years of planning and fundraising to make the new clubhouse a reality.

In 1926, a down payment was made on the $5,000 bay-front property on Dawes Street in Pacific Beach and dredging began to rid the area of the muddy waters that constantly flooded the bay when the spring tides were high. Doubts were raised about these mud flats, that perhaps the purchase approved by the board of directors had been rash and ill-advised, and some of the club members worried that the land was unsuitable for building on. Even Lena aired her concerns and nearly cried when she saw the lots: "there was nothing but water...I stood at

the edge of the lake for a long time wondering how we ever got into such a tangle and whether or not the club could get its money back." But when Lena realized that the club had its own "honest-to-goodness, college-trained architect" in its membership and that the project would be wisely placed in her competent hands, Lilian was able to allay Lena's fears and the club breathed a collective sigh of relief.

Lilian's first task was to make improvements to the lot before construction could start. Her inspection of the property in early January 1930 led to the construction of a seawall, sited fifty feet beyond the club's property line. It took almost a year to get to the point where construction could be started, helped along by financial aid from Thomas Osborn Scripps, who lived next to his parents' estate, *Braemar*, located on the northwestern part of Mission Bay (now the site of the Catamaran Resort Hotel). With the seawall in place, a sandy beach was created that stretched from Crown Point to Dawes Street. The construction project was slow to start as its unfortunate timing coincided with the onset of the Great Depression and money was very hard to come by. Undaunted, members looked to creative ways to raise funds and organized well-attended spring garden parties at *Braemar* that

ZLAC Rowing Club exterior. *PaulBodyPhoto.com*

bolstered the funds during a five-year period from 1928–1933. The Scripps family name is immortalized in San Diego today as Scripps Hospital and Scripps Institution of Oceanography, both founded by Scripps family members.

The family agreed to help ZLAC members with their fundraising by opening up their grand estate *Braemar* to the public. Guided tours were given of its beautiful grounds and a festive family occasion was created with puppet shows for the children, dancing to a live orchestra for adults, and clubmembers selling homemade candies and handcrafted items throughout the grounds. The Scripps family ties to ZLAC were cemented when Sarah Emma Jessop Scripps became an honorary member of the club. After the completion of the clubhouse in 1932, as Kate Sessions gave her expertise to the club's landscaping, Sarah also contributed the design of a decorative garden on its north side that stands today as a reminder of the Scripps family generosity and connection to the club.

Another major fundraiser was the staging of the *Rackety Packety House*, a play adapted from the book of the same name by author Frances Hodgson Burnett. Members were able to rent the recently closed San Diego's Savoy Theater located at Third and C Streets. With a cast of twenty-three ZLAC members, and eight men, the ambitious production had three acts and was accompanied by a full orchestra. The official twelve-page souvenir program offered opportunities for sponsorship with thirty-six patrons donating funds and advertising in the program, further adding to the proceeds. The U.S. Grant Hotel,

El Cortez Hotel, J. Jessops and Sons, Miss K. O. Sessions Nursery, Frost Hardwood and Lumber Co., and many more were among those businesses featured in the program.

By 1931, the ZLAC Building Committee, a group of fifteen, had recommended Lilian as the project architect. A Monterey style of design was selected for its most "suitable, attractive, and economical type of construction" with considerations that a larger building could be added at a future date. Lilian drew up her plans immediately and was able to satisfactorily incorporate as many of the ideas suggested by the ladies on the various committees while working with a limited budget, which must have been quite a challenge. The plans were approved by the committee— thirteen to two, with Lena being one of the dissenters. She would later state, "Just why I wanted the boathouse on the other side I did not know. Something about the plans made me feel dissatisfied... [But] the beauty and charm of the clubhouse grew on us and we never have become tired of it."

On March 26 1932, the club's annual meeting gave the opportunity for Lilian to unveil the model of her proposed clubhouse. All ZLAC members readily accepted her ideas as presented.

Her plans were unanimously approved and ground was broken in May 1932 with the Diamond Construction Company hired as building contractors for the clubhouse, and the Campbell Machine Company in charge of the marine architecture. Lilian visited the site daily to check on the progress and the workmen were "gently persuaded to comply with her prudent wishes."

ZLAC Rowing Club interior. *PaulBodyPhoto.com*

Lilian chose an unpretentious board and batten exterior treatment of redwood rather than the stucco finish so prevalent in her buildings she designed in Rancho Santa Fe. The organic, mellow look was "part California bungalow, part New England saltbox" according to one local historian. The structure had a boathouse, a fireplace, a large kitchen, hall, and dressing rooms. Its single-wall construction had unfinished structural wood exposed to the interior that echoed architectural forms developed in the Pacific northwest and popular in Berkeley. The interior's design had a nautical feel, the style suggestive of a ship's hold with impressive counter balancing beams that crisscrossed over a pitched ceiling of the main lounge, also reflective of the arts and crafts ideology. The budget for the interior decor and furnishings was a slim $600, so club members improvised and repurposed items where they could. Two old settles—straight-backed wooden benches with storage under the seat—were stripped, stained, and polished to look like new and were placed on each side of the large bay-view windows, and a makeshift dining table was created by laying wood panels over saw-horses. Members donated items like mirrors, pottery, coffee tables, lamps, heaters, kitchen accessories, clocks, and more. Simple rattan furniture, a comfortable sofa, and light fixtures designed by artist Gilbert Rose—that gave little illumination with their die-cut seaweed motif—added to the comfortable ambiance of the lounge area. Kate O. Sessions, a close friend of Lilian's, was landscape architect. She collaborated with club member Georgie Hardy Wright for the design of the exterior plantings. Sessions' Pacific Beach nursery provided the club with shrubs and trees, which included several exotic tea-trees, native to Australia and New Zealand. A gate made from out-of-service oars led to an outdoor brick patio, shaded by a palo verde tree, with an oversized brick-built fireplace, flanked by twin nautical wind tunnels salvaged from the ferry boat *Ramona*, which was one of the San Diego-Coronado fleet of early ferry boats; on its retirement in 1929, its steering wheel was presented to ZLAC and used by Lilian as a decorative fixture in the window that capped the double doors of the boatlaunch. It now decorates the west wall of the Trophy Room.

In 1933, the club and boathouse was selected for an Honor Award by the San Diego Chapter of the AIA and the project was featured in *California Arts and Architecture* in August 1935. The full-page spread showed photographs of the exterior west elevation, the lounge, and the exterior patio. A brief paragraph included comments on the architectural style and Kate Sessions landscaping. It also stated:

> It is rumored that there is a man or two connected with the firm of Marston and Company who were the interior decorators. If that is true, it's a pity, for it would be pleasant to think of this club, with its redwood boards and bats, and its second-story siding done in white cold water paint... as never having been defiled by the hand of man. If anything can be found to criticize it probably is the work of some persistent masculine roughneck.

6.

Almira Steele

Lilian had plenty of strong women in her life who served as excellent role models. Her great-aunt Almira was one of them. As a member of the American Missionary Association, Almira harbored a passionate calling to aid those less fortunate than herself and, like so many women of the post-Civil War era, her inner fortitude caused her to act on this calling.

A metal plaque is the sole marker that gives a hint of Almira Steele's courageous work in Post-Reconstruction Chatanooga where she founded and built the county's first orphanage for black children on that very site. From 1884–1925, this petite, spiritual woman, with the backbone of a giant, met the needs of the area's impoverished, down-trodden, and neglected black children. She not only housed, dressed, nourished, and educated them, but she also paved the road for their future employment, and as such direct descendents of these rescued waifs are, today, pillars of their respective communities and continue the work begun by this pious powerhouse. Although she suffered persecution ranging from slander to fire, Almira endured and never once wavered from what she believed was her God-given duty. For over forty years 1,600 children were aided, educated, and sheltered directly by her guiding hand. But her road to salvation had not been an easy quest and was one fraught with cruel setbacks and racial hostility.

The New England native, a white woman, was born into a respected family in the rural village of Revere in Suffolk County, five miles east of Boston. It was pre-Civil War years and the area was one of tranquility when Almira was born to the prominent Christian family on July 23, 1842. Her father, a direct descendent of the founding Puritans—Benjamin Dewing—was president of the Boston, Lynn and Wampscott Railroad and a leader in his congregational parish. With his wife, Almira Sylvester Dewing, the two raised their daughter, with her five siblings, in a strict Christian tradition.

Almira was born into privileged financial affluence and her family did not want for any material necessity; consequently, all six children were well-educated. After the completion of her schooling, she became a teacher and was appointed principal of a local elementary school. It was then, as a mature woman of twenty-eight, that she met and married Walter, the older brother of Elizur and John Steele. His sudden death, three years later, must have been a tragic blow for Almira, being left to raise her infant daughter, Mira, by herself. But Walter's death also marked a spiritual awakening for the petite widow, with a straight back and a determined countenance who, at an early age, had embraced the Abolitionist Movement. And in 1880, she threw caution to the wind, resigned her position as principal, sold her home and Walter's store, and embarked upon what she believed was her life's calling: a ministry to black children in the South.

No schools for African-Americans had been established in Hampton County in South Carolina in the 1880s. Yet Almira Steele, undeterred by the prevailing sentiment of her time—as her white neighbors could not reconcile themselves to the fact that a white woman should live, whatever the purpose, among Negroes—she founded and helped to staff eleven schools in the county. Not even the threats and resulting arson of the local Ku Klux Klan could deter her in her mission.

The *New York Times*, twenty years later, wrote of Almira's remarkable "mission of mercy" as a member of the American Missionary Association. It was after founding these schools in Hampton County that Almira packed up her meager belongings and moved to Chattanooga, Tennessee, to continue with her calling. Her arrival came shortly after the

2A 95

THE STEELE HOME FOR NEEDY CHILDREN
1884 - 1925

In post - Reconstruction Chattanooga, no orphanage existed for black children. Almira S. Steele, a white teacher from Boston, met the need by founding the Steele Home for Needy Children on this site. Mrs. Steele suffered persecution ranging from slander to fire. However, her philanthropic mission endured. Over 1600 children were aided, educated, and sheltered. Many were saved from the streets and became productive citizens. The home closed shortly after the death of Almira Steele in 1925.

Almira Steele's Home for Needy Children was once built where a plaque has been placed to memorialize her work with African-American children in Chatanooga, Tennessee. *Author's collection*

yellow fever epidemic had decimated most of the town's adults leaving many of their children helpless and literally abandoned on the streets as orphans, innocent children whom others had failed to rescue due to the color of their skin. Almira witnessed "the penury, the squalor, the suffering the ignorance, and the misery that existed in the homes of many of the Negro inhabitants," published the *Times*. "The men of these homes were generally improvident vicious,

shiftless, and often criminal, the support usually depending upon the women who worked faithfully as houses girls, nurses, washer women, and cooks for the whites."

With funds saved from her late husband's estate and through the sale of his store, Almira was able to purchase a small tract of land in a secluded part of Chattanooga. In April 1884, she founded the Steele Home for Needy Colored Children; the

Almira's original building in 1885.
Author's collection

institution opened in Fort Wood's black section. Accounts report that the wood-frame house she built on that site was furnished plainly, but adequately. Almira employed two teachers to aid in the education of the older children. At the formal dedication, a large number of citizens, mainly white, participated in the ceremonies. But from that day forward Almira was left almost entirely to her own financial resources, except for meager contributions from a few white citizens who "appreciated her zeal and sympathized with her loneliness and lack of public support."

Not surprisingly, the home immediately fell into controversy. This white proprietor with her white child living and working among its black wards was unforgivable, many claimed. It was a scandalous act of defiance that challenged an era of growing racial segregation. Almira endured verbal and physical intimidation, hate letters, and threats on her life. The threats were not empty posturing, and within a year of that dedication, intolerant racist factions, members of the Ku Klux Klan, torched the home's wood-frame buildings. Almira, with her own child, seven aides, and fifty-four children narrowly escaped with their lives.

Undaunted, and with the act of hate merely serving to strengthen her resolve, Almira saw it as an opportunity rather than a setback. She had plans drawn up for a larger, state-of-the-art brick-built structure that measured 100 feet long and 60 feet wide and had it erected on the same site. The photographs in the *New York Times* show this impressive forty-four room, four-story Queen Anne Revival structure with upper dormers, a long covered porch, and large windows that would have flooded the interior with natural light.

The basement was divided into a laundry room alongside several storerooms that contained produce and groceries and walk-in closets where supplies of new and secondhand clothing and shoes were stored. The first floor had a large reception room for visitors, a study for Almira and her teaching staff, a dining room, the babies' nursery, and a spacious hall that was furnished as a classroom. The second floor served as the grammar school and contained a prayer meeting room, the third and fourth floors had bedrooms and bathrooms for the staff, dormitories for the younger children and separate rooms for the older boys and girls.

The *Times* showed images of the rescued children with before and after shots. The white-haired Almira posed centrally in the groups. The children, once attired in rags of calico, were later photographed as impeccably dressed young men in three-piece suits, and pretty women wearing ankle-length skirts with leg o'mutton sleeved silk blouses adorned with bows and buttons.

As a Congregationalist turned Seventh-day Adventist, Almira hired cooks to prepare a vegetarian diet for the wards and church services were held on both Saturday and Sunday. Most vital was that the home was also a school and offered, what the *Times* quoted Almira describing as, "A Christian education combined with industrial training." The older students were sent to local trade schools or colleges to learn the skills to become self-supporting adults. Those fortunate enough to be "turned out from the institution" became carpenters, tailors, cooks, teachers, clerks, and missionaries. Almira actively managed the Steele Home for forty-one years. Sadly, in 1925, it foundered and closed following her death.

I first came across Almira's name as I scoured the *National City News* microfilmed archives in the National City Library. It was a few brief lines of copy that caught my attention on page one of the September 26, 1914 paper. The two paragraphs were headlined "Mrs. Steele House Guest of Mrs. Rice." Almira had traveled west to California to inspect The Children's Home, a newly opened San Diego-based institution and one no doubt she approved of wholeheartedly. It was a San Diego building project to which Lilian had close ties.

7.

Hazel Waterman

For a woman over seventy-years old, the journey west to make that visit possible was no mean feat. Almira's journey from Chattanooga to San Diego would have taken several days, but God's work never stopped, and Almira likely took the train ride with her characteristic zeal. Like many of her affluent female peers, helping those less fortunate, as commanded through the teachings of the Christian religion, was a common endeavor, and Almira's work would have been held in the highest regard

with her opinion and advice being sought by others and acted upon.

The inspection of the complex of The Children's Home on that spring day in 1914 was led by Fannie Thelan, one of the first matriarchs of National City, one who had wisely captured its early history in a handwritten chronicle archived at National City Library. At that time, Fannie was the president of the Children's Home, which was housed in a complex of four buildings located in the southern end of

The entrance to Casa de Estudillo: how it looks today. Now a popular tourist attraction in Old Town, San Diego, CA. *Photo by Diane Y. Welch*

Balboa Park in San Diego. The main building then was considered old fashioned, designed and constructed by San Diego architect C. Trotsche, who had donated his services for the plans and superintendency of construction, which was completed in 1890. To reach the Children's Home the party took a picturesque uphill walk to the top of Sixteenth and Ash Streets. Trotsche's building was then home to thirty-eight girls ranging in age from five to fourteen. At the back of the grounds were gentle, grassy, rolling hills, peppered with eucalyptus trees and to the west a panoramic view of the Pacific Ocean. Later, as the orphanage grew, due largely to the successful dedication of a corps of female volunteers and beneficiaries, three new structures were added since that founding building was dedicated in 1890 and, later, in 1926, Hazel Wood Waterman designed and added a spacious Mediterranean structure that housed the orphanage administration offices.

Two years before this spring tour in 1914—that was topical enough to warrant a lengthy two-column article in the May 4 *San Diego Union* newspaper—a cottage for babies had been added to the complex. Hazel, its designer, is now considered the first female architect of Southern California, although she never received her architect's license. A photograph of the cottage for babies published in Sally Bullard Thornton's 1987 book, *Daring To Dream: The Life of Hazel Wood Waterman*, shows the wood-frame and stucco building with a flat roof line and a shallow parapet. Minimally ornamented, its symmetrical facade, with three steps to an open arched vestibule entry, is flanked by two cubed-shaped wings with large multi-pane fenestration that would have created a bright, natural-lit interior. The style was reflective of the Mission type that was popular in 1912, when the building was designed but was surprisingly modern in its silhouette and considered so at the time of its construction.

Lilian would become a close friend and business associate of Hazel's, and she was a dear friend to her daughter Helen. The two young women rowed together at the ZLAC Rowing Club on Crew IV. In the 1910s, Lilian was retained, part-time, as a draftswoman to draw up the plans for some of Hazel's San Diego projects that coincided with Lilian's teaching work at the National City High School. An interview recorded in 1971 with Hazel's son, Waldo D. Waterman, makes note that Lilian worked in the family home on Second Street on some of the drafting for Hazel's architectural commissions. The cottage for babies was one such project.

Hazel's story is one of resiliency and determination, and no doubt she inspired Lilian, then a recent graduate. During a difficult time of financial uncertainty, when Hazel was widowed at age thirty-eight with three children to bring up, she must have wrestled with the complex problem of raising them herself while providing income for the family to stay together, a dilemma that is relevant for many women today.

When Hazel married Waldo S. Waterman in 1889, she joined a prominent family. Waldo's father, Robert Whitney Waterman, served as governor of California from 1887 to 1891. The year before the governor's tenure, his father had purchased a gold mine near Julian in San Diego County. Waldo was hired to manage the mine and the newly wedded couple moved to a ranch home next to the mining operations in the heart of rugged mining country. At it's high point, the mine is reported to have yielded $5 million worth of gold. But complications from the construction of a nearby dam plunged the once-lucrative mining business into ruin. This was compounded by Waterman's sudden death from pneumonia just two months after his governorship ended in April 1891. With the failing economy during the bust of the 1890s, Waldo struggled to get by as the Waterman estate was close to bankruptcy. Looking for opportunity Hazel and Waldo, with their three young children, moved to San Diego in 1893 living in rented accommodations. With their roller-coaster life of feast or famine, at one time the family was evicted for non-payment of rent, a shame that must have cut to the core for the family. However, when a venture to develop the harbor in San Diego Bay finally presented itself—and with it much needed steady income—Waldo was able to purchase land on Second Street between Hawthorn and Albatross in downtown San Diego where it was hoped that the family could finally settle into a more secure future.

With renewed optimism, the couple hired a renowned San Diego architect, Irving Gill, then partner in Hebbard and Gill, to design their family home. Known as The Granite Cottage, for the materials utilized in its construction, the project was an opportunity for Hazel to be a hands-on collaborator.

Casa de Estudillo in 1893 before Hazel Waterman's restoration. *Courtesy Molly McClain*

Her natural abilities in the fine arts paired with her innate sense of design gave Hazel the necessary skill to sketch out specific details of aspects of the home's design and, in so doing, impressed Gill who suggested that if she ever needed to work, she should consider architecture. That advice would prove to be prophetic when Waldo died unexpectedly in 1903.

At age thirty-nine, Hazel had to find an occupation that could provide sufficient income for the household and her young children. She followed Gill's advice and learned drafting skills through a correspondence course, an endeavor that was not unusual for the day. On completion of this course, Hazel was employed as a draftswoman in the Hebbard and Gill firm and was given a supervisory role in directing the design and construction of the Alice Lee House in San Diego. Hazel worked closely with Alice, and her close companion Katherine Teats, on various aspects of the designs. The experience gained on the project brought more work for Hazel, including a major commission that was to prove to become her magnum opus: the Casa de Estudillo.

A popular tourist attraction located on the southeast side of the plaza in Old Town San Diego

State Historic Park, the *casa* was decayed through years of neglect and decades of the tendencies of visitors to chip away chunks of the mud structure to take away as souvenirs, as well as the then-unscrupulous caretaker selling pieces for a profit. Seeing the site's tourist potential, sugar heir and local investor John D. Spreckels bought the melting adobe casa for $500 in 1906. Two years later his vice president and manager, William Clayton, hired Hazel to research and restore the historic ruin.

The site had erroneously gained regional fame due to its claim of being the marriage place of Ramona, the fictional heroine in the novel of the same name written by Helen Hunt Jackson in 1884. Her melodramatic story, set against the political backdrop of the fading Spanish Don era and the decimation of the culture of the Native Americans, follows the love match of Ramona, a half-Indian orphan born out of wedlock, with her beloved Alessandro, a full-blood Indian. Helen created several of her characters based on real people and when the two lovers eloped to marry in San Diego, she modeled the presiding priest, Father Gaspara, on Old Town's Father Ubach. Helen died in 1885, never revealing the actual place of inspiration where the marriage took place, but in 1887, a front page article of the *San Diego Union* declared the Estudillo home to be "Ramona's Marriage Place"; this was despite the fact that Jackson had never even visited the house. Visitors flocked to the building believing it was the actual location of Ramona's marriage and when graffiti, left by a tourist who had scratched the name *Alessandro* in one of the walls was made public, the myth was cemented.

By the standards of the day, Hazel had all the qualifications to undertake the restoration commission. Through Gill's support, she had an impressive mentor, then and today, Gill is considered one of San Diego's forward thinking master architects who forged the path toward what would later become the modernist movement. Hazel was an accomplished painter and had published works on adobe structures and had, according to Gill, an innate grasp of design. She also had a vision about Southern California's early Hispanic heritage and was passionate about preserving and remembering its past.

Hazel did her homework. She gathered information about adobe structures from primary sources and pored over old photographs, interviewed old timers, and spoke to promoters of the state's Spanish colonial heritage. Locally, she visited the Guajome Ranch, Rancho Santa Margarita (now on the site of Camp Pendleton), and Rancho Penasquitos and traveled to Santa Barbara and Whittier to see firsthand the De La Guerra Mansion and Pico House, respectively. Despite the appalling derelict state of the former glory seat of the Estudillo family who had moved out in 1887, Hazel, where possible, retained the original materials and built on its footprint of a one-story, U-shaped adobe with a central passageway with rooms that open onto an enclosed courtyard.

In her restoration she pioneered the use of bygone building methods and materials by employing Mexican workmen who knew how to make tiles and adobes using the traditional primitive methods. They knew how to notch the crossbeams, round the rafters, and insulate the rooflines with tule thatch. Hazel also developed innovative methods to give new timbers the aged and weathered appearance of antiquity, having them soaked in water and mud from San Diego Bay, then fixed in place with rawhide thongs rather than with nails.

Not only would Hazel's meticulous work on Casa de Estudillo later inspire and inform Lilian's own restoration project, when she was hired in 1925 by developer Alfred Barlow to make habitable the wreck of what is currently named the Silvas/Osuna Adobe in Rancho Santa Fe, it would also help launch one of California's first historic tourist attractions, albeit one that was romanticized and, when Spreckels gave promoter Tommy Getz free rein to manage it, shamelessly based on fiction, not fact. For many, visitors to the site "Ramona's Marriage Place" came to embody the romance that they imagined had existed in the "Days of the Dons." In the process, though, it helped inspire a nascent fanaticism for the state's Spanish heritage, one where myth and history collided. And an estimated 125,000 people visited the Casa de Estudillo in 1915, the same year that the Panama-California Exposition opened in Balboa Park.

8.
Panama-California Exposition
A Most Wonderful Achievement

*I*t was a beautiful afternoon, on Wednesday July 19, 1911, when the official groundbreaking took place for San Diego's Panama-California Exposition. President William Taft pressed a key in the East Room of the White House, which turned on the electric current that unfurled the US flag at the Balboa Park. The ceremony attracted 20,000 people who had gathered to witness the historic event. A tremendous unified cheer rang out as the flag flapped in the gentle breeze. Taft's representative, John Barrett, director general of the Pan American Union, addressed the audience and read an official letter from the president. With the ceremonial laying of the cornerstone of the first building, the exposition was declared official. The *Des Moines Leader* later quoted him as stating: "Every American should see the San Diego Exposition. Architecturally it is the most wonderful achievement I have ever seen."

That Wednesday morning, a spectacular military Mass took place in the park, with a replica of the altar of the Franciscan Church in Mexico City temporarily created for the occasion. On Thursday, there was a historical pageant with 800 people and ten floats, depicting the march of time. On Friday, commerce was the theme with fifty floats depicting manufacturing and local industry. That evening, the beauty queen of the carnival, Queen Ramona—Miss Helene Richards of San Diego—was crowned at a grand reception at the U. S. Grant Hotel and for three hours had a steady throng of visitors around her throne, according to one report. The climax of the four days of festivities was a mission parade—that alone cost $10,000 to create. Replicas of the state's twenty-one missions were paraded on floats and more than a thousand characters participated. This was the first time in 200 years that the world had seen anything of this kind, another news report

boasted. And for a city that had only 40,000 residents then, it was a feat of wonder and amazement.

When the Panama Canal opened, it greatly reduced the journey for ships that no longer had to navigate the waters around South America's Cape Horn. It created a reason to celebrate, especially for West Coast ports that would benefit financially from increased tourism and freight haulage. In the north of California, San Francisco, with its strategic bayside port, was selected to host the nation's official world's fair: The Panama-Pacific Exposition, in historic recognition of the canal's opening. But civic leaders in the Chamber of Commerce, from its Southern California counterpart of San Diego, not to be outdone by San Francisco, were also intent on showcasing their region's possibilities. With the assured opportunity for widespread media attention, chamber members voted to support the funding for the Panama-California Exposition.

On July 9, 1909, G. Aubrey Davidson, president of the San Diego Chamber of Commerce, urged his fellow chamber members to help create an exposition that would put the city in the national spotlight and bolster its lagging economy. Members authorized him to appoint a committee to look into his idea. Because of his initial suggestion, Aubrey Davidson has gone down in history as "the father of the exposition."

Within two months, a committee was formed with Ulysses S. Grant Jr. elected president and John D. Spreckels as first vice president. Grant, the son of the former US president, co-owned the U.S. Grant Hotel. Spreckels owned San Diego real estate, hotels, newspapers, banks, and other commercial ventures,

An illustration of Bertram Goodhue's California Buildings for the 1915 Panama-California Exposition. *Author's collection*

including a local electric-run railway. Both had a vested interest in drawing tourism dollars to the area and both poured their own money into the project. Lilian's brother was married to Grant's daughter, Miriam, so it's probable that the Rice family had inside knowledge of the plans for the exposition, which may have been the source of animated family conversation. Perhaps their commentary became even more animated on hearing news of Grant's unexpected resignation on November 22, 1911, just four months after the exposition's elaborate groundbreaking ceremonies had taken place which had spanned a whole four days.

The fair officially opened at midnight on New Year's Eve, December 1914. President Woodrow Wilson echoed Taft's actions and ceremoniously pushed a button in Washington, DC, while simultaneously 3,000 miles away, in San Diego, the power was activated in the park. The electric charge illuminated a dramatic arc of light, which covered an area of three miles in the sky, signaling news that the Panama-California Exposition had been officially opened. From the planning to the grand opening and every step along the way, newspapers throughout California reported widely of the exposition's success. One article described how an important party of assemblymen from Sacramento were en route to visit the exposition in early April. The trip was a direct result of a speech made by Assemblyman Grant Conard to his colleagues in which he outlined the chief points and beauties of the exposition.

I ask you, gentlemen, to accept this invitation to visit this great Exposition of California...I want you to see the buildings, this magic city of old Spain that has been erected here on the shores of the Harbor of the Sun; I want you to see the California State building and the great exhibits of archaeology and ethnology, which we are going to donate to California. I want you to see the Science of Man building. We want you to see the California building; we want you to partake of the hospitality of the people of San Diego. San Diego and the Pan-American Exposition invites the state of California through her representatives to come and see what she has accomplished. Gentlemen...I ask you to accept this invitation.

The delegation was moved by Grant Conard's speech, reported in the *San Diego Union* newspaper. They did accept the invitation to visit, along with a staggering half-a-million people in those first three months who must have marveled at the impressive architecture and the extensive landscaping that earned it the moniker "Garden Fair." Decorated with over two million plants, of 1,200 different types, the park was a glorious horticultural spectacle. The exposition proved a huge success and attracted worldwide visitors, government officials, and prominent civic leaders. Franklin D. Roosevelt, then assistant secretary of the Navy—with G. Aubrey Davidson and Mayor Charles F. O'Neall as his passengers—was the first to drive across the elegant seven-arched Cabrillo Bridge, which was completed on April 12, 1914. Former president William Howard Taft was a visitor as was President Theodore Roosevelt who brought his wife, Edith. In July 1915, their attendance attracted media coverage in a short, silent film and Roosevelt took the opportunity to address San Diegans at the Spreckels Organ Pavilion, where he made a public request that San Diego keep the exhibition buildings permanently, though in the original design much of the architecture was temporary.

The park had taken five-and-a-half years to come to completion, since Aubrey Davidson shared his idea in July 1909. Even before work could start on its design, a suitable location was essential. San Diego's City Park—open space set aside in 1868 by San Diego civic leaders—was the obvious choice. The natural parklands, sited 300 feet from sea-level, were then 1,400 acres of scrub-filled mesa that today overlook downtown San Diego. The sparse park was beautified largely due to the efforts of Kate Sessions, who was a close friend to the Rice family and actively followed Lilian's career in the field of architecture and would later collaborate with Lilian on some of her landscaping projects. In 1892, Kate planted a hundred trees and donated shrubs and decorative plantings for the park in exchange for a thirty-two acre parcel within its boundaries to be used for her nursery. Some of those plants included birds of paradise and poinsettias, which transformed the once-dull vegetation into a blaze of color. Today, Kate Sessions is known as the Mother of Balboa Park because of her efforts, and some of the original trees she planted still stand.

Ten years before the exposition opened, park commissioners announced plans to rename the park. Its prior name of City Park seemed too prosaic and not fitting for a prestigious statewide fair. After months of discussion, with members of the public chiming in, the name of Balboa Park was chosen in honor of Vasco Nunez de Balboa, who was the first European in the New World to see the Pacific Ocean. With the new name in place, plans soon got underway to design the fair complex. January 1911, the Chamber of Commerce's Building and Grounds Committee engaged Frank P. Allen Jr. of Seattle as director of works and landscape architects John C. Olmsted and Frederick Law Olmsted Jr. of Brookline, Massachusetts, were invited to lay out the exposition grounds.

The committee asked John Galen Howard to serve as lead supervisory architect. But with his time still devoted to the building of the campus for the University of California at Berkeley and working as head of the architectural department, he declined. Likely he had neither the time nor the inclination to devote to a project of this magnitude after the rigor of building the University of California campus. Instead, New York City architect Bertram Grosvenor Goodhue was chosen as lead architect of the park's prominent buildings. He had applied for the position at the prompting of the Olmsted brothers and would be assisted by San Diego architect Irving Gill. And so the architectural team was complete.

Original plans called for Indian, Mission, and Pueblo styles of architecture, in contrast to the formal

West Gate to Panama-California Exposition showing Tower and Dome of California Building.

An illustration of Bertram Goodhue's California Buildings for the 1915 Panama-California Exposition seen from the Cabrillo Bridge. *Author's collection*

Kate Sessions, known as the Mother of Balboa Park for hundreds of trees that she planted there. *Author's collection*

neoclassical styles regularly used at international expositions. However, Goodhue's familiarity with Spanish baroque relegated the simpler vernacular styles of the American southwest to second place. Initially, there was uncertainty and conflict with regard to the design styles considered suitable for the exposition. As a result of marked differences in philosophy, the Olmsted brothers offered their resignation, followed swiftly by Irving Gill. The three felt strongly, like Lilian did, that buildings should harmonize with the environment rather than overpower it. But Goodhue was intoxicated by the more elaborate Spanish-colonial architecture and formal Muslim gardens that he had seen firsthand during his trips to Mexico and Persia. In his replacement of Gill and the Olmsteds, Goodhue was aided by Carleton M. Winslow, Clarence Stein, and Frank Allen Jr., a dynamic team that created a romantic city within the acres of Balboa Park. Bertram personally designed the permanent California Quadrangle and sketched the Home Economy and Southern California Countries Buildings. He supplied his team with drawings and photographs of buildings in Mexico and Spain, and reviewed their designs for the temporary buildings. Palatial in scope, the buildings contained reminiscences of Mexican, Spanish, and Italian palaces, yet drew inspiration from missions and churches in Southern California and Mexico. Goodhue incorporated dramatic churrigueresque and plateresque design embellishments in his creation of the centerpiece California Building. It served as a focal point with its brightly tiled dome and dramatic tower in a classic Spanish-Renaissance style that contributed greatly to the region's Spanish myth.

However, the exposition's theme also highlighted the diversity of the culture, commerce and arts of the region and recognized the southwest's native origins. The Atchison, Topeka and Santa Fe Railroad Company showcased the scenic wonders of California and the southwest by their exhibit of an Indian Village and the Painted Desert on a five-acre mesa at the northern end of the exposition. These buildings resembled Taos and Zuni pueblos of New Mexico. The railroad made no secret that its aim was to entice potential future passengers to points along their rail route from east to west, through the exotic Southwestern regions of New Mexico and Arizona. Mary Colter, a lady architect who was a contemporary of Lilian's, was commissioned to design the Painted Desert, the railroad's exhibit that was a replica of an Indian village. She prepared a wax model, which was later recast in plaster, that was sent to San Diego the year before the exposition opened. It was placed on display in the window of the Santa Fe offices in the U. S. Grant Hotel in downtown San Diego, with copies sent to other Santa Fe offices across the nation. It would be interesting to know if Lilian personally had connections with Mary Colter, but she would most certainly have known of her, as Lilian would have attended the exposition—likely more than once—and seen Mary's work for herself. While the aftermath of the exposition ushered in a new regional identity for Southern California's built environment, with the newly created style of Spanish colonial revival—favored by many of the local architects—Lilian preferred to design her own version of what she thought represented Southern California. Like Mary Colter, her work conveyed an understated simplicity. And in this way she was more in step with a style that would develop after World War II: modernism, and as such, she was clearly ahead of her time. The style was one of contradiction. Ironically, Lilian's modern approach took its inspiration from antiquated rustic adobes. But it was an approach that would bring her to the attention of a major railroad corporation and would divert her career path from high school teacher to licensed architect.

PART II

The Professional Years

9.
A Soulless Corporation

When I first drove along Linea del Cielo, a narrow, winding two-lane road that meanders its way into the heart of Rancho Santa Fe, just four miles inland from Solana Beach where I live, the journey was memorable. The roadside was flanked by eucalyptus trees, bougainvillea, tropical palms, and bamboo: a colorful expanse of exotic horticultural plantings. Glimpses of red-tiled rooftops and white stucco chimneys gave hints of the architecture that was almost lost behind high hedges. And, as I drove, I wondered about the people who had the means to live in such a beautiful, private community. Little did I know then that I would be doing this same drive repeatedly for over a decade, and each time it would be as lovely as the first.

Rancho Santa Fe was purposefully planned to be this lovely. In 1922, when the community development was first conceived in the minds of railroad executive W. E. Hodges and San Diego land developer Colonel Ed Fletcher, it is doubtful that they could have truly envisioned the sheer enormity of the future conspicuous wealth that represents Rancho Santa Fe in the twenty-first century. However, it was then, and remains today, a beautiful and exclusive, restricted enclave.

Lilian would be spending the last sixteen years of her working life consumed by Rancho Santa Fe. With its wealthy, discerning residents, its ambitious realtors and its residential workforce, she was the hub in the orchestrated machine that made it all happen. It was the blank canvas for her artistic expression, but it also became her home and her community. Planning its development from a defunct working ranch, to an impressive new state-of-the-art community steeped in the lore of its past—designed to attract wealthy retirees and movie stars—the project was an opportunity of a lifetime, and most would say poetically was the jewel in Lilian's crown.

The road from the coast that pushes eastward into Rancho Santa Fe is dominated by trees—thousands of them. I soon discovered that the recent history of the Ranch in fact has its roots in trees. English walnuts, citrus, but mostly eucalyptus trees. Their seemingly fragile trunks with peeling bark defy their true robust nature. Leaves of blue green, silver green, gray green, and every verdant shade in between, the Australian eucalypti, were brought to the Americas by well-intentioned horticulturists, and in Rancho Santa Fe's case, by a commissioned Scottish railroad employee, Edwin Ogilvie Faulkner. Over three million seedlings planted with purpose, transformed into three million trees, bark to bough, crammed into the two square leagues forming an aromatic forest, appearing for all intents and purposes less like an agricultural experiment for creating inexpensive railroad ties, and more like the backdrop for a slice of paradise. Walter Edward Hodges, the vice president of the Atchison, Topeka and Santa Fe Railway Company (ATSF) had chosen this remote, idyllic California location, twenty-five miles north of San Diego, with an eye for future development. Spending part of the year in Chicago, and part in his newly acquired Ranch, he would have found solitude in the natural beauty of these remote environs and doubtless would have been formulating a plan in his mind how best to capitalize on this beauty.

When the West had opened up to rapid development, and California had emerged as the thirty-first state in the Union on June 10, 1850, spawned by the Gold Rush of 1849, the railroad companies had turned their attention to the land. Quick to seize the potential for increased passenger and freight loads, and diversifying to make even more profit, they joined the ranks of real estate developers. With Edward Payson Ripley in the railroad president's seat in 1895, following the reorganization of the

A eucalyptus-lined road leading into Rancho Santa Fe, CA. *Author's collection*

ATSF Railway, Hodges became his right-hand man. Between them, the decision to purchase the former Spanish land grant was solidified. In 1906, using their newly formed subsidiary, the Santa Fe Land Improvement Company (SFLIC), with the sole purpose to buy, subdivide, and sell land, Hodges, as president of the subsidiary company, took ownership of what was once Don Juan Maria Osuna's Rancho. An idyllic 8,000-plus acres of frostless land, two square leagues of spectacular coastal rolling Rancho, it had immeasurable potential and the dollar signs must have dazzled. A plan to develop it was no doubt building in Hodges' imagination. But first, the history of this land grant needed to be studied and understood, then romanticized and retold as part of a cleverly conceived advertizing campaign.

Lee Shippey, a *Los Angeles Times* contributor, wrote an article in 1923 that retold the roots of what became Rancho Santa Fe and in an opinioned essay waxed lyrically about "The Old Spanish Estate." He made a reference that the newly developed Ranch, a park-like region, would be preserved as a "shrine to California's historic past" a place that "teemed with an association of princely days when the old dons lived in California in almost feudal splendor." More surprising, wrote Shippey, was that this idealistic undertaking was being carried out "by a soulless corporation," the Atchison Topeka Santa Fe Railroad Company.

Despite the florid language, the article does give an accurate overview of the Mission-era history of the former Spanish Land Grant once owned by Don Juan Maria Osuna. By 1830, times were changing in California and the Spanish missions were undergoing secularization. The civic-minded Don Juan Maria Osuna became the administrator for the San Diego Mission, a justice of the peace, and was elected to the public office of alcalde, San Diego's first mayor. Voted into office in 1834, he was the town's first elected official. The King of Spain was rewarding former loyalists with generous grants of land as a way of both populating the region and working the farmlands. These ranches provided much-needed beef and hides from their free-roaming cattle, wool and mutton from their sheep, and grains as well as fruit and vegetables from their land, and also the source of much-needed transportation: horses. In 1836, Osuna took possession of Rancho San Dieguito, one of the largest tracts of land in San Diego County to be transferred to one person.

The 4,000 hectares of land granted to Osuna had the San Dieguito River running through it, fertile land for crops and cattle grazing, and was just four miles from the coast to its west and guarded by mountains to its east. The old military road from San Diego to Los Angeles passed through that land and the Ranch played an important part in the war with Mexico.

Much has been recorded in historic journals, newspaper accounts like Shippey's, and books about this romantic era of the Spanish Dons, and the newly landed gentry of Alta California, who by the turn of the century became the stuff of legends. Helen Hunt Jackson's 1884 book *Ramona*, described as the first novel about Southern California, it inspired a myth that has indelibly marked the California landscape, and one that is evident today.

Similarly, the Osuna story weaves a tale of mythic dimensions, with a plot that incorporates intrigue, gambling, poisoning, treachery, and ultimately, suicide, according to San Diego folklore. By the time Juan Maria Osuna died, in 1847, much of his 8,824.71 land-grant acres had passed out of his family. An article appearing in a local newspaper, published in 1959, cited an account by Ramon Osuna, Juan Maria Osuna's surviving great-grandson, that explained how Osuna lost his possessions, in part, to the lure of gambling. Ramon Osuna recalled that his great-grandfather had been known to trudge home after a night of gambling, with his saddle weighing heavy on his shoulder, having lost his horse in a wager. This weakness paired with a love of horses often resulted in losses for Osuna. Wagering on horse racing at a nearby track would not only render him horseless, but often left him cash poor.

Leaving his two adobe homes and what was left of his dwindling estate to his son, Leandro, Juan Osuna ultimately sealed the fate of his family's assets. Described in news accounts as a hot-headed, bad-tempered individual, the egotistical Leandro was despised by the American Indians who were practically slaves to the Spanish land-grant owners and to the padres who built the mission system on the backs of Native Indian labor. A local myth retells

that natives allegedly tried to poison Leandro with a deadly cocktail of ground human bones blended with cactus pulp and juice. The mix worked its magic as he took his own life rather than suffer the possible slow death that the perpetrators promised would surely follow. Whether the ingredients were poisonous is doubtful, but the mere suggestion that Leandro had consumed the deadly brew, coupled with his emotionally volatile temperament, had the desired effect, and Leandro shot himself in the heart. Thus, dramatically, the Osuna chapter was essentially over for Rancho San Dieguito and, as heavy mortgages on the family assets depleted their fortune still further, and with little land left, they were forced to move away. Juliana Osuna, Don Juan Maria Osuna's widow, and her daughter Felipa were the last Osuna family members to remain in what must have been an idyllic setting. It surely was paradise lost when the remnants of the Osuna family sold their holdings to George N. Gilbert and James E. and Marie L. Connell, as title to the land was transferred following Leandro's death. At the same time that Lilian Rice settled into her freshman year at the University of California, a new chapter was about to be written in the annals of the once-thriving Rancho. And within twelve years, the Osuna Ranch and Lilian Rice would become very closely acquainted.

On October 22, 1906, the Santa Fe Land Improvement Company, filed their title deed for the purchase of the Ranch, having secured the sale for $100,000, owning all but the 374 acres within the original boundaries of the Spanish land grant. Named for the winding river that runs through it, Hodges had plans for this newly made purchase. A man with a sharp attention to detail, he had a no-nonsense approach to business and an edge that had enabled him to climb the railroad corporate ladder to stardom in what people casually called "the Santa Fe." Hodges was clearly a shrewd businessman. Outwardly polite, Hodges had a duplicitous nature that was reflected in his appearance. Gaunt in the face, yet strong jawed; powerful, yet slight of frame; white, thinning hair, but sporting a full moustache, Hodges' aging exterior belied his inner force. Not surprisingly, he did not suffer fools gladly and preferred to be in control.

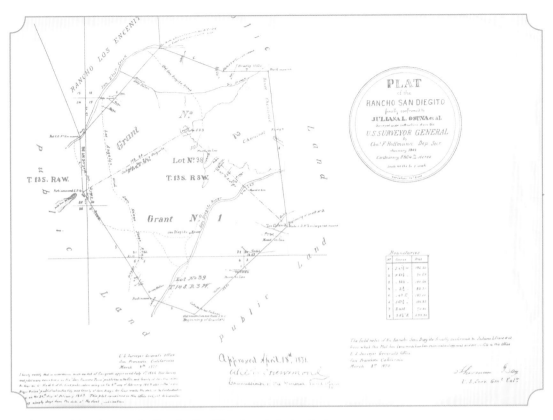

A copy of the plat map for Rancho San Dieguito. *Author's collection*

Hodges' initial use for the Ranch land has subsequently been the subject of much speculation. For some, the use of the land became the brunt of jokes and sniggering asides. It was assumed that Hodges led a team of entrepreneurs too inept to figure out how to grow suitable lumber for railroad ties. The much publicized story retells that Hodges acquired Rancho San Dieguito in order to stage a bold experiment, an undertaking inspired by the reforestation program, initiated to secure the future of the nation's forests, a project created by Gifford Pinochet, head of the US Forest Service during the presidency of Theodore Roosevelt. Under the guise of this program, Hodges opted to plant trees on his two-square leagues. The trees would be grown to maturity and would then be fashioned into suitable cross ties to facilitate the railroad's expansion. The eucalyptus tree-planting project began with over twelve varieties of seedlings brought back from Australia by Faulkner. Whether Hodges' intentions were to help reforest the land or whether he covertly had a less environmental purpose in mind, we shall never know.

Despite Faulkner's efforts and his thorough scientific process to study the wood of the eucalyptus for the necessary attributes for railroad ties, mother nature interfered with his plan to plant 700 acres over a ten-year period for a total of 7,000 acres dedicated to this massive undertaking. But seven long years of continual drought had left the trees starved for water and resulted in lack of growth, with a width that was insufficient for their conversion into railroad ties. Evidently, no one told Faulkner that "it never rains in Southern California."

As the land languished, local developer Colonel Ed Fletcher appeared to save the day. An imposing figure of influence, broad shouldered and straight backed, standing over six-foot-two, he was a self-made man. At the age of sixteen, Fletcher had come to San Diego from Littleton, Massachusetts. In 1888, with only five dollars in his pocket, he first scraped a living by selling fruit and vegetables to customers in remote regions of San Diego's back country. Equipped with only a bike for transportation, Fletcher would navigate the boulder-strewn hilly terrain, often carrying his bike across creeks and rocks when the way became unnavigable for its rigid frame. These humble beginnings led to Fletcher's ultimate financial success. He earned the use of the title "Colonel" when, in 1907, he was appointed lieutenant colonel of the National Guard and, in 1934, he was elected to the California State Senate. He was a much-respected local figure and a major player in the development of San Diego. Today, he is memorialized there with street names like Fletcher Parkway, the community of Fletcher Hills, and Fletcher Cove, a coastal inlet in Solana Beach.

In business correspondence between Walter Hodges and Ed Fletcher, the latter, who was acting as his sales agent during the early development of the Ranch lands, evidence of Hodges' business acuity is presented. Hodges was more than willing to allow Fletcher the privilege of clearing some of the land of many of the now-defunct eucalyptus trees, white elephants that had become a nuisance, shedding their bark, dropping their leaves, and with no redeeming features, other than their languid beauty and pungent fragrance. The land company purchased a caterpillar tractor for Fletcher's use and consequently thousands of acres were cleared. The eucalyptus once so painstakingly transported from a continent that must have seemed a world apart, then planted scientifically in perfect formation, were unceremoniously ripped apart limb from limb. Like a freshly shorn head, large sweeps of the land were laid bare for the next phase of the Ranch's history.

With Fletcher as manager, this newly trans-formed acreage was leased to local farmers, most of them Japanese, who grew beets, tomatoes, beans, and grain. Wells had been bored, ditches dug, and irrigation implemented, and a pumping plant, "the largest in the county" had been constructed. In all, Fletcher had spent about three years overseeing the Ranch, making improvements and bringing in val-uable rents. The company also profited from a percentage of the takings from the sale of harvested goods. Undoubtedly, the Ranch was a potential gold mine, but despite Fletcher's optimistic ploy, Hodges was not willing to allow Fletcher to purchase the Ranch and make a profit by selling the land himself.

In response to one of Fletcher's letters, Hodges wrote on company letterhead, June 1, 1915, the following strongly stated objection:

> It does not appeal to me...to give you the option that you request. It is one thing to give an option to a probable purchaser it is quite another thing to give it to you, which would be in effect simply giving you the exclusive agency for sale. This latter I am not prepared to do...

By 1921, the value of the Ranch land was estimated at $450,000—a massive amount of money by today's standards, and a more than a four-fold return on the SFLIC's initial investment in 1906, when the Ranch was originally purchased. And so it was decided that the Ranch would be developed into a restricted master-planned community—the finest ever conceived. It would be fit for the most discerning of customers, fit for Hollywood's elite, the newly rising superstars in the West. And while Fletcher was granted a contract to act as agent in selling the subdivided homesites, he had no part in the control of the development of the community.

To make the dream of a high-class community a reality, sufficient water would first have to be pumped in. Without irrigation, due to the arid coastal desert climate, large acres devoted to citrus and avocados would be a futile exercise. By 1918, the ATSF Railway had paid for, and built, a dam at the site of the Carroll reservoir, which was then owned by William G. Henshaw, who also had the riparian rights of the surrounding acreage, but who ultimately agreed to sell out to the railroad company. At a cost of $2,000,000 the multiple arch dam was constructed and, although initially known as Carroll Dam, it was later renamed Hodges Dam, a politically correct nod to Walter E. Hodges.

A holding company was formed, the San Dieguito Mutual Water Company, with Fletcher as president of the board, and, subsequently, local water districts were organized. A flume was constructed that brought the water down from Lake Hodges into the nearby coastal communities. Trenches were dug, pipes were installed, and an infrastructure began to take shape that would provide the necessary foundation for the community development.

Commencement of construction of Santa Fe Park - San Dieguito Ranch 8800 Acres on June 7 1922.
ED FLETCHER COMPANY AGENT.

1922. Ed Fletcher, center, with his team captured during the official commencement of construction of Santa Fe Park, now known as Rancho Santa Fe. *Author's collection*

And so with this activity the landscape began to change: once a cattle ranch, then agrarian, and now a construction zone. The metamorphosis created a buzz of frenzied activity. A team of top-rated supervisory specialists were hired to facilitate the transformation. Joseph Barlow Lippincott was named chief engineer. He appointed Kenneth Q. Volk as his on-site resident engineer. U. L. Voris was chosen as the horticultural contractor, Robert McKenna and W. D. McFadden directed and installed the water pipes, and Ralph E. Badger was hired as orchard manager. The SFLIC chose the prickly Leone Sinnard as the project manager of the development. He would become the lead player for the orchestrated efforts of all involved and a celestial force in the railroad's newfound universe. One writer said that he had "the wand of a genius" to create this "seemingly perfect project" and he was not far from the truth as Leone worked his magic to get the job underway.

It was Leone who singled out the San Diego-based firm of Requa and Jackson as architectural designers. Requa's prior work in Ojai in 1919 had caught his eye. Designing in the Spanish revival style, Requa's work fit the railroad's paradigm of re-creating the romance of Alta California's storied past. During those early years of the 1920s, however, Richard Requa was too busy to supervise construction himself and coinciding with the start of the project, his business partner and engineer Herbert Jackson was sick and had been hospitalized. It is also probable that the offered compensation of six percent was too low a commission to support Requa's city office and warrant the hour and a half trip each way from his office in downtown San Diego. For these reasons, Lilian, at the time a respected and most capable female associate in Requa's busy office, was given control of the initial design and supervised the construction of the community center, the first phase of the Ranch's development.

The year was 1922, and Lilian was at the point in life as a thirty-three year-old woman—mature, unattached, free spirited—when she was more than ready for a challenge. Richard Requa, no doubt knew this. Displaying a mildness of manner, yet possessing the essential qualities for a lead architect, Lilian could professionally direct and supervise the teams of workers who would support the architectural development and bring into reality her designs. No doubt her prior experience in the Mare Island Shipping yards in San Francisco in 1918 would serve her well working with teams of men.

Already underway were the grading of the roads and the laying of the water pipes. Massive trenches had been sliced deep into the landscape. Surveyor's spikes and lengths of string forming the division of blocks, crisscrossed the terrain like a patchwork-quilt design. Teams of mules pulled wooden sleds, smoothing out the dusty land, arid from the heat of the California climate and the distinct lack of water. Rain had been sparse these last few years. Soon, like a carefully orchestrated collective, teams of workers, many of them Mexican, scoured the landscape. The aroma of the spicy Mexican fare drifting from the commissary tent would have signaled a welcome respite for the manual workforce as mealtime rolled around. Laboring over adobe bricks, and tile and lumber, the Ranch bustled with work crews and their equipment. The task was monumental.

10.
Leone George Sinnard

*T*his monumental task was placed under the management of a man perfectly suited for the challenge: Leone Sinnard. His many talents would be tested and the variety of his undertakings do seem unreasonable for one man to carry out, but clearly Leone steadfastly faced the demands. He designed the roads and the conceptual layout of the community civic center; he conducted scientific analysis of the soils for optimum plantings; he was engaged in the sales of estate lots, and created the marketing and promotional literature for these lots; and not the least, served as the manager of the guest house, which was the first structure to be completed in the civic center. No wonder he was a tad testy. Accounts paint Sinnard as an irascible individual, quick to temper, and hard to get along with. A slender man with an impeccably erect back, he appears as the picture of perfection in his neatly pressed suit, white shirt, and tie, and with a meticulously trimmed moustache that bridges a mouth that does not smile, at least not for photographs. When I delved into Sinnard's background, I uncovered a fiercely independent individual who, heeding the cry of "Go west young man," followed in the tracks of many migrants who journeyed to the Golden State in the second half of the nineteenth century to start a new life and to reinvent themselves.

An Indiana native, Leone George Sinnard was one of four children: three boys and a girl. Born in 1869 to John and Georgiana Sinnard, he was the youngest boy and must have felt the burden of contributing to the family coffers from an early age, as census records show that when he was only ten years old he was working as a cash boy in a local store. His family background indicates upheaval and possible emotional trauma. A news report from 1866, published in the *Crawfordsville Weekly Review*, gave notice of the tragic drowning of Leone's then-four-

year-old brother, who had crawled into a cistern behind the large family home. The effect on Georgiana must have been devastating, as shortly after Leone's birth she moved with her remaining three children from Indiana to Ohio, without the father, an herbalist and homeopathic physician who, despite the apparent estrangement from his wife and children had significant social standing in Crawsfordsville.

With her ties severed from the eminent Doctor Sinnard, life must have been full of hardship and struggle for the single mother who alone raised her two boys and a daughter. By the time Leone had turned sixteen, the family was residing in Olympia in Washington Territory, and he had landed a plum job as secretary to the then-Governor Watson Carvosso Squire. Perhaps it was family connections that created the opportunity for young Leone, maybe Squire was taken with the teenager's mature and meticulous work ethic, or perhaps it was his knowledge and talent—we will likely never know. In 1886, Leone was paid five dollars per day for his work as secretary, a princely sum worth $125 a day in today's money, and the family's situation must have improved significantly.

In his adult years, another notable characteristic of Leone's was his tendency to remarry. The *Oakland Tribune* published brief details of Leone's divorce from Lottie, his first wife, when by 1898, the two had parted ways. The report alleged the cause for divorce was Leone's "desertion, failure to provide," and "galling matrimonial chains." It was during this period that Leone had traveled south to Oakland, where he and Lottie starred at the acclaimed MacDonough Theatre. His wife, a concert pianist and vocalist, and Leone, a violinist of some acclaim, the couple were often featured in the entertainment columns of the local paper for their virtuoso performances. They also gave private concerts at garden parties and church events, but evidently the common bond of music was not enough to prevent a marital rift. As the new century began, the Sinnard family had moved to Paso Robles in San Luis Obispo County, possibly to escape the grief following the death of Leone's younger sister, Grace, who had passed away from tuberculosis in 1898, coinciding with Leone's new career in the passenger department of the Southern Pacific Railroad, based in San Francisco. His new position would lead him into the company of a sultry raven-haired beauty, Hazel Henderson, who shared Leone's love of the violin, and who played it equally as well.

Not long after the two met, their engagement announcement made the *San Francisco Chronicle* newspaper, as did the wedding affair, a year later. Hazel was a young woman of social standing and also the daughter of Leone's boss. At the time Leone had risen in the ranks of the railroad company and held a position as a promoter for the Colonization Department and was in charge of the western region's publicity and marketing; his articles were often published in the *Sunset Magazine* and depicted travels westward on the railroad in a romantic light. However, the same could not be said about his marital partnership. A published photograph of Hazel doesn't depict the blissful fiancé that we would expect to find, rather she appears dull with a sullen expression. Perhaps it foreshadowed the inevitable rift between the two, as Hazel filed for a divorce within six years of their wedding day. For Leone, that meant not only the loss of a wife, but also the loss of his job.

Leone remained single until he met Ruth Craig, a stenographer from Oakland, who was twenty-two years his junior. The two married in Yolo County in 1918. This marriage was also doomed and lasted less than five years, and when Leone was given a promising career break in San Diego County, the long distance relationship proved to be fatal to the union. His estranged wife told the *Oakland Tribune* reporters that Leone was "sulky and morose" and refused to take her to any "amusements or have anything to do with her friends."

By all accounts, Leone was not a good husband, fathered no children, and from evidence published in California-based newspapers, he appears to have been constantly reinventing himself. Aside from being a former promoter of the MacDonough Theatre,

Leone George Sinnard, project manager for Rancho Santa Fe, CA, circa 1924. *Author's collection*

(a place that Lilian visited often when she was at university), and one of its stars, his potpourri of professions included real estate agent, land developer, marketer, promoter, irrigation (hydrologist), and agronomist (soils expert). Often highlighted in the society columns of the local papers, we get a hint at Leone's chameleon lifestyle. The same year that he married Hazel Henderson, he was secretary for the then newly formed National Irrigation Committee, a national association of water experts that advised on the proper use of water irrigation and dam construction, especially for arid regions like Arizona and Nevada. Leone wrote and distributed informational pamphlets from his office in the Flood Building in San Francisco, and attended newsworthy inspections of newly built dams with senators and public officials. Within two years, he was in charge of "an immense colonization scheme embracing one million acres of Mexico lands for John Hays Hammond and his associates." Apparently impressed by his achievement, the *San Luis Obispo Daily Telegram* added: "[he] is drawing a salary of $8,000 a year (over $200,000 in today's dollars) and is a hard worker and deserving of success."

It's unknown how Leone perfected all of these talents, but it is a common trait for the era in which he came of age. There were ample opportunities for men of above average intelligence to learn new trades and to put the knowledge to practical use. While the papers are eager to report of the opportunities afforded people of note, there is little or nothing to answer the question: Then what happened? There are no academic or university records of Leone ever going to higher education to learn about the complexity of soil analysis, for example, and why he apparently changed tack so often in his career, but it is possible that his passion for soil analysis was fueled and honed by his association with Edwin Wickson, who headed the agricultural department of the University of California in the late 1800s.

It was shortly after his divorce from Hazel that Leone became an expert agronomist, perhaps severing ties with the railroad company meant that Leone had no choice but to reinvent himself. In 1913, we find him collaborating with Wickson on a project in San Luis Obispo County, California, when the two men joined a team of dedicated followers of Edward C. Lewis, an innovator famed during his day for the creation of a master-planned city in St. Louis: University City. Not only did Lewis conceive the idea and oversee the development of this city, he also included in its master plan one of the largest printing operations in the world with a press that in just three hours spat out one million copies of his own publication: the *Women's National Weekly Magazine*. Lewis planned to make his city of Atascadero in San Luis Obispo County the

headquarters for his publishing business, to expand his national reach and influence. Millions of dollars and thousands of people would be involved, he told reporters: "Only experts in their respective lines will be hired…this will be the most beautiful city in the world. We will build a little paradise." One of these experts was Leone Sinnard.

Lewis's $800,000 purchase of 20,000 acres of former California Spanish land grant from J. H. Henry was big news in San Luis Obispo County. His intent was to re-create a master-planned community in Central California on the same scale as his University City in St. Louis. The fact that this "spectacular operator" to quote the *San Luis Obispo Telegram*, had been mired in litigation with that project, did not seem to dampen the enthusiasm for his "latest great coup." He was described in the local news as "a small man of diminutive stature but with mammoth ideas and aspirations." The man with the boyish face and an infectious smile was also famed for his bold motto:

Why think small when you can think big? It is just as easy and much better to launch a tremendous enterprise involving millions of dollars than it is to waste time and worry over a small affair.

In February 1913, soil tests were started by Leone, who was by then a single man and free to enlist in Lewis's mastermind of a project without the encumbrances of a spouse. He joined an elite team known as the Communities Foundation. Wickson was placed in charge of agriculture and horticulture, H. T. Cory was the project engineer, Walter D. Bliss was the lead architect, G. H. Hudson was in charge of irrigation and general superintendency, and Leone was the soils expert. A month later, Leone Sinnard was struck with a debilitating illness and was rushed to a San Francisco hospital for an emergency appendectomy. A serious condition by itself, it was complicated by peritonitis caused by infection following the rupture and Leone was confined to his bed for several months. But his infirmity did not halt the project's progress. The soils he had analyzed proved suitable for the initial plantings, which were stands of roses that lined the carefully planned walkable streets of the colony, and dense groves of citrus and avocado orchards.

Leone George Sinnard, far right, with irrigation officials, circa 1912. *Author's collection*

Atascadero was troubled with false starts and financial hurdles, but ultimately the colony attracted enough funding from public bonds to become a viable community, with families living in a tent city before they moved into more permanent dwellings that were built in 1915. Thousands of acres of orchards were planted, a water system was installed, and construction began on an eighteen-mile road that ran through the rugged Santa Lucia Mountains to Morro Bay. The first civic building housed the Printery, which had the first rotogravure presses west of Chicago. Lewis published the *Atascadero News* publication and the *Illustrated Review*, a photo-news magazine. The centerpiece of his community was an impressive Italian Renaissance-style building that housed the colony administration offices. Completed by 1918 with bricks made from local clay, this unique structure, The Rotunda Building—inspired by the 1904 World's Fair in St. Louis—is one of the few buildings that have survived from the colony and today it is recognized as a California Historical Landmark.

Initially, sales of individual lots were slow and the anticipated 50,000 people that Lewis hoped to attract to the colony fell short by about 45,000. Plagued by jealous enemies who were intent on bringing him down—a major disgruntled foe being the postmaster general—Lewis was tried and accused of mail fraud through his banking-by-mail scheme, which vexed the US Government Post Office. Further reports retold how some were more concerned with Lewis's support of women's suffrage, which would lead to them getting the vote and having too much power. Ahead of his time, he was a vocal male advocate for women's rights—he and his wife were viewed as heroes by women suffragettes. Lewis founded the American Women's League in 1908 to promote educational, cultural, and business opportunities for women and created a plan for a network of institutions and businesses to serve them. By 1910, there were approximately 100,000 members and, a year later, the league was renamed the American Women's Republic with a mission to prepare women for an expanded role in government. Sure enough, women did get the vote in 1920, but within four years, Lewis was forced into involuntary receivership in December 1924. Despite his charisma and his grandiose plans, he was not a businessman. Lewis's Utopian dream was just that: a dream.

Lilian Rice would have no doubt approved of Lewis's support for women—she herself represented the modern woman of her era: she was well-educated, motivated, and fiercely independent. By 1924, as Lewis filed for bankruptcy, Lilian Rice was a rising star as the supervising resident architect for the newly planned community of Rancho Santa Fe in San Diego County. As Leone Sinnard had been hired too as project manager to oversee this Southern California version of paradise 500 miles to the south of Atascadero, he no doubt would have been greatly influenced by the Central California colony. Except with the funding that did not rely on East Coast investors and local bonds, coming instead directly from the deep pockets of the Atchison, Topeka and Santa Fe Railroad Company, his success was assured.

On June 11, 1922, the *San Diego Union* reported of the "Great Development Project" in San Diego County on former Spanish land-grant acreage between inland Escondido and coastal Del Mar. The Santa Fe railroad had set aside half a million dollars for the project and Vice President Walter E. Hodges ceremoniously "piloted the big tractor" that started the road work on Wednesday, June 7, as ground was broken, marking the development of almost 9,000 acres of land. The reporter had interviewed noted local developer Colonel Ed Fletcher on the Saturday before. Fletcher said that he was "seeing a dream come true."

Fletcher was instrumental in securing the riparian rights for the Santa Fe Railroad through his association with Mr. Henshaw, who at the time not only owned the rights to the Carroll Lake, but also to segments of the San Dieguito River, which ran through four miles of the Ranch lands. The railroad agreed to finance the dam development, which supported the irrigation of 20,000 acres of virgin, frostless land. About half a million dollars was devoted to financing the project development and within days of the groundbreaking, Leone began his task of designing the fifty miles of winding roads and the prime estate tracts, which ranged from twenty- to forty-acre lots. He had already supplied a comprehensive soil analysis of the tract and shown

that the land was perfectly suited for citrus, avocado, and walnut groves.

The *San Diego Union* paper noted that Professor Wickson of the University of California had recommended Leone Sinnard to Walter Hodges and, as the two had worked together on the Atascadero Colony, the professor was well-apprised of Leone's ability. Joseph Barlow Lippencott was retained by the railroad company to direct the irrigation system that made the entire project feasible; Leone and Lippencott had served together on the National Irrigation Committee. So these men of might and high importance, who knew each other well, teamed together to begin what would become known as Rancho Santa Fe, a community that today is one of the wealthiest zip codes in the nation and that was born from humble beginnings as a cattle ranch on a former Spanish land grant. How surprising then that a woman should be the supervisory architect who served as the general contractor and architectural designer of the lion's share of the fledgling community's civic buildings and residences.

In 1922, the *San Diego Union* reported the breaking news about the Ranch development on the front pages of the June 11 Sunday edition. Not then officially named, the article made note that local architect W. H. Wheeler was already drawing plans for the guest house, the first building to be designed and constructed in the new community's civic center, which was to be started within six weeks of the story running.

> This is the largest project that has ever been developed at one time in Southern California under one ownership...

boasted the reporter whose byline was not included in the article. Perhaps the writer got his facts wrong, or maybe his source was unreliable, but a report published a few weeks later shows that it was Richard Requa and Herbert Jackson who were chosen as the architectural firm for the project. Likely Leone was feeling the responsibilities of all the aspects of the project that were laid on his slim shoulders, and tensions must have been felt during this initial phase of planning, engineering and the creation of the infrastructure on which to build the dream community. We'll never know if Leone kept his cool under this stress, but when I read letters held in Ed Fletcher's archived collection at UCSD's Mandeville Library, there was a hint that the two men didn't exactly see eye to eye and that there was evidently discord between them. Fletcher wrote a note to Walter Hodges with a formal complaint that Leone had rented a typewriter—for the purposes of writing promotional literature—without the boss's permission and had used company funds to pay for it. Hodges wrote back that the typewriter must be returned.

Lilian perhaps was the calming, unflappable influence for Leone that Richard Requa could not be, or did not want to be, or perhaps being a woman she was more likely to defer to his demands. This kind of intimate detail will never be known as no written documentation between the two exists. Despite Leone's dictatorial management style, it appears that someone appreciated his talent and didn't begrudge him well-earned accolades. A promotional pamphlet titled *The Endless Miracle* published around 1927 gushed romantically about the Ranch, which was born from "brave old days of happiness and contentment, of peace and plenty." The copy was provided by John Steven McGroarty famed throughout the state for his Mission Play and his book, *California: It's History and Romance*. McGroarty praises Walter Hodges, who "inspired to weave imperishably into the fabric of his beloved railway the romance and the beauty of this historic region." He also gives credit to Hodges for finding Leone:

> A man of incalculable potentialities…who knew for many years in his heart and soul as a devotee knows his prayers, the endless miracle of California. Sinnard laid before Mr. Hodges and his associates of the Santa Fe the inspiration concerning the abandoned Rancho of old Don Maria Osuna, waiting in its splendid solitude for the footsteps of the dreamer. For like Theodore Judah who dreamed his first railway across the high Sierras, Sinnard had his own dream tucked away in a sunny corner of his soul.

McGroarty dedicates the pamphlet: "To L. G. Sinnard whose inspired vision, high ideals, and unfailing courage conceived and builded Rancho Santa Fe this book is dedicated."

The pamphlet has no publication date, but contains sepia photographs of the civic center, estates, and residences, orchards, La Morada Hotel, the restored original Osuna adobe hacienda, and the Joers/Ketchum store and apartment building completed in 1926. It is interesting then that McGroarty refers in his written essay to the Osuna adobe as a ruin; it strongly suggests that he wasn't actually at the site of Rancho Santa Fe, as in 1925 Lilian had restored the adobe. Perhaps McGroarty had given Leone such glowing acknowledgment of his accomplishments as by March 1927, he was gravely ill and was confined in the hospital as a result of his ailment. Because of his infirmity, Leone retired from the Rancho Santa Fe project and, after his recovery, purchased his own ranch: Zanja Rancho, in Mentone in Riverside County, California. But within five years, the *Riverside Chronicle* published notice of his death in February 1932; with no children from his three marriages, Leone George Sinnard faded into a forgotten past.

11.
Richard Requa

As the civic center of Rancho Santa Fe was taking shape, Richard Requa's attention was turned toward the development of Kensington Heights, a subdivision of the City of San Diego some twenty-five miles to the south, one of San Diego's first suburbs. Located on the southern rim of Mission Valley, which was former mission land, the subdivision was created in 1910 by G. Aubrey Davidson, who named the sixty-six acres Kensington Park. Like Rancho Santa Fe, the purchase of land in Kensington Park came with deed restrictions. Only single-family homes could be built; apartments, duplexes, and hotels were not allowed; and ownership was restricted to whites.

A booming economy in the 1920s meant that the sale of smaller lots on which to build more modest-sized homes was a practical approach. Davidson's acreage was further split into five subdivisions with Kensington Heights being the first to establish architectural design restrictions like those in Rancho Santa Fe. The developer, Davis-Baker—a Pasadena-based company—hired Richard Requa to join its design committee to create a neighborhood that reflected the newly created aesthetic of "Southern California Style." Richard had traveled overseas and had seen firsthand the architecture of countries with climates that mirrored that of San Diego County. This knowledge of the colonial Spanish style informed his work in San Diego, as it did Lilian's.

In an effort to promote sales of lots, the Davis-Baker Company devised a promotional competition for readers of the *San Diego Union* newspaper to submit design ideas for a single-family home that would be built in Kensington Heights. Announced in the home section of the paper, the contest attracted about 400 entries, and each week the anticipation of the winning design was ramped up as some of the entry ideas—sketched-out floor plans that showed

the room arrangements and interior and exterior details—were published. In one such article published on March 14, 1926, Requa included an illustration of how he visualized the completed home would appear next to a photograph of himself poring over design entries with a caption that read that he had "found many laudable designs in the mail." The winner would receive $100 for first place, which in today's money represents about $1,500.

The home was to be built for a Mr. George T. Forbes, who requested a Spanish-type design and offered the prize money. Ostensibly he was unable to select a set of plans that met his satisfaction, and when he suggested the contest, "The *Union* gladly cooperated" offering to receive and submit the designs to an architectural committee. Why members of the committee could not have created their own plans that met the approval of Mr. Forbes must have seemed a mystery to the *Union* readers. The house was limited to having six rooms or less and represented a modest residence with charm and an economy of design, but "no expense [should] be spared in making it an ideal dwelling well-suited to its fine setting of Kensington Heights," Forbes instructed. A week later, the winning plan was announced with Mrs. Margaret Fickeisen as the winner and architect Lloyd Ruocco in second place (although the contest was intended for the lay person).

On March 28, a *San Diego Union* feature story was published with the headline, "Woman Who Draws Plans for Fun Finds She Has Home Idea That Pays." It was enhanced with photographs of Richard Davis and Harrison Baker of the Davis-Baker company along with their sales manager Alfred T. Herrick, subdivision owner George Forbes, Richard Requa, and the winning contestants. "I just went out to Kensington Heights and looked at that beautiful lot where the model Southern California

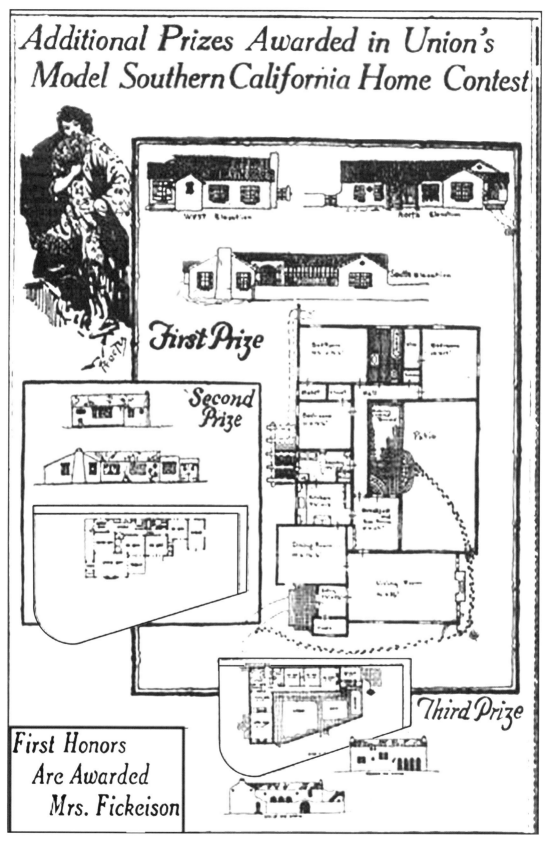

Additional Prizes Awarded in Union's Model Southern California Home Contest

First Prize

Second Prize

Third Prize

First Honors Are Awarded Mrs. Fickeison

The results of the contest for a home design in Kensington Heights, 1926. *Author's collection*

home is to be built," said Mrs. Margaret Fickeisen to the reporter.

> I knew that it would require a perfect home for that exquisite setting—and I did my best. I drew the plans of just such a home as I or any other woman would love to have, one that would be appropriate to southern California and particularly to that part of it overlooking Mission Valley and the home of the Mission fathers. The judges were good enough to tell me that my plans were the best and, needless to say, I am delighted with the honor of having formed the plans for this gem of a home.

Requa was quoted as saying: "The young woman certainly showed a fine conception of what is required for the ideal southern California type of home. And she has a splendid grasp of the possibilities of the Kensington Heights location."

The contest was deemed a great success and certainly brought attention to the new subdivision, with increased interest in Kensington Heights and subsequent sales. But there was one major issue that came out later and was quietly brushed under the proverbial carpet. Mrs. Fickeisen had not created that design; Richard Requa had. The contest was a publicity stunt and a sham.

In the 1930s, Richard Requa was a prominent member of the local chapter of the American Institute of Architects and a visible and involved citizen in San Diego County. He was a regular contributor to the *San Diego Union* newspaper for approximately ten years during the 1920s and '30s writing lengthy and informative articles on architecture, mostly lauding his design concepts that promoted the Southern California style that used wood frame with concrete stucco, which also benefited his sponsor, the Portland Monolith Cement Company.

Richard had learned his craft of architectural design from other notable San Diego architects through the time honored tradition of apprenticeship. The son of Edward H. and Sarah J. Requa, he was born at Rock Island, Illinois, on March 27, 1881, his father, a merchant at Rock Island. Four years

later, the family moved to Norfolk, Nebraska, where Richard grew up with his five siblings. The family relocated to San Diego when Requa was nineteen. Trained as an electrical engineer in Nebraska, he continued in that line of work in California and, in 1902, was teaching night classes in electricity for the San Diego YMCA, as noted in an *Evening Tribune* article published September 19 of that year. Within five years, he became associated with famed architect Irving J. Gill—lauded as an early pioneer of the modernist movement—and learned the craft of architectural design with Gill as his mentor. It was a good year for Richard. On the morning of February 21, 1907, he married his sweetheart Viola Hust. At the time he was working for the Kirby Realty Company, which must have been part-time work that he engaged in while learning his craft with Gill. Viola and Richard Requa were a handsome, popular couple and very involved in social and civic affairs in San Diego, their names appearing weekly in the society pages of the local press.

By 1912, Requa had opened his own architectural office and one of his early commissions was an apartment complex in La Jolla designed for George A. Bane and B. B. Harlan. "It is the largest and said to be the best equipped building of its kind in La Jolla," noted the writer in the March 1913 article in the *San Diego Union*, providing commentary on the project's many innovations. With all the luxurious conveniences of a modern hotel, it still conveyed the privacy and simplicity of a home. With steam heat, electric lights, telephone service, and running hot and cold water, it was a marvel of modernity and designed aesthetically with sun porches that afforded views to the Pacific Ocean.

Richard Requa partnered with Frank Mead as commissions steadily grew. One major undertaking for the team was the Chapin apartment complex located at Sixth and Maple in San Diego. In December, when the designs were drawn up for Mrs. Cornelia Chapin, the permit cost was $50,000, but by the following March, San Diego building department issued an additional permit for a total of $60,000. The wealthy New York lady desiring a winter home commissioned the architectural firm to design and build a three-story apartment complex that overlooked Balboa Park. There were eight apartments per floor with an "elaborate tea garden occupying the roof" with Mrs. Chapin taking possession of the ground-floor apartment with its Maple Street entry. Later they would be known as the "Palomar Apartments." Like Richard Requa's La Jolla apartment complex, there was every modern convenience, including an automatic electric elevator, an electric central vacuum cleaning plant, and steam heat.

The exterior design was of Spanish type with Moorish elements. There were balconies and white stuccoed arches around an interior sunken-pool garden modeled after the Alhambra palace in Granada, Spain. Mead had visited there a few months earlier and reportedly measured the palace perimeter and gardens, then used the exact specifications for this project. Arched corridors decorated with richly colored tiles, manufactured at the National City China Clay Products Company, added a colorful accent to the Moorish-style interior courtyard. It was lauded as being "one of the finest specimens of Moorish Architecture on the Pacific Coast if not the entire country." Of historic note is that world-famous aviator Charles Lindbergh was a resident there in 1927, living in unit number 201 while he waited for his plane, *The Spirit of St. Louis,* to be built by nearby Ryan Aeronautical Co., and Wallis Simpson, the American divorcé for whom Edward VIII of England abdicated, lived in unit number 104.

Requa's reputation would steadily rise after he and Mead, in 1913, undertook the rebuilding of the town of Ojai in Ventura County, which primarily consisted of the structures on the south side of Ojai Avenue. Under the direction of wealthy local businessman Mr. Edward Libbey, who had purchased the entire block for refurbishment, Mead and Requa designed a civic center with a Mission-style colonnade and post office tower with a vine-covered pergola joining the two. This project would come into the radar of Leone Sinnard, who at the time was engaged in the development of Atascadero. Its architectural features would later inspire those of the civic center administration block in Rancho Santa Fe, designs that were modified by Lilian to create a simplified aesthetic favored by Leone.

By May 1920 Richard had parted company with Mead (although some claim that they did not officially dissolve the partnership until 1923) and joining up with structural engineer Herbert L. Jackson—who had also been in Gill's office—they created the firm of Requa and Jackson. Landscape architect Milton P. Sessions, nephew of Kate Sessions,

worked closely with Requa on many of his major projects. Throughout the 1920s, San Diego witnessed a building boom, architects enjoyed celebrity status, and there was plenty of work for the many practices that had been formed in San Diego County during that period. It was a prosperous era that ended abruptly in October 1929 with the stock market crash and its economic aftermath.

As part of a local effort in San Diego to put people to work, Frank Drugan, a newcomer to the area in 1933, recognized the potential of the buildings in Balboa Park left over from the 1915–1916 exposition. Some of the structures were designed to be temporary, but having been refurbished and upgraded several times—largely due to the tireless efforts of Miss Gilbert of San Diego—were available for use. "Why not stage another exposition?" suggested Drugan. Richard Requa had been an active figure in the rehabilitation work of Balboa Park for some time and, in 1934, he was appointed as the consulting architect for the California Pacific International Exposition that would rival the original Panama-California Exposition. Drugan took on the role of promotions manager, then became executive secretary for a newly formed exposition committee, gaining financial backing from local businessmen and the Chamber of Commerce. The project, aided financially by FDR's Work Relief fund, stretched Richard and his team to maximum capacity and, under a rigorous deadline, they worked feverishly to complete the restoration in a fierce fight against time. But all was completed by exposition's opening day on May 29, 1935, and through their efforts over seven million people visited the park, bringing renewed hope and much-needed tourist dollars into the beautiful, but economically depressed, San Diego area.

12.

La Morada
A Home-Away-from-Home

The morning was beautiful as I arrived at The Inn at Rancho Santa Fe on this midweek day in July 2013; fortunately there are so many mornings like this in San Diego county and I felt gratitude for my circumstances. I waited in The Inn's aptly named "living room" with its comfortable couches and easy chairs, for a special meeting with Duncan Hadden who agreed to join me to share his childhood memories. It was a personal history that was set against the backdrop of The Inn as it had been his home, and later his place of work, for half a century. As Duncan strode along the foyer, my eyes were drawn downward to the pitted tiles that showed the chipped patina of ninety years of wear and bore the ghostly memories of many thousands of guests' footsteps who had walked, glided, or stumbled across that same threshold.

Duncan Hadden, a tall handsome man, walked confidently toward me, his six-four frame with a straight back moved with a steady pace. Relaxed in khaki pants and a powder blue Hawaiian shirt, Duncan looked like a man on vacation and, for him, the sale of The Inn a year earlier must have been positive with the effects reflected in his casual demeanor. We strolled the grounds of The Inn, which today is owned by J. M. I. Realty, that had purchased the boutique hotel a couple of years earlier from Duncan's family, the Royces. Until that point, it had been in the Royce family for just over fifty years and the memories for Duncan were fond ones.

"This is the cottage where we lived," said Duncan singling out one of several on the hotel's grounds. These quaint cottages resemble Mediterranean village dwellings and are each named in a Spanish vernacular. He pointed to Manzanita, on the south side of The Inn, which was added in the 1930s by Lilian. With his mother Dorothy Royce Hadden, his father Wesley, and five other siblings, the little cottage must have bursted with the exuberant energy of a growing family.

Bougainvillea is also one of the earliest guest cottages built in the early 1940s, with others being added over the decades, with names like Mariposa, Honeysuckle Cottage, and Wisteria Cottage, the latter being Lilian's former residence she built for herself in 1924. These charming cottages sited independently of the main structure of the hotel look less like temporary places to stay and more like a village transplanted from the Spanish Pyrenees. On the grounds were fifteen residential cottages leased to permanent longtime residents who had gravitated to the serenity and beauty of the location of The Inn, which are now being rebuilt. The road leading to the cottages was renamed Stephen Wheeler Royce Lane in memory of Duncan's grandfather, who had previously owned the Huntington Hotel in Pasadena. When he sold it in 1958, he was able to purchase The Inn for his daughter Dorothy with the proceeds.

There is a sole two-story building on the hotel's property. "This was formerly a room dormitory for male hotel workers. When I took over management, I had the dorm converted into seven luxury suites," said Duncan as we strode through the hotel's grounds enjoying the fragrance of jasmine that attracted several hummingbirds darting across our path leading up to the suites. The structure sits on a knoll in the grounds and is artfully sited to enjoy cooling breezes and views of the Ranch. "The 1990s remodel stayed true to the original Lilian Rice features, like the deeply recessed windows, varied roof line, and asymmetrical exterior wall placement, which were left intact," said Duncan. "We wanted to maintain that rustic impression."

Duncan shared stories about the horse corral that was once sited in the rear of The Inn, how the garden at the back of the main building once held a glorious stand of roses, and how the Mexican female staff were chauffeured back and forth daily to their homes in nearby Solana Beach because

La Morada in 1923, a rustic yet charming guest house where potential purchasers of land stayed in Rancho Santa Fe, CA. *Author's collection*

La Morada, now The Inn at Rancho Santa Fe. *Courtesy The Inn at Rancho Santa Fe*

it was considered "improper" for them to stay away from home overnight. It was a generous gesture by Duncan to give me this guided tour of the hotel and its grounds and his statement about recent remodels staying true to Lilian's designs played in my mind. For him at least there wasn't a question as to who designed The Inn. But the debate remains divided.

The preliminary sketch and the final presentation drawing of the guest house were both crafted by Lilian's easily distinguishable hand. Her pencil work shows deliberate contrast with heavy black strokes paired with the fine gray strokes, and a distinctive gauze-like crosshatching that gives an impression of depth and creates an overall appearance of a three-dimensional building with perfect perspective. The nature of the design itself is that of a simple, rustic single-story building, constructed from adobe bricks and wood frame. The structure has an asymmetrical footprint, with a main entryway aesthetically sited to overlook a dramatic view of the civic center. There's a wing to the north with twelve rooms for guests, and to the south an exterior patio, with a low adobe wall that hugs its perimeter, canopied by a trellis fashioned from split logs adorned with creeping crimson bougainvillea vines.

Photographer Herbert Fitch was commissioned by the land developers to capture early images during the 1920s as the civic center was under construction. Hauling his large box camera through the gritty dirt roads of the emergent village, he created a portfolio of real-time photographs that faithfully, and artfully, documented the newly built hotel, the civic center, and several residential structures as they were completed. Many of these images found their way into the sales booklet *The Endless Miracle* that served

The Hadden family on the steps of The Inn at Rancho Santa Fe, 1961. Left to right, top to bottom: Alex Hadden, Wesley Hadden, Dorothy Hadden; Linn Hadden, Marne Hadden, Duncan Hadden; Marion Hadden. *Courtesy Duncan Hadden*

to create a sense of romantic history derived from the earlier days of the Spanish dons.

It didn't take long for me to seek out Tom Clotfelter, an individual who had firsthand knowledge of Lilian's work and whose parents were closely connected to Rancho Santa Fe. I found him at his desk in a soft-pink-tinged stucco building on the north side of Paseo Delicias, which had once housed the offices of his father Reginald Clotfelter, a former sales agent for Rancho Santa Fe and at one time the manager of The Inn. Tom had taken over the family realty business and, with that responsibility, his father's former office. Tom was an organized, fastidious businessman—not a scrap of clutter anywhere—and he had a clear affinity for the Ranch's history with

large copies of Fitch's sepia photographs framed and adorning the walls of his office. I soon discovered he was also a walking history book of Rancho Santa Fe. Tom, I proclaimed, was my time lord. After brief introductions, he handed to me two publications which I treasure to this day: an almost perfect copy of *The Endless Miracle,* and a signed and dated copy of a book that his mother self-published in the 1980s. Tom was also generous with his knowledge and having an indisputable steel-trap memory, he answered many of my questions that I fired at him during that pleasant office visit.

Born in 1932, Tom showed the visible signs of his years. Tall and slender, yet still youthful in his energy, his face held the memories of a lifelong outdoor adventurer and keen sportsman. But those deep brown eyes still held a boyish mischief, and it was evident that Tom still had an enormous zest for

Wisteria cottage, one of the guest rooms at The Inn at Rancho Santa Fe,
formerly Lilian's home from 1924–1938. *Photo by Diane Y. Welch*

A guest bedroom in La Morada would have looked like
this in 1923. *Photo by Diane Y. Welch*

life. He was the first child born to Constance and Reginald Clotfelter who came to Rancho Santa Fe from Pasadena. Two siblings would follow. With their family stories and with Tom's own recollections, the Clotfelters literally wrote the history book on these early days of Rancho Santa Fe as Connie self-published her collection of essays, titled *Echoes of Rancho Santa Fe* that chronicled Ranch life during the 1920s and '30s.

Tom spoke effortlessly about distant memories that would tax the minds of most septuagenarians, and he also suggested others who I might interview: *Los Ancianos*, as they called themselves, a group of old timers who had kept in touch over the many decades since they had met and grown up in the Ranch and had become lifelong friends. I scratched down the list of names and was eager to follow up to meet new portals to the past, a past that I could only imagine. Tom also told me of his parents coming to Rancho Santa Fe in 1931 and the role they played in the running of the Ranch's only hotel, Reg as manager and Connie as hostess of what was then La Morada.

Leone had been the hotel's first manager and witnessed the ground breaking of the guest house (as it was first named) in November 1922. Workmen housed temporarily in tents erected close to the site labored around the clock to meet a spring deadline for its official opening. It had taken only three months to complete the guest house, and the work had represented a boom for some of the residents in nearby coastal Solana Beach. Five miles to the west of the Ranch, a section of the coastal community was specifically developed as a low-income neighborhood to house the labor force, now known as La Colonia de Eden Gardens. Today, it is an historic enclave with descendants of many of those first families still calling it home. These laborers, many of them Mexican masons, manufactured adobe bricks, by hand, at the site. Laid over a wood-frame structure, the bricks created a time-worn, rough exterior that harkened back to old Spain. Glenn A. Moore, resident landscape architect, designed and developed its lush gardens that created a Mediterranean setting, and Lilian designed the building and supervised the construction. By the time of the guest house opening in the early spring of 1923, the hotel

was renamed La Morada, which simply translates to "home."

Prospective buyers now had a place to stay while they perused the exclusive lots in the Ranch. Marketed widely on the East Coast, the concept attracted retired men of means from New York, Massachusetts, Pennsylvania, and other northern East Coast states. La Morada would symbolize their first impression of the community. It was less a hotel, more a home-away-from-home. Majestically appointed, it represented the signature architectural gateway to the Ranch.

Constructed on a gently sloping knoll, it also became the first sales center for prospective buyers to purchase large lots of land in the newly forming community. One report stated that the hotel:

> was not for tourists or for guests in the ordinary hotel sense. One may not drive up to its door and register and stay as long as one may wish on payment of a fee. One comes here as a selected guest, to stay a limited time, to study the proposition of whether one wishes to build a home pure and simple or to undertake the fruitful cultivation of the land. Guests are selected because of their likeliness financially and otherwise, to become permanent residents of the Rancho Santa Fe.

These affluent guests were met at the Del Mar train station, then chauffeured via the company's Cadillac into Rancho Santa Fe. Guided tours were then given in an open-top Cadillac bus that afforded ample visibility to survey prime estate lots that had been carefully selected by Leone Sinnard two years earlier. The guest house offered all the comforts of a high-class hotel for these discerning clients, yet it presented a simple charm that resembled a European hostelry, rather than the luxurious grandeur of the Ritz Carlton Hotel in New York. Guest house rooms were furnished in a Spanish motif with dark-stained, carved, solid-wood bed frames and colorful bed linens and accessories. The foyer was furnished like a comfortable room in a home and, early on, was named the living room to emphasize the casual nature of the setting. It had easy chairs with side tables, free-standing lamps, and a large-breasted fireplace. But the simple room was capped by an

The Living Room at The Inn at Rancho Santa Fe, as it looks today.
Courtesy The Inn at Rancho Santa Fe

expansive, hand-carved, heavy, wood-beamed vaulted ceiling that soared to the roof, adding the touch of majesty reminiscent of an inn from antiquity.

It was during the research on The Inn that I learned of a celebrity visitor who had an unusual request of the hotel's hostess, and an even more unusual request of a local clergyman. In one of our conversations, Tom told me about Evelyn Weatherall and suggested how she might be able to tell me more about this bizarre midnight vigil held at La Morada in the summer of 1928. After a few phone calls, I was able to locate Evelyn, who lived in nearby Morgan Run. She was a remarkable picture of healthy living and was still able to drive her car, a fact that she was very proud of: "as I'm ninety-three years old, you know," she commented. This lovely, elegant lady, who topped six feet in height, sat me down and handed me a glass of ice tea, which I set down on a side table next to a copy of her father's self-published book. She began to tell me about the day that her father received a flamboyant

visitor, a treasured family memory that was recounted in the Reverend's memoirs.

Quite unexpectedly and unannounced a gentleman, short of stature, dressed in a black suit with a black tie and sporting a black porkpie hat rapped on our front door with his silver-topped walking cane, Evelyn recalled. My father, Reverend Charles Knight, was a little taken aback, especially when he realized that standing in front of him was the architect Frank Lloyd Wright. "I'd like to hire you to preside over my wedding," he asked of my father. "But it needs to be kept secret and done at precisely midnight on August 25."

While the request seemed eccentric, Wright told her father that at exactly midnight the court's mandated one-year cooling off period for his divorce to his ex-wife, Miriam Noel Wright, would be over and he would be free to marry the new love of his life, Olgivanna Lazovich. Evelyn said:

> My father agreed to officiate at the wedding and Frank Lloyd Wright sent a chauffeured car to drive us from La Jolla into Rancho Santa Fe on that Saturday night. My father took both me and my mother with him.

The two were the only witnesses to the ceremony along with Iovanna, the Wright's three-year-old daughter, and the hotel's hostess. The vows were taken on the grounds of La Morada with only the visible light provided by the moon.

> My father wrote in his memoir that he had trouble reading the exact wording for the wedding vows but was able to ad lib sufficiently to make it legal and at about ten minutes after midnight Frank and Olgivanna were officially married.

> With the marriage ceremony taken care of, Wright immediately asked where the nearest phone was. He wanted to call the newspapers to report of the event. "Won't I give them something to write about!" he told my father, Evelyn recalled.

The stormy and tragic relationships of the world-renowned celebrity architect had given the reporters something to write about for decades. On August 15, 1914, one of Wright's recently hired domestic workers at his compound, Taliesin in Wisconsin, murdered Mamah Borthwick Cheney, the beautiful wife of a former client and the second love in Wright's life. She tragically perished along with her two children and four others in the slashing hatchet murder at the hands of Julien Carlton, who slaughtered seven people as they tried to escape a fire that he had deliberately set. When the divorce was finally granted from his first wife, Kitty, in 1922, Wright was free to marry Miriam Noel, the third love in his life. He was required to wait one year and on November 19, 1923 at midnight, Miriam and Wright were married in Spring Green, Wisconsin.

Their relationship was tumultuous. Marriage resulted in ruin for both. "Instead of improving with marriage, as I had hoped, our relationship became worse," Wright wrote in his autobiography. Miriam was addicted to morphine and had epic outbursts, the two quarreled a great deal and in less than a year they were separated. In 1924, after the separation, but while still married, Wright met Olgivanna at the Petrograd Ballet in Chicago. On November 27, 1925, Miriam filed for a divorce, alleging desertion and cruelty and a legal battle ensued that captivated the media. In August 1926, Miriam was barred from entering the Taliesin estate that Wright had built in Wisconsin as an architect's colony. She filed a suit for $100,000, a massive amount of money then, claiming that she suffered "great bodily injury" when she was prevented from entering Taliesen, according to news accounts. Miriam further charged that Olga "having appealed to the vanity and senility" of Wright (who was fifty-five) induced him to separate wrongfully from his wife and to refuse to provide her the "necessities of life," as reported in the *Union*. Miriam was charged with malicious mischief after she ransacked Wright's La Jolla home, destroying about $1,000 worth of household furnishings, chinaware, books, and clothing, tearing them up and tossing them into the street. She was arrested and placed in jail overnight then released on $250 bail. After a three-year legal battle, the two were divorced on August 26, 1927, and a year later Wright was free to marry Olga, which he did—to the exact minute—in the grounds of La Morada.

Naturally reporters were quick to break the news and the marriage did make the local newspapers and would prove, in future decades, to have started a trend of weddings in the grounds of the hotel. However, after the onset of the economic Depression, the hotel was in financial uncertainty, was sparsely occupied, and was available for sale to interested parties. Attorney Alexander Krisel showed some interest and, in 1935, made an offer to purchase La Morada during a visit to Rancho Santa Fe from Shanghai, China, but his wife Cecilia would not agree to the sale. The hotel closed briefly in the late 1930s, then passed into the ownership of Colonel George Roslington in 1939. Luke Kibler, Del Mar realtor, finalized the sale while Roslington, a world traveler, was in Bombay, India. On his return, Roslington changed the name to the Hacienda Hotel, and made several updates and alterations. A fifty-foot swimming pool was built, as was a cocktail

The advertisement for the opening of the Hacienda Hotel,
formerly La Morada. *Author's collection*

lounge, and two tile porches were added to the front of the building, "for the purpose of dignifying the structure." Proud of the new acquisition and taking the opportunity to run a full-page advertisement in the *Union* newspaper on August 5, 1939, the modern, updated hotel offered "five acres of fairyland gardens open all year" with room rates at $7 for single occupancy and $12 for double. Landscape architect Paul Avery beautified the grounds and modified the entrance roadway. Subcontractors who worked on the project also ran advertisements on the same page. August Anderson from Encinitas was the building contractor; Herschell Larrick, manager of Barr Lumber Company, provided much of the lumber in the remodel; Ace Tile provided the tiling in the pool and bungalow bathrooms; and Tanner Nurseries supplied the plantings.

For New Year's Eve that year the local paper gave notice that the Hacienda had a special weekend arranged for guests with a party planned that included a fine spread of food, Spanish music in the living room, and decorations of 300 luminaries—tea candles in paper bags—placed around the perimeter of the grounds "to make the little inn a truly different and atmospheric spot." An early morning hunt on New Year's Day was scheduled using Dave Willoughby's horses. The party was to ride out to nearby Spook's Canyon in search of a young lion that had been sighted out there. The

evening would not only usher in a new year, but also a new decade as 1939 gave way to 1940 and everyone must have been relieved to leave behind the decade that brought the Great Depression. Unfortunately for George Roslington, the new decade would not be auspicious, at least for him in his role as hotelier and, on August 20, 1941, the *Union* newspaper published notice that George Richardson of Chicago had purchased the Hacienda Hotel, which he immediately closed for beautification. By fall of 1941, advertisements for the hotel carried its new name: "The Inn at Rancho Santa Fe." Under new management, it had been completely redecorated and remodeled.

Richardson kept ownership of The Inn until 1958, when Stephen Wheeler Royce made his purchase for his daughter Dorothy and her husband Wesley to run. On a bright July morning in 1958, probably not unlike the day that I met Duncan fifty-five years later, the Royces "were feted" when Mr. and Mrs. Stephen Royce, and their daughter and son-in-law were introduced to residents of The Inn at a lively poolside cocktail party. The occasion would prove to be the launching of a long, successful period of ownership for the Royce family, passing the half-century mark and only ending when The Inn was sold to J. M. I Realty in the spring of 2012. As was the historic custom, after the sale, the hotel underwent further beautification.

13.
1923: A Turning Point

During the one-year period from 1922 to 1923, work in Rancho Santa Fe's civic center progressed at a rapid pace. There was evidently a well-planned timeline to uphold, and Lilian was not about to have it interrupted by a team of truck drivers who thought themselves above this schedule. Water pipes were still being laid in the late summer of 1923 and their timely installation was critical to the workload moving forward in the next phase of orchard development. Word got out swiftly to the local press that the drivers who were employed to haul material from the building yard to the installation site had called an impromptu strike. A reporter from a local branch office of the *Los Angeles Times* immediately showed up on the site to document the labor conflict, and took what has become an iconic photograph of Lilian posing about to step foot into the cab of a Mack lift truck. As he observed Lilian and three other women take charge of the potential breakdown in smooth operations, he took advantage of the occasion and staged a full photo shoot.

The article noted, "Miss Rice is resident architectural designer at Rancho Santa Fe, 'the most perfectly-planned land project in the world.'" The writer stated that he thought Lilian should receive "a prize for versatility" due to her actions on that sunny September morning.

She can draw pictures, boss building construction, plan flower gardens, drive a truck or operate a steam shovel, and do all these well enough to earn good pay. She has just gained new laurels here by organizing a volunteer corps of girl truck drivers and making a bunch of striking truck drivers so ashamed of themselves that they quickly returned to work.

The article continued:

People planning handsome country homes consult her. The Spanish garden that transforms the garage in the civic center into a place of artistic beauty was her idea. She is familiar with every bit of construction work in the twenty square miles of the project.

What caused the truck drivers to strike was an incident that occurred while they were charged with moving water pipes from the materials yard to the concrete camp for installation and, as that road was being surfaced, a detour was necessary. The drivers declared the new route impracticable for heavily loaded trucks, which they arrogantly walked away from. The halt in progress threatened to completely tie up the concrete camp with the pipes needed for the irrigation of 5,000 acres of avocados and citrus groves. Lilian called a meeting at the site with Leone and suggested that three of the female staff who worked in the civic center, and who could drive, could more than likely master the workings of a truck and do the jobs of the striking men. Leone spoke to railroad executives by phone who gave the solution their approval, and so the four women dressed themselves in riding and hiking gear to tackle the job at hand. Lilian stepped into the largest of the trucks and the others followed behind: Bertha Kreuziger (secretary for the irrigation district), Doris Chaney (Leone Sinnard's secretary), and Virginia Smith (the hostess of La Morada). All day they worked, driving the pipes back and forth, over that impassable road, until every one was delivered to its appropriate site. "And even a striking truck driver could not argue with that," commented a *LA Times* reporter.

Lilian Rice stands by a Mack truck in Rancho Santa Fe, CA. At this time, during the construction phase of the civic center in 1923, a truck driver's strike meant Lilian had to also master the operation of the dump truck to keep the work on schedule. *Author's collection*

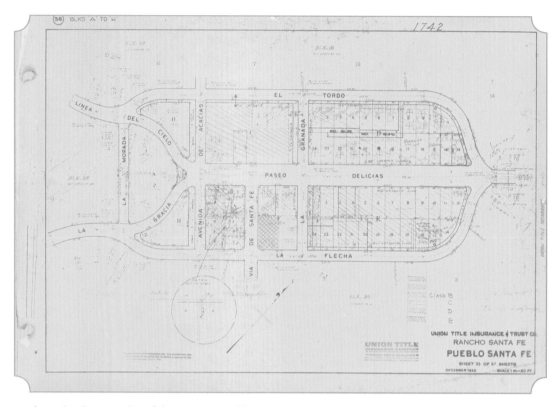

An early schematic plan of the civic center of Rancho Santa Fe, then called Pueblo Santa Fe. *Author's collection*

The incident also made the Sunday *San Francisco Chronicle* along with two posed photographs of the women, who looked ebullient in their temporary roles, sitting astride the hood and on the running board of the big Mack truck. Its headlines stated, "Capable young women keep tons of material moving over bad roads" and "Accomplishment of pretty chauffeurs puts an end to threatened walkout."

When asked by the reporter how she felt about her new role as truck driver, Bertha Kreuziger replied, "I feel truck-ulent myself!"

This published report solved a nagging mystery for me as I had seen the vintage photographs of this incident decorating the hallways in The Inn at Rancho Santa Fe, and wondered what had transpired. It was often assumed that this was Lilian's work

crew, but the facts prove otherwise, that the other women worked in support roles in the Ranch. There is another iconic photograph that shows Lilian at the center of a group of Ranch employees in front of the double doors to her office in the administration block; it is also dated 1923. She is flanked by the three women and a large group of men. A copy of this photograph was sent to me by one of the daughters of Bertha Kreuziger; I was able to seek her out through an online genealogy site and she was willing to talk to me by phone. In a group photograph of land company staff, to Bertha's left stands Vinent Smale, who was then her fiancé. He was hired as the irrigation district treasurer, replacing Wilfred Boetigger who had been promoted to superintendent. But it wasn't long until Vinent, a

cocky, self-assured individual with illusions of grandeur was fired.

What I heard from Bertha's daughter, Phoeobe Marrall, shocked me, but it was not uncommon then, or now, for some women to endure a controlling spouse with an undiagnosed psychiatric condition. With no alternate means of support, they become trapped into the role of wife and mother and forced to live with the abuse. The couple had met in Rancho Santa Fe in 1923 and were married two years later. "He had a murderous temper," Phoebe told me, "Vinent would walk around the house with a loaded shotgun and we were all deathly afraid of him." Bertha had five girls and only one was able to speak to me of this terrible childhood as it was too painful to remember. When the children were growing up, the

family lived on a small-holding in a modest house in El Cajon where they witnessed the daily abuse that their mother endured. Ironically, Vinent was a health fanatic; a vegetarian, he kept a large barrel of olives in brine handy for snacking. Bertha became morbidly ill from eating some of those olives, which had subsequently spoiled, and she died a painful death on December 21, 1941, from acute poisoning from the toxins. There was a hint that perhaps Bertha knew that the olives were spoiled and intended to end her misery, but it was not investigated. The girls were expected to take care of their father after Bertha's death and had to take turns missing school to see to his needs when he became sick with chronic bronchitis. A burden was lifted for the children when he died less than four months after his wife.

The three women, support staff for the development of Rancho Santa Fe, and Lilian with their trucks parked at the material yard, during a driver's strike in 1923. *Author's collection*

Lilian would never know the pain of being married and trapped in an abusive relationship; she remained single throughout her life, being more focused on her career, which she was not willing to give up to become a homemaker. However, her single status did not prevent her from living a fulfilled life. Besides her architectural work, Lilian still had an active social life, kept in contact with her friends from ZLAC, and stayed in close communications with Grace Morin. In 1925, she prepared for an adventurous three-month trip overseas that would immerse her in the exotic Spanish environs.

In the early 1920s, Californians who visited Europe traveled by train across country then embarked from New York to sail to Liverpool or Southampton in England. From there they journeyed to points beyond into France then by train into other European countries. The trip was long, but with the means to enjoy first-class service, the leisurely journey would have been a pleasant vacation (providing the seas were not too rough) for affluent travelers. Lilian took such a trip when the land company, most likely prompted by Leone, agreed to sponsor her travel to Spain to see firsthand the vernacular architecture in the region where the climate mirrored that of Southern California: the province of Andalusia.

Details of Lilian's outbound travel dates have not been found, but an online document tells of her return journey. A copy of the ship's manifest shows that Lilian traveled back to the US on the SS *Aquatania*, of the famed Cunard Line, which sailed from Cherbourg, France, on November 21, 1925, then arrived in New York six days later. It's unfortunate that there are no records of this landmark trip, other than this prosaic document. Lilian is listed as a single

Rancho Santa Fe, civic center buildings, the administration block, as it looks today. Mille Fleurs restaurant now stands where landscape designers and orchardists had their offices. *Photo by Half Full Photography*

woman who appears to be unaccompanied, although it would have been more appropriate for an unmarried woman to take such a trip with a trusted travel companion. A brief paragraph in the Sunday *San Diego Union* paper reported on December 27, 1925:

> Miss Lillian [*sic*] Rice motored down from Santa Fe Rancho [*sic*] the first of the week for a short visit at the home of her parents, Mr. and Mrs. J. C. [*sic*] Rice on East Second Street, National City. Miss Rice recently returned from a three-month tour abroad and reports an interesting and delightful trip.

Lilian evidently packed her box camera, as on her trip she did take photographs—hundreds of them—that captured the everyday dwellings and farmhouses in Tarifa, Spain, and nearby villages and tourist attractions. Out of those hundreds of photographs, only a handful of prints have survived, copies that Lilian gave to her friend Ruth Nelson. These are snapshots that show a long shot of the Alhambra in Granada with its iconic tower visible in the distant landscape, and images of typical Andalusian farmhouses and rowhouses. About two years after this trip, Lilian included a series of her photographs in the monthly edition of the *Rancho Santa Fe Progress*. Some of them were taken in Havana, Cuba, which at the time was a popular tourist resort and clearly Lilian had traveled there, too. The idea was for Lilian to use both trips as design inspiration for homes in the Ranch. One photograph showed the facade of a two-story residence with an upper window embellished with a wrought-iron grille, above an impressive entryway encasing a heavy, solid-wood door. Two ladies pose in the entryway, formally dressed, with another to their right who is more modestly attired, and must be their maid. The caption under the photograph reads:

> Doorway, Tarifa, Spain. From a collection of several hundred photographs especially taken by Lilian J. Rice so authentic details and architectural treatment in the old Spanish World could be available for those who build in Rancho Santa Fe. Through this small town of Tarifa the

Moors entered Spain and it was the last town to be surrendered by them on their retreat to Africa.

The first major project that Lilian designed on her return to the US was four homes on vacant lots in Block D on the north side of Paseo Delicias heading eastward out of the civic center. Preliminary plans were drawn up for the modest rowhouses that were designed as a contiguous structure, but with each being a unique variation on a Mediterranean theme derived from Lilian's travel experiences in Spain. Like Lilian's photograph published in the *Progress*, these residences had front entryways that opened directly onto the street, a novel idea at the time and yet each home was quite different. The homes were named simply A, B, C, and D. Cottage A and D were designed with entry doors that immediately opened into a spacious patio that would have been used as an outside dining area enhanced with creeping vines and potted tropical plantings, also a novelty at the time. Cottage C, had a small, two-roomed guest apartment constructed at the rear of the lot, while the other three homes had garages built at the rear. Flat roof lines alternated with tiled roofs and distinct changes in stucco color, from light ivory to deep tan, added visual interest. Doorways varied as did the window treatments, some with turned wooden grilles, one with twin florid, decorative wrought iron grilles, and another with more simplified window grillwork. Each home had much of the lot devoted to private garden space, and their facades were set back slightly to create an impression that each dwelling stood independent of the other. As it was pre-planned for the project to be realized on Lilian's return from Spain, the land company sold the lots prior to her departure to locals who worked in the Ranch, with the intent that each residence could be tailored for each client, and they were.

Currently, the rowhouses are known for the historic families who lived there when the homes were completed by the beginning of 1927: from A to D, Louise Spurr and Reginald and Connie Clotfelter, Sydney and Ruth Nelson, Pearl Baker and John Megrew, and Glenn and Ida May Moore, and today with both buildings A and C being listed on the National Register of Historic Places. In 1927, the homes had no landscaping in the front, just a narrow concrete footpath, although today that area

Plans for the four rowhouses that Lilian designed after a landmark trip to Spain. *Re-created by Christopher Real and Monique Parsons.*

ROW HOUSES - PASEO DELICIAS

REPRODUCTION OF FLOOR PLAN BY CHRISTOPHER REAL AND MONIQUE PARSONS

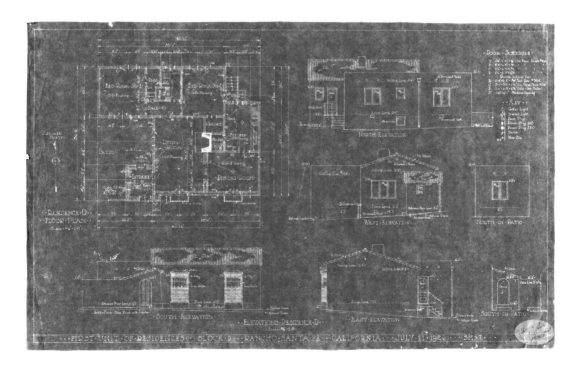

Lilian's blueprint for Rowhouse D, Paseo Delicias, Rancho Santa Fe, CA. Approved, dated, and signed by Lilian J. Rice, July 11, 1926. *Courtesy International Archive of Women in Architecture*

Vintage photograph of the civic center rowhouses, looking east. *Courtesy the Spurr Family*

has been widened and drought-tolerant landscaping beautifies the space.

After the rowhouses were completed, two Ranch residents, former Beverly Hills realtor Fred W. Joers, and contractor Harold Ketchum, formerly from Long Beach, retained Lilian to design a mixed-use two-story structure also in Block D of the civic center. This was the center's first commercial project to be built that was not owned by the land company and so has its special place in the civic center history. Located on the corner of Paseo Delicias and La Granada, the building created a commanding focal point and made full-use of some of the design features that Lilian saw in Spain. The lower level was designed to be a storeroom, the upper level had two studio apartments with two single-story units adjoining the main structure at 6108 Paseo Delicias and 6016 La Granada; it was so notable that the *Evening Tribune* published notice of its completion in August 1927. The exterior has an unusual herringbone brick

wainscot not seen in other buildings, making its design unique. There is an upper balcony with a wrought iron rail, large grilled windows, stucco chimneys, and turned wooden eave supports. In May 1928, the lower storeroom was transformed into a tea room and the *San Diego Union* wrote a piece about a group of ladies who were the first to frequent it, and the article painted a genteel picture of a simpler time.

The ladies, members of the San Diego Writing Club, were Ruth Nelson's guests on Saturday morning, May 15, 1928. Several of them had taken the train to Del Mar, were picked up in the land company touring Cadillac, then chauffeured to Ruth and Sydney's new home on Paseo Delicias in the civic center. The group enjoyed Ruth's "lovely garden," then walked the few steps to the tea room that had recently opened and had "been hastened in compliment to Mrs. Nelson's guests." The tea room, named La Amapola for the decorative poppy artwork on the

One of hundreds of photographs taken by Lilian during her trip to Spain in 1925. This image is of the Alhambra visible in the distance. *Author's collection*

interior walls, had small tables with linen cloths decorated with floral centerpieces and orange-colored candles. The writing club members read poems, excerpts from an Indian opera *Sun Maid* and Ruth's son Robert read a description of the Osuna garden that had been beautified by horticulturist Dr. A. R. Sprague, famed for his hybridized orchid gladioli. After the readings, there was a driving tour of the Ranch to view the elegant estate homes, the new golf course, Rancho Zorro, and to generally enjoy the gorgeous scenery. The ladies must have felt privileged for their unique peek into the private world of these hidden estates.

This second phase of the civic center complemented the first phase of buildings, which included La Morada, the administration block, and the garage block. Then, in 1924, the schoolhouse was built followed by the Santa Fe Irrigation District office complex in 1925. Wilfred Ott Boetigger had been the superintendent of the irrigation district during the early years of development in the Ranch. I was introduced to his son Bill, then eighty-seven, by Tom Clotfelter.

The family arrived in Rancho Santa Fe in August 1923. Bill's father was an engineer and had been hired by the irrigation district first as treasurer and then superintendent. The Boetiggers, having recently relocated from Chicago, moved into a house in Del Mar awaiting a home to be built at the Ranch. Within two years, the Boetiggers had settled into their new home designed by Lilian and located along the top road into the Ranch, Linea del Cielo. Their home was part of a small complex of buildings sited next to the irrigation district office, which had been created by Lilian as part of the cohesive design of the civic center. The office resembled a house with no hint of commercial use, an important approach

One of the Rancho Santa Fe rowhouses, formerly owned by the Nelson family, as it looks today.
Photo by Half Full Photography

The offices of the Santa Fe Irrigation District as they look today.
Photo by Half Full Photography

for the overall master plan of the community. Both the office building and the Boetigger's home were designed in a Spanish colonial revival style; the latter had a simple charm that the family of six enjoyed. It had two bedrooms, one for the parents and baby Bea, the other for Bill and his sister Claire and younger brother Bud, who shared his bunk bed. Bill described how the view from his window spanned miles across open arid terrain, as the Ranch was just beginning to be developed. "There was a barranca, a deep ditch, next to the Irrigation District offices. Some of the workmen, road builders, and pipe layers, would camp down by there. There were tents set up for them and a mess kitchen. It was a hive of activity," he told me. "Crews worked around the clock."

Between the mid- and late-1920s, sales of estate lots naturally brought new faces to the Ranch, and Lilian's workload increased; within time, the Ranch would represent the lion's share of commissions for Lilian's office until her career ended. The land company's marketing was clearly successful, and its target prospects—East Coast retirees—began to arrive and most importantly bought into the concept of large estate lots with agricultural acreage. It wouldn't be long before the Boetiggers had plenty of new neighbors, some of them families with children.

Beyond the civic center, the first residence built, for Bowly and Ethel Le Huray, was a modest single-story house with an attached garage. Le Huray had recently retired as president of his own commercial lithography company in New York City. When he left the corporate world, Rancho Santa Fe must have seemed the ideal community to relocate to, leaving the harsh winters and humid summers of New York City far behind. Like so many of these retired gentlemen, he was eager to take on a new life and a new role. Bowly became the Ranch's first postmaster in 1924, and also lists himself as a rancher in voting records with his acreage devoted to avocados. This particular home underwent a major remodel in 1968 by local building contractor Samuel Gross when it was rescued from certain demolition.

The discovery of this home, that was integrated into the remodel of a master-recycler, who used doors, beams, and balcony supports from the Del Mar Hotel (that was in the process of demolition in the late 1960s) solved a frustrating puzzle for me. It was the exact home that was captured in a photograph of Lilian and her mother, one that came into my private collection via family descendent Mim Sellgren, who gifted me many Rice family photographs. The image, although not dated, must have been taken in 1923 and suggests that Lilian treasured this moment with her mother, who would have traveled up from National City to see the tangible expression of her daughter's artistry. Although the house was unrecognizable in 2013 when it came into my radar, by tracking down family descendents of the Le Huray's and receiving a photograph from them of the exact house, I was able to make a positive identification. The family's image showed a modest single-story house with minimal, restrained decorative treatment, a tan stucco exterior, a flat roof, with a distinctive chimney topped with a tiled spark-arrester, and Mediterranean type landscaping with drought-tolerant plantings. The puzzle piece slotted perfectly into place and now I have a location for the building, its entire history over a ninety-year period, and the biography of the family who commissioned Lilian to design the home.

Another notable home designed by Lilian during this initial phase when the civic center was being completed was a pueblo-style structure owned by the land company. It was used as a temporary stay for visiting company executives, then later as a rental for company employees. Today, that home is known as La Flecha house and serves as the Rancho Santa Fe Historical Society headquarters and museum and is the repository for its archives. The structure was part of the south side of the administration block and, despite its rustic adobe exterior with twelve-inch thick, uneven walls and deep-set windows protected by spindled wooden grilles, it had every modern convenience, including electric lighting and heating, and telephone service. There was an outside patio entered through an archway and canales grouped in threes, a common Lilian Rice design touch, that were both functional, to drain water, and ornamental, adding a subtle splash of color and interest to the rectangular mass of the exterior wall.

One of the first people to rent the home was the Nelson family. Sydney Nelson had been hired as the assistant manager to Leone Sinnard in 1922, and by 1923, Sydney had made arrangements for his wife Ruth and his son Robert to join him. I corresponded with Robert, and we also chatted by phone; he was about to turn ninety years old

The home of Bowly and Ethel Le Huray, the first residence built in 1923, just beyond the civic center of Rancho Santa Fe, CA, photo dated 1926. *Author's collection*

The same home with Lilian and her mother visiting the site, 1923. *Author's collection*

when we spoke. In his adult life, he took to using his first name of Charles. Like Bill Boetigger, although advanced in years, Charles' memory was still razor sharp. One of the first things I asked was about the early days of Lilian's involvement in the Ranch. His response was disappointing, "About Lilian Rice, you have a difficult problem due to scarcity of documentation," he said, a fact of which I was painfully aware. But Charles was able to send some copies of photographs that his

mother had in her collection that showed the interior of La Morada, and three that Lilian had snapped during her landmark trip to Spain. Charles was also eager to describe to me the adobe home on La Flecha and how, despite its modest size and tiny kitchen his mother Ruth was able to manage her small family of three. She made good use of a small patch of soil by growing vegetables and like most of her neighbors shopped daily for other food items.

La Flecha House in the village of Rancho Santa Fe, now home to the Rancho Santa Fe Historical Society. *Photo by Half Full Photography*

In 1924, Ruth, an avid writer and a dedicated member of the San Diego Writing Club, (a talent that would transform her into the Ranch's first historian), started a branch library in the home. The family would live there until 1926, when Lilian designed and completed the four rowhouses in the civic center, which served as permanent homes for some of the land company employees. The Nelsons stayed in the rowhouse for many years and, like Connie and Reg Clotfelter, both Ruth and Sydney were very active in the community. Charles mostly remembered the close friendship that Ruth had with Lilian, a fact that later would shed some light on how Lilian became the chief architect for a project that was initially contracted to Requa and Jackson.

In 2005, I was fortunate to receive a hand-written letter from John Minchin—he also had memories of the Rice family, stories that had been retold by his mother. His letter contained valuable information. John's mother was Margery Smith, deceased for some years when he sent me the letter. Margery's family had several ties to the Rice family and, in her twilight years, she lived to be ninety-six, she was still very acute mentally and had vivid memory of

the period in the early 1920s. Lilian, who would frequently travel back to National City to see her parents, would occasionally allow Margery, seventeen at that time, to ride out with her to Rancho Santa Fe. They drove via the back roads together, a trip that in 1923 took about two hours. "Upon arrival in Rancho Santa Fe, Margery would sit on the porch of La Morada for several hours while Lilian checked in on the construction projects in early Rancho Santa Fe," wrote John in his letter. He also recalled that his mother told him that Lilian's mother Laura was a talented artist. As a gesture of friendship, Laura gave Margery one of her miniature oil paintings, which was later donated to the Rancho Santa Fe Historical Society; it is still on display there today. Of further interest was that John was a retired architect. In fact, his firm at one time was located in the La Flecha House, renting the space from the owners, E. I. (Bud) and Marguerita Reitz who had bought the property and, in 1962, remodeled the interior for commercial use. In 1988, the Reitzes donated the home to the historical society, and John was called upon again to remodel the structure, this time to take it back close to its original Lilian Rice design of 1923, which is how it stands today.

More Building Than Ever Before

The Claude and Florence Terwilliger House in Rancho Santa Fe as it looked circa 1925. *Courtesy Don Terwilliger*

My friend Charles Larrick also had crystal-clear recollections of the 1920s in Rancho Santa Fe and, over the course of several visits, we talked at length about his memories, specifically about his father's lumber business and the Rancho Santa Fe home that he commissioned Lilian to design in 1928. Chuck, as he prefers to be known, self-published a memoir that traced the Larrick family from its very early pre-Roman roots to current times, and in it he included a chapter about this home.

Sited just outside the civic center, on the corner of La Flecha and Paseo Delicias, the Larrick's estate home held a most prominent location; the grounds were artfully landscaped by Glenn A. Moore, who included a bowling green, a rose garden, and a citrus orchard in its design. In 1928, Herschell Larrick's Solana Beach-based business—the Lumber and Builders Supply Company—was at the height of its success. The development of nearby Rancho Santa Fe had meant a boom in business and the lumberyard on North Cedros Avenue steadily grew. The business was started by Larrick in 1924, when the community of Solana Beach had just twenty-two residents. Ed Fletcher owned much of the land and had commissioned Requa and Jackson to design the buildings in a central plaza that included a gas station, a post office, and a small hotel and bank sited on the top of the coastal bluffs. Larrick's business was just across the tracks from the plaza and, like Fletcher, he also used Requa's design services to build his company store. Larrick was so assured that his lumber business would continue to prosper that he borrowed heavily for both the business and his estate home in Rancho Santa Fe, but as Chuck told me, they considered themselves, "living in high cotton" with no reason to believe that anything would change. At the same time that Annabel and Herschell planned the design of their dream home with Lilian as architect, a "big, black, seven-passenger Cadillac" was purchased. The family drove around town like royalty, and with Herschell's many civic roles that he happily took on during this period, he became an important leading figure in local community affairs.

Consequently, when their Rancho Santa Fe estate home and its grounds were completed, the local newspaper showed interest. The Larricks agreed to an open house on Sunday August 12, 1928. Herschell and his wife Annabel must have been very proud of their recently completed residence that was open for "public inspection" for all to view the "interesting structure." An in-depth article published in the *San Diego Union's* home and garden section wrote glowingly of the home's many features, which likely helped showcase some of Larrick's exotic woods from his own lumber business and gave visibility to Lilian's architectural services.

"Evidences of her special talent are not lacking and the visitor will get a thrill of delight at her special conceptions," the writer commented about Lilian, who had used J. M. Wilson as contractor. Of interest is that Wilson had built the foundations for Requa's Open Air Theater in Mount Helix in La Mesa, in San Diego's east county in 1924, so he and Lilian must have been closely acquainted. The home's exterior met the covenant design restrictions of Mediterranean type, but like all of Lilian's homes, with each having unique character-defining features, this home was no exception and was unlike any other. What notably set it apart was a solid-wood balcony that spanned the entire front elevation of the structure. Known as "Monterey-type," the two-story home also featured the typical Spanish-style red-tiled roof and white-washed stucco on frame construction. As one would imagine for a lumberman, the interior featured an array of woods. The walls of the living room, entrance hall, and dining room were

Herschell Larrick Sr. outside his lumber business in Solana Beach, CA, circa 1925. *Author's collection.*

finished in knotted redwood boards, wire brushed, waxed, then coated in paraffin oil following the traditions of early California colonial carpentry, which gave the interior a look and feel, and no doubt a slight aroma, of antiquity. Doors were hand-carved in solid redwood, and Bataan mahogany was used for wall accents like the baseboards, picture molding, and window casing, which were then finished in a lacquer to bring out the natural deep red tones in the wood and to add a protective coating.

An innovation used in the wall construction was acoustic plaster, which absorbed up to twenty-five percent of noise, making it a unique feature that likely suited the Larricks due to their four children, plus their inlaws, making a large family of eight. The living room had a Bataan mahogany floor treatment with planks laid expertly and fixed in place with wooden plugs, and the stair treads were of Orion mahogany. The staircase was enhanced with an elegant, yet simple wrought iron handrail that complemented the color of the wood. The flooring throughout the rest of the house was waterproofed Brucelized oak and therefore unaffected by humidity, which was useful in the bathrooms and the kitchen.

One of the bathrooms was finished in a fashionable satin-black tile and the other in abalone-shell pink tile; the kitchen had a state-of-the-art refrigerator, which was lacquered in red to match the wood trim and counters, and a dish-washing machine, a modern luxury, "for reducing this drudgery to a minimum."

Unfortunately for Annabel, she would not escape this drudgery for long, and within five years, practically everything she had was repossessed by the bank: the home, the car, the hi-tech gadgets. With Larrick's company losing ninety percent of its business, the family moved back to Solana Beach into a small two-bedroom home on Barbara Street, with one inadequate bathroom.

Chuck's written record of this period shows no hint of bitterness, and as I spoke with him, he had pride in his parents' resiliency to pick themselves up, dust themselves off, and to continue to make a wonderful life for themselves, their four children, and the grandparents. Herschell Larrick was able to continue to work in the lumber business when the Barr family took it over in lieu of payments on the loan that Herschell had originally signed with them when he founded his business in 1924. The Barrs retained him as manager with three other people as employees. Despite the struggles, Chuck was never aware of his father's anxieties. "He surely must have had them—a man with only one leg and this large family to feed, house, and clothe."

Herschell Larrick Sr. was constantly irritated by his wooden prosthetic leg. He had lost the limb following a tragic accident when slipped under a trolley car in San Diego when the pavement was slick, due to a heavy downpour. A young woman, a nurse, happened to be a bystander and had the foresight to apply a tourniquet that saved his life. Despite the loss of limb, Larrick was a force of character and was in no way impeded by his wooden leg; in fact, Chuck said that it was "the making of him" as his reduced mobility meant he was moved out of the Benson Lumber yard and into the administration side of operations where he learned the business from the ground up. In his later adult years, Larrick's civic service included successfully lobbying for a separate local high school district and then becoming one of its first trustees, being elected to the local water board, and perhaps his most important feat, heading up a movement to stop an ill-informed plan to build a freeway that cut off local coastal communities to their beaches, which would have been certain death for nearby businesses. Local people agreed with Larrick, and together they raised funds to hire an engineer to create a plan that was better and cheaper than the one proposed by the state. Today, Highway Interstate 5 follows that plan almost exactly. Herschell Larrick Sr. passed away in 1963, before the freeway was officially dedicated, but Annabel was invited to cut the ribbon that opened the section of I-5 from Carlsbad to Del Mar. And after his death she destroyed all his love letters to her and had her sons burn the wooden leg that had caused him so much pain.

The Larrick estate home in Rancho Santa Fe went through various owners and, in the 1980s, it was purchased by Carl Cato, a real estate entrepreneur who "for a while built and moved houses in the area like pieces in a chess game," to quote one writer. He decided he didn't like its original location at the end of Paseo Delicias. So, in the dark of night, the home was literally split in two, heaved onto portable platforms, and wheeled unceremoniously through the village center to a lot on the corner of Puerto del Sol and Linea del Cielo where it stands today. The main structure was flip-flopped with the front becoming the rear. Changing hands again, the current owners have remodeled the original structure, but the home has a timeless elegance and has retained many of the original defining features of Lilian's design.

The 1920s was a prosperous decade for the land company as sales in Rancho Santa Fe were brisk, attracting many out-of-state purchasers—just as its marketing plan had set out to achieve. The concept of gentlemen ranchos had caught on and, by 1927, seventy-five percent of the approximate 9,000 acres had been sold as noted by Sydney Nelson in the land company's monthly publication. A list of home owners was published in 1928, which exceeded those of the prior year's, and several were women: Mrs. Mary Campbell (whose former residence is now home to the Rancho Santa Fe Senior Center), Mrs. Pearl Baker, Mrs. Belle Claggett, Mrs. Florence J. Corbus, and sisters Alice L. and Florence E. Wilson. All but a few of the estate homes and more modest dwellings built close to the civic center were designed

The patio of the Christiancy House, now the Black House, in Rancho Santa Fe.
Photo by Diane Y. Welch

by Lilian; her office must have been in perpetual motion producing floor plans, presentation drawings, and in some cases three-dimensional clay models of the proposed home. One such home was highlighted in the *San Diego Union* paper with the headline: "Hollywood couple to build fine home on commanding site of Rancho Santa Fe." Lilian is referred to from this point on as the resident architect, and generally there is no doubt as to her authority in the design of buildings from 1928 forward, although she did not officially receive her license until 1929.

Elmer and Louise Cord had purchased several acres on one of the Ranch's premium lots with a unique site chosen for the home along the ridge of a hill on Los Morros. Lilian had drawn up detailed plans to the house, which had a pronounced, horizontal aspect, almost like it had been laid down, then stretched out along the land's natural topography. To give a more concrete concept of the design, she created a clay model to exact scale. The siting allowed the home to take full advantage of panoramic views.

A steep road led up to the home site where an auto circle had been created for vehicles to turn around and journey back down the hill, along with four garages for parking. Guests would drive through a dramatic arched entry to the auto circle, then parking their vehicles there, they would then be led to a walled exterior patio, which dropped down via a few tiled steps with colorful ceramic risers. They would enter the house through an oversized, arched wooden door, reminiscent of old world Spain.

The living room was large with high ceilings, with an irregular-shaped alcove at one end and an immense fireplace at the other. Spectacular views that opened up through an exterior rustic pergola that seemed to frame the vista, spanned from Olivenhain to the ocean. The house had varied floor levels, with an open staircase leading to two upper bedrooms and a lower staircase leading down to two more bedrooms. One of the bedrooms had an "attractive balcony overlooking miles and miles of attractive landscaping." Off the dining room was

The rear elevation of the former Belle Claggett house in Rancho Santa Fe, CA.
Author's collection

another walled exterior patio with an outside fireplace, in signature Lilian-style, extending an interior space into an outside living space.

The clay model was prominently displayed in Lilian's office and would have attracted a lot of attention from clients. By the early summer of 1928, it was likely hard to keep up with the demands of new property owners; the land company was now boasting that eighty percent of all acreage had been sold. Spanish architecture prevailed and the homes were almost without exception surrounded by plentiful orchards of oranges, avocados, lemons, walnuts, apricots, and other deciduous fruit. Most of the homeowners contracted with orchardist U. L. Voris, who had the on-site facilities to attend to every phase of his work from ground preparation, planting, picking, and marketing the produce. The land company was more than pleased with its successes and the freight tonnage gathered from these large estate lots exceeded their expectations.

Claude Terwilliger and his wife Florence were early purchasers of a prime estate lot on the knoll of a steep hill affording panoramic views over a sweeping picturesque valley. Their grandson, Don Terwilliger, is a dear friend of mine, who lives in coastal Del Mar, just four miles west of Rancho Santa Fe. Together we pored over his family album that contained period photographs that with evident pride had captured the estate home built in 1925 by Lilian. Naturally, Don remembered this home in Rancho Santa Fe, even though he was very young when his grandparents lived there. The sepia images in the album prompted his memories and later conversations that his parents had shared about the estate. His grandfather, born in 1881, was a successful grain broker in Alberta, Canada, with farmland exceeding 600 acres. "He had about fifty grain elevators and a ranch where he raised Belgian work horses," said Don. "At age forty, he had made a million-dollar fortune, was restless, and was ready to retire." So Claude looked to the sunny climes of California to pursue this dream, purchasing scenic property in Rancho Santa Fe.

Each year Claude, Florence, and their only child Ted—Don's father—had spent the winter months in California, vacationing in both Point Loma and Coronado. They also vacationed in Long Beach. Eager to invest his fortune, Claude placed an option to purchase property there. But at the

The front elevation of the former Hamilton Carpenter house in Rancho Santa Fe, CA. *Photo by DarrenEdwards.com*

same time, in 1922, land in San Diego County seemed more appealing. Torn between the two locations, Don's grandfather "decided to sell his Canadian property and chose to invest in Rancho Santa Fe," said Don. The role of gentleman rancher attracted him, and Claude felt that the land there was more suitable for growing citrus, which was known by then to be transforming seemingly worthless backwood acreage into a highly profitable venture. Ironically, his expired purchase option in Long Beach was on land in Signal Hill where huge reserves of oil were later discovered, a realization that must have had Claude cursing the direction that he fatefully took. But Claude and Florence had already purchased their prime piece of property that bordered the winding roads of San Elijo Avenue and Rambla de las Flores and were pleased with their choice. A residential site was selected that overlooked a picturesque pond. Lilian designed the exterior of the estate home with wood frame covered in light-toned, roughly applied stucco. It was a modest structure that reflected perfectly her ideal of its harmony with the land. The flow of the architecture followed the slope of the steep hillside, and designed in a simple U shape, it was evocative of old world Mexico. The rear of the home afforded

unhampered views over a vast expanse of untamed arroyos. On his cultivated land Claude planted groves of oranges, lemons, and walnuts tended by Mexican workers hired from nearby Eden Gardens in Solana Beach.

Traversing unpaved roads made horses an essential mode of transportation in the 1920s in Rancho Santa Fe. Claude and Florence bought two racehorses, Wyzation and Hand Sweep, from Agua Caliente in Tijuana. Claude hoped to make them into saddle horses but they were too spirited, Don told me. After a few years, Claude Terwilliger's restless nature would cause him to sell off all but sixty acres of his Rancho Santa Fe property and build luxury apartments in Golden Hill in the city of San Diego. In 1944, when Franklin D. Roosevelt was reelected president for a fourth term, Claude Terwilliger, a staunch Republican, refused to pay property taxes on his remaining acreage in Rancho Santa Fe, which he "walked away from" and was subsequently repossessed. Following the death of Florence, then a succession of three failed marriages, Claude Terwilliger, at the age of seventy-five took his own life. His body was found in the kitchen of his home in Riverside, with the stove's unlit gas burners full on.

Today, the name of Terwilliger lives on in Rancho Santa Fe. In 1993, the family home, the fifth oldest residence in Rancho Santa Fe, was listed on the National Registry of Historic Places as "The Claude and Florence Terwilliger House." I asked Don if he had any documented proof that Lilian was the architect of his grandparents' home. From his recollection there was no question that Lilian was the architect as she and his grandmother became friends and Lilian often socialized with the Terwilligers and other Ranch residents. Unfortunately, the original floor plans and elevations had not been kept in the family. But there is one document, dated 1925, that has survived the years, one that would support the case for Lilian's rightful authority to her architectural work completed in Rancho Santa Fe before she received her license. It was the building permit application to the Santa Fe Land Improvement Company, which had been originally submitted by Lilian for approval with a plot plan and a set of blueprints. It was signed by Claude Terwilliger and dated June 25, 1925, then approved in Lilian's distinct hand thus: "By Requa & Jackson, Architect per L. J. R." This was a big clue that even though Lilian did not have her architectural license during this period, she did have the authority to sign off on these legal documents. "Per L. J. R." translates to "through" or "via" Lilian J. Rice," it is evident then that Lilian was engaged as the architectural designer for buildings completed during this contested period of 1923 through 1927. Although the legal aspect of the paperwork held Requa and Jackson's name, it was Lilian who was on site, working closely with the clients, not only building homes for them, but also building relationships with them, and most importantly signing off on critical permits.

Some of Lilian's most notable architectural design work was done during this four-year period as wealthy clients were able to afford the high cost of the land and the estate home that was mandated to be built on that acreage. However, a large estate home did not necessarily translate into an ostentatious structure. Lilian understood the simple aesthetic of unadorned cubes, arches, and wall surfaces that her residential buildings were designed around, and many of her grand homes reflected this simple approach. Like her former colleagues, who were members of the Hillside Club, Lilian believed firmly that structures must be in subordination with the landscape, that they should "conform to the setting of nature." After 1928, the walls of new buildings in Rancho Santa Fe were required to be white, but Lilian still incorporated a simplicity, with restrained decoration, using minimal tile work and carefully thought-out design embellishments that set her apart from other architects. She built homes that welcomed in the landscape just beyond their walled patios, homes infused with light, and a quality of domesticity that Lilian herself claimed was her contribution as a woman architect.

In March 1928, it was reported that new homes valued together at $60,000 had been completed in the Ranch for that year. Plans were under way for an anticipated $300,000 in total value, for the remainder of the year. Due to large lots, and therefore relatively small number of transactions, the numbers were impressive. Practically each week the *Union* published up-to-date figures on the Ranch. One of the most ambitious estate homes was commissioned by Charles F. Pease. It took two years for the retired millionaire to reach completion of the home, although his lot had been planted to citrus and the landscaping begun in 1926. With a headline "Novelty Seen in Buildings," his home was described in some detail:

> Approaching the home by a winding road that skirts a tiny lake ingeniously created in a small barranca below the house, the visitor drives under an archway and finds the entrance just off an arcaded loggia that extends nearly the full length of the lower floor. The principal rooms are on a higher floor which is reached from the entrance by way of a wide stairway. Just off the hall at the top of these steps is a magnificent living room, 23 feet x 32 feet in a size with antiqued beam ceiling and fireplaces...two solar water heating plants are cleverly built into the roof.

In that same year, retired New York banker George A. C. Christiancy used Lilian's services to build his bluff-top estate home with dramatic views of the valley below and rolling hills on the horizon. Built on the street named "El Mirador," the two-and-a-half-story structure has a northern exposure for its front elevation and is sited to naturally fit the topography. A rising driveway leads to a tiled auto court in front of the home. The façade has a central double stairway that leads to an arched doorway that leads to an interior patio with small steps up into the living area. Decorative tile, wood balconies, wrought-iron grillwork, and a signature varied roof line capped with barrel, red tiles are typical Lilian Rice design elements that, while restrained, added a touch of the romance of old world Spain with mission revival.

Christiancy also purchased a vacant lot on Paseo Delicias, across from the Joers-Ketchum building. Lilian drew up floor plans and presentation drawings for this mixed-use project, the second in the civic center in private ownership. The Monterrey-type building contained offices on the lower level, Christiancy's son-in-law Barton Millard leased one of them, and Lilian leased the other when she opened her own firm in 1928, as the land company divested itself of the Rancho Santa Fe project. The upper level was dedicated to three apartments that were accessed by a curved exterior stairwell leading to a wood balcony that stretched the whole length of the front elevation. Lilian would put these arrangements to good use to house her draftsmen as her work load increased in the mid 1930s; the complex became known as La Valenciana and still stands today, much as it did in the late 1920s, although in recent years the front of the complex has seen additional commercial building.

Architectural restrictions set down by the land company mandated that all buildings within the geographical area of the original land grant boundaries should conform to this Mediterranean type, a compliance that had a ten year cap. Other regulations included minimum building costs: the larger the estate, the greater the amount of funds that should be devoted to the construction of the home. Property owners were required to sign this covenant that aimed to uphold the value of their property and restrict those with lesser financial means from making purchases. In the busy sales period of the mid-1920s,

Mixed-use commercial and residential complex, La Valenciana, built by Lilian in 1928 in the civic center of Rancho Santa Fe, CA. The project won Lilian an AIA honor award in 1933. *Photo by Half Full Photography*

Lilian completed homes for retired executives, single women of means, bankers, lawyers, realtors, company employees, and Hollywood elite.

By 1927, a more permanent protective covenant was authored by a consultant named Charles H. Cheney, a city planner of some note. A 1904 graduate in architecture at the University of California, Berkeley, Lilian's alma mater, he had served as one of its founding members of the architectural association and no doubt was known personally to Lilian. In 1922, Cheney had drawn up a set of protective restrictions for Palos Verdes Estate, a planned community outside Los Angeles. Following Cheney's recommendation, a nonprofit organization, the Rancho Santa Fe Association, was formed in 1927 to oversee the new covenant mandated restrictions and to extend the time frame of the binding covenant. These new regulations were adopted by the Rancho Santa Fe Association on July 14, 1927. A subcommittee—the art jury—ensured that architectural restrictions were adhered to. Comprised of manager Sydney Nelson, Lilian as resident architectural expert who served as secretary, and Briggs C. Keck, as the representative resident, the art jury held its first recorded meeting on March 6, 1928. In her capacity as a member of this elite trio, Lilian had a great deal of power and used it judiciously to approve or reject projects, or aspects of the project, as she deemed fit.

16.
The Osuna Adobe

*T*his postcard-sized oil painting of the white-washed, single-story adobe hacienda was a pleasant image that captured the restoration of a historically important landmark in Rancho Santa Fe, undertaken by Lilian in 1925. It was a project that she must have surely relished, one that had noble roots that reached back to the "days of the Spanish Dons" as the era of the Californios was then romantically referred to in published accounts.

The hand that had skillfully laid down the oil paint in the visual recreation of this hacienda, using a fine brush with delicate strokes, belonged to Laura, Lilian's mother. The composition was the same one used by Padilla as he photographed the restored adobe at about the same time, in 1927, when the once derelict ruin had become a comfortable, beloved home to the Barlow family and a summer retreat for aunts, uncles, and cousins.

The miniature painting is in the private collection of Mim Sellgren, who agreed to generously loan it to me, so that I could scan it and share it with others. It is plain to see from where Lilian inherited her artistic aptitude and the remnants of Laura's art pieces offer proof that the artistic gene ran along the Rice female line. I could imagine Laura's interest and pride in her daughter's ground-breaking work at Rancho Santa Fe and how the two must have enjoyed animated conversations about the design and development of the community, and especially how Lilian invited her mother to visit, enjoy the scenery, and express her own artistry influenced by its romantic ambiance.

Rustic, yet comfortable, this restored adobe, labeled benignly as Adobe #1 by local historians (to differentiate it from Adobe #2 which was built later for Juan Maria Osuna) has caused a great deal of confusion in the written record. Most recently the adobe has been renamed simply the Osuna Adobe, according to a report by the new owners of the adobe and its surrounding acreage and horse ranch: the Rancho Santa Fe Association. The property was purchased in June 2006 by the association for $11.9 million, in efforts to preserve it and to prevent possible development. Land in Rancho Santa Fe comes with a premium price tag and this property, with its close proximity to the Ranch's village, situated on a knoll overlooking the San Dieguito River Valley, could bring millions of dollars more than the association's purchase price, if subdivided and developed into luxury estates. Most importantly they were preserving a precious slice of Californio history.

The original adobe was built circa 1831 by Jose Manuel Silvas, a member of an historic family whose documented history in San Diego goes back to the 1700s, according to Abel Silvas, a surviving descendent. Ten years after Mexico gained its independence from Spain, Silvas was given this provisional land grant for Rancho San Dieguito. However, five years later, both the simple adobe, then comprising just two rooms with rammed, earth flooring; an open exterior front porch that stretched the length of the structure, a thatched roof of light pole framework, lashed together with rawhide strips; and the surrounding two-square leagues of acreage were further granted to Juan Maria Osuna, a principal figure in the history of San Diego County. Lost to history are the reasons why this occurred, although Osuna held a great deal of political sway in the region being San Diego's first alcalde or mayor, as well as Major Domo—officer in charge—for the San Diego Mission D'Alcala and San Luis Rey Mission. The land grant was considered then, and now, a jewel in the Southern California landscape and has been described in the Osuna family written archives as

Laura Rice's miniature oil painting on canvas board that depicts the Osuna Adobe, circa 1927. *Courtesy Miriam Sellgren*

having within its boundaries, "luxuriant little valleys, ample lengths of mesa, and a bubbling river."

Adobe #2 was constructed in Rancho San Dieguito, along the historic route leading east from the coast, now known as Via de la Valle, and was designed as a more elegant and, therefore, a more fitting residence for Juan Maria Osuna and his wife Juliana. The exact date of construction is unknown, but reports allude to within a few years of the Osunas's taking claim to Adobe #1, which was subsequently inhabited by Osuna's son, Leandro. However, as the family holdings were depleted through a period of economic uncertainty, and as Southern California succumbed to western migration as it earned its statehood, the integrity of the land grant was undermined. With the death of Juan Maria Osuna in 1851, and Leandro's death in 1859, the land grant was chipped away, pieces sold to speculative businessmen, and the adobe stood merely as a reminder of the earlier lifestyle and culture of the former inhabitants who grew crops and raised cattle and sheep.

There is no verifiable record of the adobe's later residents, although they were likely descendants of the Osunas. What is known, however, is that by the late 1800s, the adobe structure had been altered with the addition of a living room, an extra room in the rear, and two bedrooms. The original roof had been replaced with milled lumber and shingles. The rustic home still offered the bare, basic accommodations with no bathroom facilities or kitchen. All food preparations would have been done outside using a clay-fired chiminea (an adobe oven) and bathing may well have taken place in the San Dieguito River. From the late 1800s until the purchase of the rancho by the railroad company in 1906, known as the adobe's American Period, the adobe fell into prolonged neglect and was a ruin when real estate developer Alfred Henry Barlow viewed the historic property.

It was in 1924 that Alfred and his wife Blanche visited Rancho Santa Fe with an eye to purchase the derelict adobe and the surrounding grounds. Today, that parcel of land amounts to 24.5 acres, which includes a horse boarding facility and a private residence, constructed in 1982, within its boundaries. However, when the Barlows viewed those grounds, they were home to an ancient pepper tree, cactus, and a pile of decaying adobe bricks literally melting back into the earth from whence they originated.

On viewing the property, the couple purchased the estate from the Santa Fe Land Improvement Company in 1924, but rather than developing it into an estate home with citrus and avocado orchards, the Barlows hired Lilian to restore the wreck of a structure and to transform it into a pleasant, simply designed *casa* for their family of five. Alfred Barlow was a successful businessman in nearby coastal La Jolla and had made a name for himself as a local developer. For one of his projects, the Country Club Heights development, Lilian later designed a Spanish Colonial Revival estate home in 1927 for a Mr. Turner, no doubt with recommendation from Alfred Barlow. But this adobe would not be torn down and replaced with a stylish, luxury home; rather, it would stand as a reminder of its former humble roots.

I met Laurie Barlow through social media. An architect based in Pasadena, she had an interest in the Osuna adobe, its storied past, and its future restoration. She also had a more personal interest in the adobe as she is a direct descendent of Alfred and Blanche Barlow being the granddaughter of Alfred's brother Robert Barlow. We initially communicated virtually via email and then eventually met in person in July 2011 in Rancho Santa Fe.

Laurie's cousins, Steve and Gale Barlow and Susan Barlow Loyd, came with us as we toured the former Osuna property now located on Via de Santa Fe in the village of Rancho Santa Fe. Susan's father was William Barlow, Alfred and Blanche's son. Born in October 1924, William was only a baby as the restoration of the adobe was taking shape and is captured in several of the family photographs. He had three older siblings—Betty, John, and Mary—although sadly, Betty died before the Barlows purchased the property. Susan is the only surviving

direct link to Alfred and Blanche Barlow. The day of our tour was one of brilliant sunshine and the rays beat down on us as we parked up in the sandy parking area that is now part of a horse-boarding facility. The telltale signs of gopher activity were evident as we strolled toward the adobe, and carefully avoided the uneven ground in front of the sagging structure with its white-washed walls peeling limply from an overall state of disrepair.

On entering the adobe structure, the heat of that July day was quelled by the adobe's interior coolness. The clay walls, at points up to forty-four inches thick, and small window openings, did exactly what they were designed to do: keep out the heat. The most striking feature of the interior was a large-breasted asymmetrical fireplace. This is a signature Lilian Rice feature and was added during her restoration in 1925. In the Barlow family's past, Blanche evidently, purposefully, and carefully documented the transformation of the derelict shell of the adobe into a lovely home for the family of five. The dates written onto photographs in the album begin in January 1925 and trace the steady construction of the project until its completion and beyond into 1927, as local photographer Padilla shot the newly restored home, its interior with that notable fireplace, and the grounds for the land company's promotional brochures and marketing materials, copies of which were given to the Barlow family and included in their album.

These unique photographs have captured the idyllic times enjoyed by a California family with the children exploring the natural beauty of Rancho Santa Fe, when extended family visited to enjoy summers there and "to come home" to a ranch house made comfortable and habitable by a lady architect. It has been reported that Lilian, like Hazel Waterman before her (as she restored the Casa de Estudillo), delved into the history of the adobe and, while transforming the structure to reflect a Spanish Colonial type, was mindful of the area's historic roots. She hired a team of Mexican craftsmen to manufacture the adobe bricks on site, using traditional methods passed down through generations, to replace missing or damaged wall sections. In addition to preserving the original structure, she constructed heavy beams to support a roof of red, barrel tiles, re-purposing original tiles salvaged from the Pala Mission. She added decorative shutters and erected a pergola over the open-air kitchen in the rear of

The Osuna Adobe in the heart of Rancho Santa Fe, as it lay in a ruinous state of decay, dated January 10, 1925. *Courtesy the Barlow Family*

Members of the Barlow family in front of the Osuna Adobe, 1925. Left to right, Unidentified, Alfred Barlow with William, Blanche Barlow with Mary. *Courtesy the Barlow Family*

Interior of the Osuna Adobe with Lilian Rice's signature fireplace built in 1925. *Photograph by PaulBodyPhoto.com*

the adobe. The long front porch, already destroyed, was instead replaced with a smaller porch that served as a welcome into the main entryway of the home. Lilian also restored a well-head in the grounds that was both functional and created visual interest, added native plantings along with bougainvillea vines, and created a rustic, adobe brick chiminea that rose several feet into the air.

Exterior walls were white-washed, and interior closets were built, with the added convenience of electricity and a much-needed bathroom. But there was still no interior kitchen, the Barlows preferred the traditional methods of outdoor food preparation as used by the Silvas and the Osuna women.

During my conversations with Tom Clotfelter, I learned that following the stock market crash of 1929, Alfred and Blanche were unable to financially keep the adobe and its estate in Rancho Santa Fe, and so it reverted back to the Santa Fe Land Improvement Company. Consequently, when Reginald

and Connie Clotfelter arrived in the Ranch in 1931, the adobe estate was for sale. Initially living for a few months in one of the upper apartments in the mixed-use complex in the civic center, as neighbors of Lilian's, they were asked by the land company to live in the adobe to help maintain it and show it to prospective buyers. In my meetings with Tom, he retold with a wry chuckle how the adobe was "cool in the summer, and wet and cool in the winter" and never quite warmed up, much to the chagrin of his mother who tried to dry his freshly washed diapers. The Clotfelter family lived in the adobe for three years in a bucolic setting with a gold fish pond, open space dominated by native flora, and the ancient pepper tree as a witness to quieter times when Connie, like Blanche and those before her, prepared dinner in an out-door kitchen.

For the Barlow family, today the adobe represents a link to a past when its forbears, Blanche and Alfred, Pennsylvania natives, migrated west with their family to start a new life. The fact that the couple had the foresight to rescue the historic Osuna ruin is an act to be especially proud of. The family photographic album, that so meticulously documented the construction of this wreck into a livable home, ironically is not in the hands of the Barlow descendants where it should rightfully be kept, treasured and passed down through the generations. Instead, the album has, by some unknown source and without the consent of the family, found its way into the archives of the California State Library in Sacramento. It is hoped that this chapter will bring this error to light and return Blanche and Alfred's priceless and irreplaceable property to their heirs.

For Lilian Rice, in 1925, the adobe represented a significant addition to her roster of work in Rancho Santa Fe and, at that time, it was acclaimed in several contemporaneous news reports as an important and sensitive remodel of a ruin that not only was an eyesore in the fledgling community of Rancho Santa Fe, but was destined to be hidden in the shadows of time without her intervening hand. This is a fact that is not lost on the Rancho Santa Fe Association that is striving to preserve the adobe and its surrounding acreage. By including Lilian Rice's historic contributions, that were so timely that the neglected adobe was rescued from certain obscurity, they are also paying homage to the lady architect who is largely responsible for the unique allure of the community of Ranch Santa Fe.

17.
Ed Spurr

*I*t was in the small hours of the morning when Ed Spurr heard an intruder stumbling about in the kitchens of his mother's Rancho Santa Fe eatery, known as Louise Badger's Fountain Lunch. As the Ranch's main watering hole, it was the local gathering spot for residents as well as serving as the local library. Ed's bedroom backed onto the kitchen, and at the age of ten he wasn't bold enough to venture out of his room to investigate the break in. Instead he lay frozen in his bed not daring to make a sound. In the morning, Ed knew that his fears had been groundless. He soon found out what had transpired when he walked into the kitchen during daylight hours and saw a hastily written note on the kitchen counter, "Put the beer on my account!" signed, "Bing Crosby."

Ed told me this story along with others about the early days of the Ranch when sightings of celebrities were commonplace. As with Bill Boetigger, Tom Clotfelter had introduced us. We met at Ed's home in Valley Center, in northeast San Diego; he was aging and infirm due to decades of smoking cigarettes, a habit picked up when he was in the Navy, and the emphysema he suffered as a consequence meant that he walked with his constant companion, an oxygen tank. Despite his failing health, Ed's mind was sharp and he was able to recall details that have not been published in newspaper records, the type of source that is invaluable: a firsthand account. His recollections brought to the fore the fledgling years of Rancho Santa Fe:

My father, Charlie Spurr, was hired by the land company to come down to manage the service station, as he'd been in that business in Santa Monica. I was a baby at the time. For my early years, before I was old enough to go to school, there was little for me to do.

Within a few years of the family's arrival in the Ranch, Charlie decided he didn't want anything to do with the new position he'd been offered and, without advance warning, abandoned his wife Louise to manage the service station and to raise her son by herself.

It was a difficult time for her, and as there were few families in the area, and as I wasn't old enough to attend the new school that had been built, there was no one to babysit me. My mother asked Lilian if she would keep an eye on me, and she gladly agreed.

Lilian's office was conveniently located close-by on Paseo Delicias in the civic center, and she accommodated her young charge by setting up a small table in her office, equipped with paper, set square, colored pencils, and chalks. Ed happily busied himself with "his projects at his drafting table."

It wouldn't be the last time that Lilian's services would be sought to babysit. When Tom Clotfelter was a baby, his mother Connie asked Lilian to watch him, which she gladly did. And when the MacDonalds moved into the Ranch, Lilian babysat their son Robert. It's clear that Lilian was a close part of this burgeoning community and that other women sought her friendship, but more importantly, they trusted her with their small children.

Ed remembered Lilian as a very kind woman who showed exemplary character by watching over him while his mother worked, especially as Lilian had so much responsibility to not only superintend the building development in the Ranch, but to also create new residential and commercial designs. She worked closely with her affluent and discerning clients, along with a team of subcontractors, who made their homes just as they visualized them. In addition to keeping her designs always fresh and unique, Lilian also had the extra burden of the running and management of a successful business, working long hours to complete the necessary specification sheets and other fine details that go into the design of a building. Telling of Lilian's position in the community, she was asked to serve as a school board trustee for the Aliso School District, to which she agreed. As the resident architectural designer, she also had the responsibility, as mentioned earlier, to be a part of the art jury board. One of only three board members, she vetted all the design work from architecture to landscape, to signage, before it was accepted and approved for construction, a role that was naturally of great benefit to the vetting of her own designs.

In the early 1930s, when a second school in the Ranch was in the final stages of construction by Lilian, in partnership with architect Hammond Whitsett, she "hired" Ed to count its rafters when a building superintendent had come to the site to inspect the construction. "She paid me forty cents an hour for the job, which took several hours to do. Boy, I thought it was fantastic money," Ed recalled.

Ed Spurr standing outside the school that he was not old enough to attend, Rancho Santa Fe, CA, circa 1927. *Courtesy the Spurr family*

When he became old enough, Ed attended that newly built school, which now houses the administration offices of the Rancho Santa Fe Association. These childhood memories stayed with Ed all his life and he held them dear. I was touched by his obvious fondness for Lilian. In later years, Ed honed his drawing skills by inventing humorous caricatures and comic strips, but as a hobby, not as a profession. And as an adult, he artfully designed three residences for his own family.

During my visit with Ed, we thumbed through his family album of vintage photos that had captured moments in time when the village of Rancho Santa Fe was in its infancy and the architecture was freshly constructed in the early 1920s. The images are monochrome, in high contrast, and have an artistic quality that provides a romantic veil over the scene. It gave me a tangible sense of the historic nature of those moments, especially the photograph in which Ed was standing in front of the school that he was not yet old enough to attend. Even though the photographs are not in color, it is obvious that the hues of the stucco used to coat the wood-frame structures were of varying shades of earth tones, not the whitewashed look that we see today. Ed recalled that the architectural style then was more Southwestern in its design type, with its thick, uneven walls, deep-set windows with rough hand-hewn timber lintels and exposed log vigas, roofed with red barrel tiles: signature Lilian Rice.

A treasured family photograph was one that was framed and hung on the wall; this image had been skillfully hand-colorized with oil paints. The photograph captures the entrance to the service station where Louise and her second husband Hal Badger worked for many years and where Ed helped out as a teenager, pumping gas, filling tanks with oil, and checking tires. A notable romantic feature of the service station was the gasoline pump, housed in a wishing-well-type structure, flanked by planters with cascading vines that both disguised and enhanced the prosaic nature of the pumps. It is an iconic image that represents how the design of the civic center did not in any way suggest a commercial purpose, rather its design created a pleasant ambiance for people to stroll along its three short blocks. In later years, the pump structure was torn down and the space filled in with a red brick office where a real estate business is now located. Likely, at that same

Ed Spurr in front of the house of his mother, Louise Badger, in the garage block of the civic center, Rancho Santa Fe, CA, circa 1927. *Courtesy the Spurr family*

time, the patio of Louise Badger's home was also filled in with a similar building, which for many years was home to the showroom of McNally's Silver and Antiques.

My conversation with Ed meandered to his recollections of some of the people who would come and go through the fountain lunch, and although Ed was a child, he had to help in the restaurant and was often called on to pitch in at the service station. The fountain lunch had one wall devoted exclusively to shelves brimming with books, that served as a branch library, taken over from Ruth Nelson. Ed said that Louise was particularly fond of her role as branch librarian as it meant that she had a close rapport with many of the Ranch residents who wandered in looking for a good read. Ed recalled Betty Davis coming in one time and he was surprised at how petite she was. When Bing Crosby drove into town, Ed helped service his car. In 1935, Bing drove a Lincoln Coupe, then in 1936, he switched to a Dodge, "He hated that car and drove it so hard it needed four quarts of oil after the trip down from Los Angeles," Ed told me. I understood why Bing

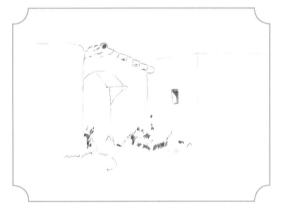

Sketch of the entrance to the garage service station quadrangle, re-created by Carol Beth Rodriguez. *Courtesy Carol Beth Rodriguez*

had little regard for his new Dodge, as the car was given to him for publicity reasons. I found an advertisement in the San Francisco Chronicle that boasted of the notable men who drove the new Dodge models, among them was Bing Crosby. With his classic Hollywood headshot, a direct quotation

A colorized vintage photograph that captures the simple beauty of a prosaic service station in the civic center, beautified by Lilian's artistic hand, circa 1927. *Courtesy the Spurr family*

The administration block, on the corner of Paseo Delicias and Via de Santa Fe, in the civic center of Rancho Santa Fe, California, as it looks today. Lilian Rice had her first office in this building. *Photo by Half Full Photography*

was published, "You're asking how I like my new Dodge? Well, I'd just like to see a car that offers so much driving satisfaction at such a low driving cost." Naturally, Bing had to say something positive about it, but Ed Spurr knew the truth.

Despite its rustic appearances, the civic center was on the cutting edge of technology and was designed specifically for the automobile. With its modern amenities, yet designed as garden city, it was a welcome retreat from Los Angeles, which by the 1920s, was succumbing to rapid development. So it was not surprising that several movie stars and directors visited Rancho Santa Fe, purchased land, and made it home. Many of them frequented the fountain lunch, much to the amusement of Ed.

During that period, Louise and Lilian became close friends, as the busy architect watched over Ed, allowing Louise to run the service station and fountain lunch and, as far as Ed knew, their friendship lasted until Lilian passed away in 1938. Seven years later, Louise retired from her business but stayed in Rancho Santa Fe and, in the 1950s, befriended actress Corinne Griffith, who had purchased the administration block in the civic center, with her then-husband George Preston Marshall, owner of the Washington Redskins. Corinne was famed in her early career as a silent movie star and was considered the most beautiful actress of her day, being known as the *Orchid Lady of the Screen*, due to her pale complexion, dark hair, and piercing blue eyes. She had been signed to the Vitagraph Company of America in 1916, when movie director King Vidor, who also bought property in the Ranch, discovered her at a West Texas health resort; she soon became its top star. Corinne also became known for her astute business acumen. In 1926, she paid $185,000 for two properties in downtown Beverly Hills, a purchase that would become the basis for her second career in commercial real estate. It's not known what she paid for the administration block—the price was not revealed in subsequent reports, but it must have been a princely sum. However, on September 28, 1941, an article in the *San Diego Union* reported news of the transaction. Headlined "Rancho Santa Fe Business Block Sold to Former Star," the story reported how Corinne planned to "make a little Wilshire Boulevard in Rancho Santa Fe." Her plans included a theater, a new service station, and alterations in the post office building (now home to Caldwell

Banker). But like many well-intentioned plans, Corinne did not realize them, and today there is no theater or new service station located on Paseo Delicias.

By the 1970s, it was clear that property values in Rancho Santa Fe were on the rise and the past few decades have secured its place in the nation as a most exclusive community of private expansive estates, just as the railroad company had originally planned it to be. Of interest is that both Louise and Corinne were devout Christian Scientists and attended church together, and were charter members of the First Church of Christ in Rancho Santa Fe. While Corinne evidently benefited from her investment in the civic center of Rancho Santa Fe, Louise did not fair so well. Unlike her movie star friend, Ed told me that Louise donated her property on Paseo Delicias to the First Church of Christ. Ed showed me the documents, signed by his mother and her accountant, that proved this transference of the property to the church. He also showed me Louise's original will, that left everything to her only son, that had gone unsigned and unfulfilled.

The Endless Miracle brochure was mailed from coast to coast, and satellite sales offices for the land improvement company were opened in Los Angeles and Pasadena to service potential clients there. An idyllic retreat in the backwoods of San Diego County was very appealing and caught the attention of that novel phenomenon, the movie star. At the turn of the century, silent movies were beginning to attract more audiences than live theater and, with the broad distribution of film made possible, actors and actresses became international sensations almost overnight and the "stars of the silver screen" were born. Artists flocked to the nerve center of the movie industry, Hollywood, and production companies rapidly expanded. However, as Hollywood morphed from its agrarian roots into a commercial and densely populated, residential landscape, those with the means to escape the overcrowding did so and purchased hidden ranches that primarily served as weekend retreats.

The first high-profile couple who ventured south to tour the estate lots of Rancho Santa Fe and secure one of its prime locations were Pauline Neff and her aviator husband Frank Coffyn. Pauline had starred in several silent films, as had Frank, and their hectic lives brought them to the tranquility of the Ranch where they purchased hilltop acreage, two-thirds of it devoted to citrus. Lilian, as the land company's architect, designed them an impressive estate home on Linea del Cielo, at the peak of a rise in the terrain that afforded panoramic views from the coast of nearby Solana Beach to the west and the mountains and arroyos to the east.

While scant written documentation has survived from that year of 1926 when Mr. and Mrs. Coffyn took title of their new purchase, stories have been passed down about the entertaining that the Coffyns did in that elegant home that they named "Olvidar"

which translates from Spanish to English to mean "*a place to forget*." Despite prohibition, alcohol was plentiful in the Ranch, and rumor had it that there was some serious "private socializing" taking place in these quiet and secluded backwoods. The *Rancho Santa Fe Progress* newspaper noted on several occasions that the Coffyns entertained out-of-town guests and that Lilian was often present. It's not hard to imagine the glamor and the prestige of these affairs as the famous couple opened up their home to guests. With its dramatic living room space dominated on one side by a solid wood balcony on the upper story, and capped with massive redwood roof beams that had been designed to mirror those in the living room of La Morada, the interior was impressive. The home's rear outside patio had smooth tile paving that made an ideal dance floor and a Victrola would have provided party-goers with dance music of the day recorded by popular artists like George Olson and Louis Armstrong. There was an exterior fireplace that provided ample warmth and ambiance for chilly evenings, and it's easy to visualize the social affairs that took place there organized by the attractive hostess, who must have relished in her new role as a homemaker, something world's apart from her prior role as an actress.

Pauline Neff rose to stardom acting in silent movies, but before that she was a stage actress. She was thrust into the national media spotlight when she married the wealthiest man in Pennsylvania, Dr. James Munyon, a multi-millionaire who had made his fortune initially by writing popular songs and then in the manufacture, patenting, and distribution of pharmaceuticals. Notice of the wedding appeared in regional newspapers from coast to coast, each article emphasizing the fact that Dr. Munyon was sixty and Pauline only twenty-four. The *Kansas City Star* reported in July 1908 that the newlyweds created

Again, Lilian makes a prosaic building look attractive through her use of Spanish colonial-type design. This building housed the pumps that irrigated the vast orange groves owned by Douglas Fairbanks Sr. and Mary Pickford. *Author's collection*

a sensation when they were sighted in Atlantic City with the three-month bride sporting a body-hugging sheath gown; the couple were mobbed by a crowd as they strolled along the boardwalk. The dress, so daring for the era, caused "promenaders to cluster around the couple," who were forced to call a cab to take them back to their hotel.

This was Pauline's second marriage; she had divorced her first husband—who she'd met and married when she was just sixteen—to make her union with Dr. Munyon possible. But like her first, this one did not last. Within six years, divorce papers were being drawn up. Evidently, the couple did not see eye-to-eye and often their heated outbursts were the brunt of public gossip. Naturally, the legal proceedings made newspaper headlines, this time with crowds gawking as Pauline tore up her soon to

be ex-husband's clothing in a spiteful rage. Munyon claimed the divorce on the grounds of desertion as Pauline spent most of her time traveling across the states starring in musical comedies and in vaudeville, refusing to stay put in Philadelphia. Her ex-husband told reporters that he wouldn't be marrying again; he'd rather just enjoy his friends.

However, by 1925, Pauline's star was rising and she was being cast in silent movies. In December of that year, she played an aristocratic beauty in a Metro-Goldwyn-Mayer (MGM) film *The Masked Bride* and by spring of 1926 she was starring alongside Frank Coffyn—who had become her third husband in 1919 —in *Ranson's Folly*. Frank was a pioneer aviator, as well as an actor, and he also served as an aviation consultant for the film industry. He had learned to fly from the Wright Brothers in Dayton,

Ohio, and was a member of the original Wright Flying Team—he was acclaimed as their "best man." At the Minnesota Fair, in the fall of 1911, flying a bi-plane, the *Grand Forks Daily Herald* reported he, "battled with wind and gravity and won." The following year, Frank displayed his aeronautic skills when he piloted a hydro-aeroplane over New York harbor. He climbed to heights of 800 feet, then dipped under the Brooklyn and Manhattan Bridges creating a spectacular stunt for the thrilled crowds below.

The handsome pilot and the beautiful actress must have been a charismatic couple and, as the first to purchase land in Rancho Santa Fe, they paved the way for other Hollywood stars to buy into the secluded estates of the Ranch. Lilian's relationship with the Coffyns would have boosted her professional reputation, and more commissions followed as a result with Lilian's roster of clients steadily increasing even through the Depression years. For the couple, though, the romance of the Ranch was short-lived. Despite outside appearances, their union was doomed and, on March 2, 1929, the *San Diego Evening Tribune* published notice that their divorce decree had been granted. They sold the estate home in the Ranch and Pauline Neff moved to nearby Del Mar as a single woman.

Frank Coffyn went on to reach greater heights with his flying career and, in 1930, he joined the staff of the General Development Company. It had plans to build the largest airliner in the world and Frank was hired as the test pilot. The story ran January 12, on page sixteen of the *Rockford Illinois Morning Star*. A smaller article adjacent to Coffyn's story showed the photograph of an attractive young woman with a broad smile framed with a flying helmet and goggles. The woman was eighteen-year-old Miss Mildred Stinaff from Akron, Ohio. "Life is just a series of ups and downs," quipped the writer who described Mildred's day job as an aerial test pilot. Hired by a local tire company, it was her task to undertake multiple take-offs and landings, often in hazardous conditions, to test the tires' maximum efficiencies. In 1930, she was the nation's only girl test pilot, yet today that accomplishment is forgotten. Like so many women of her era, she probably looked to other women as role models and likely followed the lead of Amelia Earhart, who received her pilot's license at age twenty-six in 1923. While the world

knows of the fate of Miss Earhart, as her flight across the Atlantic in 1938 resulted in her mysterious disappearance, Mildred Stinaff's name has been lost in the past, but we may remember her here despite her lack of celebrity.

Of note is the rise in film celebrity that skyrocketed in the early 1920s as silent movies gave way to talkies. In Los Angeles, film studios and Hollywood grew, as filmmakers gravitated to Southern California during the period of the industry's early development. Attracted by the mild climate and perpetual sunshine, movies could be filmed outdoors, year-round. In 1910, D. W. Griffith had filmed the first movie ever shot in Hollywood, *In Old California*, a melodrama about California in the nineteenth century when it was under Mexican rule. That movie would also spark a novel trend for the state to become enamored with its Spanish colonial roots. Griffith had come to the West Coast from New York and brought with him his acting troupe; among the team was a an attractive, petite actress, Mary Pickford. This opened the floodgates for others in the film industry and, by the second decade of the twentieth century, Hollywood became the movie capital of the world.

But as Hollywood became more crowded, actors and directors sought the quietude of a simpler life and looked south for real estate investment opportunities, and perhaps more importantly, for its close proximity to Tijuana, the border town in Mexico where gambling and drinking alcohol was legal during the Prohibition era. Independent movie producer and director Joseph Schenck and his actress wife Norma Talmadge, like the Coffyns, heard about the beauty, and, more importantly, the seclusion, of Rancho Santa Fe. The couple moved to Rancho Santa Fe in 1926, where they leased the home of retired New York banker D. M. Richards. His estate home on Las Colinas had been designed and built by Lilian in 1925. In an opposite tack to his famous tenants, Richards often spent his time in Los Angeles and enjoyed extended stays in the Biltmore Hotel, using his Rancho Santa Fe home mostly as a weekend retreat and then as an income property when he leased it out. The home had a simple elegance more rustic in design than the Coffyn's Olvidar. In Lilian's hallmark Spanish eclectic style, the home was constructed as a single-story dwelling with a varied roof line topped by red barrel tiles. Its windows were deep set and grilled, the exterior walls in tan stucco were complemented with window boxes and creeping vines. There was an attached garage and an outside walled patio. The spacious home was sited on a gentle rise in the terrain, surrounded by acres of citrus and avocados and is still lovely today.

By 1923, Joseph Schenck had agreed to a partnership with Douglas Fairbanks Sr., Mary Pickford, Charlie Chaplin, Norma and Constance Talmadge, D. W. Griffith, Pola Negri, and Harold Lloyd merging his company, the Norma Talmadge Film Corporation, with United Artists, and he was elected as president. With the boom of the movie business, actors became some of the highest paid people in the world and many invested their worth in real estate. Joseph Schenck, in 1925, invested in the Southern California Realty Corporation by financially backing the development of Talmadge Park, a San Diego city subdivision just north of El Cajon Boulevard and east of Kensington Avenue. Several of the district's streets were named for his wife and her sisters and still are today. The community was dedicated January 3, 1926, with the sisters in attendance along with Buster Keaton and Louis B. Mayer, which created quite a local sensation with people lining up to purchase lots in the subdivision.

At the same time that Talmadge Park was being built, work was begun on the modernization of Fairbanks and Pickford's studios in Hollywood. The *San Francisco Chronicle* reported that one million dollars would be spent on improvements on the compound. Douglas Fairbanks Sr. and Mary Pickford were the most famed of all the movie star couples in their era during the height of silent movies in the early 1920s and their earnings were immense. While their studios were undergoing a major facelift, their first movie theater was being created. United Artists' Theatre was designed by C. Howard Crane through architects Walker and Eisen, located on Broadway in downtown Los Angeles. A crowd of about 5,000 gathered to witness the groundbreaking on May 5, 1927. Mary Pickford ceremoniously lifted out the first scoop of earth from the lot having on the fly successfully mastered the controls of an industrial steam shovel. Director Fred Niblo

was master of ceremonies with Douglas Fairbanks Sr. and John Barrymore by Mary's side.

A *Los Angeles Times* reporter quoted Douglas as saying he hoped the theatre "will always be a reminder of the fact that Los Angeles is the center of production of the film industry," in what now proves to be a prophetic statement.

The theatre officially opened on December 26, 1927, with the silent film *My Best Girl* starring Mary Pickford and Buddy Rogers. John Barrymore emceed the grand opening and participating in the festivities—relayed by loudspeakers along Broadway for the large crowd of onlookers who had gathered—were Mary Pickford, Douglas Fairbanks Sr., Charlie Chaplin, Norma Talmadge, Gloria Swanson, D. W. Griffith, and Ronald Colman.

Douglas Fairbanks met actress Mary Pickford at a party in 1916 and, as they were both married then (but had fallen in love with each other), they began an affair. Eventually released from the bonds of their respective spouses, the couple were free to marry on March 28, 1920. They lived in their Beverly Hills estate, "Pickfair," becoming one of Hollywood's earliest super couples, much like today's Angelina Jolie and Brad Pitt. Douglas, born in Denver in 1883, was a child stage actor. He worked with an English acting company in New York as a young adult, then moved to Los Angeles in 1915 where he starred in silent movies, establishing his own company a year later. Within three years, Douglas was Hollywood's most popular actor and was the third-highest paid industry-wide. In 1917, he published a self-help book, *Laugh and Live,* which extolled the power of positive thinking and self-confidence in raising one's health, business, and social prospects, in hopes of sharing the secret of his success.

Mary was also a child actor. Born Gladys Mary Smith in 1892, in Toronto, Canada, she began performing at age five with family members and was known as *Baby Gladys.* She took the name Mary Pickford when she made her 1907 Broadway debut in the stage show *The Warrens of Virginia.* Within two years, she had joined the D. W. Griffith's Biograph Company and, by 1909, was appearing in a silent movie a week. Within seven years, Mary became an international star, beloved for her beauty and charm, and was known as "America's Sweetheart" and over the years, her fame grew as well as her worth.

It would be interesting to know what Lilian thought of Mary Pickford, who, according to one movie reporter in 1916, was: "The best known woman who has ever lived, the woman who was known to more people and loved by more people than any other woman that has been in all history." Lilian had often taken part in stage plays during her years at Cal and even afterward had played roles in local San Diego productions. Perhaps she was in awe of this megastar whose appeal was described in the trade magazine *Photoplay* as "luminous tenderness in a steel band of gutter ferocity," or perhaps the two had a mutual respect and admiration when in 1926 their paths crossed.

As groundsman for La Morada, Earnest Maddux made his regular rounds to supervise and protect the newly planted turf that lay in front of the guest house, a lawn that served both as a pleasant place to stroll and a croquet lawn for guests to while away their time. His indignation by the sight Earnest came upon when he saw Douglas Fairbanks practicing his golf swing with great gusto—using a riding whip in place of a club—on that newly planted lawn was understandable. The force of his swing caused chunks of grass to be whipped out by its roots and Earnest had to bite his tongue, unable to verbally chastise Douglas for his thoughtless actions.

But the land company management had no quarrel with Douglas Fairbanks; rather it was eager to capitalize on his and Mary's connection to Rancho Santa Fe. When the two secured their financial interests by their purchase of Block K, on the southeast side of the development, their names became a valuable addition to the marketing materials. One quarter-page newspaper advertisement in 1927 asked the rhetorical question, "Who are the owners at Rancho Santa Fe? Where do they come from?" With 200 families from across America buying property there, and with eighty percent of the land sold, the list read like a "Who's Who of America's Most Wealthy" and included the production manager of one of the largest motion picture studios in Hollywood and America's most-famous motion picture couple, along with bankers, capitalists, railroad officials, developers, corporate executives, hoteliers, and even an AIA architect from Illinois.

Land sales documents show that the Fairbankses purchased 800 acres of land in 1926, then added at least 2,000 acres more from the adjoining Lusardi Ranch. The *San Diego Evening Tribune* wrote: "After looking at many places the actor and his wife decided upon Rancho Santa Fe as the place for the building of an estate the like of which probably will not be equalled anywhere." According to the article, they'd planned to create an entire Spanish village on their vast holdings. At the time of its publication, in October 1927, they had made improvements totalling a quarter of a million dollars—over three and a half million dollars in today's money—part of the expense going solely to the construction of a dam, which captured the waters from the Lusardi Creek, at a cost of $25,000. The water held in the dam fed a high-tech irrigation system that ensured the healthy growth of swaths of Valencia orange groves and other crops.

Through my contact with the Rancho Santa Fe Historical Society, I was soon introduced to Jean Smart Barnes, then a resident in the nearby golf resort of Morgan Run. With vivid clarity, she recollected the role her father, William Smart, played as manager to the Fairbanks's property, and was able to supply firsthand accounts of these years when Mary and Douglas spent time on their ranch, which became known as "Rancho Zorro" after one of Douglas's famous films, *The Mark of Zorro*. Jean was just two years old when the family came to Rancho Santa Fe. Initially hired by the land company, Bill was educated in the new horticultural methods for cultivating citrus and avocados. The Smart family moved temporarily into the company's rental home, La Flecha House. When Bill was hired by Douglas Fairbanks, the family moved into a Spanish revival house designed by architect Wallace Neff, built on the grounds of Rancho Zorro. Wallace and Douglas were close friends and the Los Angeles-based architect had done a major remodel to Pickfair to transform it from a modest home into a luxurious mansion. It was fitting that he would be the architect of record for the couple's buildings on Rancho Zorro.

When Bill Smart was hired as estate manager, Douglas had largely retired from his career in acting, but would go on to star in few more movies until 1934. "How my father got to work for Douglas

Fairbanks is kind of a mystery," Jean told me. "We think that it was while my father was attending Occidental College he knew the man who later became Douglas Fairbanks's personal trainer." Douglas did many of his own stunts in movies like *The Three Musketeers* and *Robin Hood* and needed a trainer to help him learn acrobatic techniques. "In fact, at one time he had a small trampoline in the yard and he would practice jumping very gracefully onto the top of a high wall," said Jean.

There were hundreds of acres of citrus, as well as herds of cattle, and Bill oversaw all the operations of both and supervised Ranch staff. While Lilian did not design the manager's house, she did design the ancillary buildings: the pump house, which contained the equipment that irrigated the land, the well stations, and the company headquarter's offices. What is so notable about these prosaic structures is that, like the civic center buildings, Lilian gave them the same aesthetic treatment as a residential structure and, as such, their Spanish style exteriors artfully disguised their utilitarian purpose.

It was rumored that Douglas courted the new love of his life, Lady Sylvia Ashley, in the pump house when his relationship with Mary had soured, their legal partnership finally ending in divorce in 1936 after a three-year separation. In a typical Hollywood-style show of their union, the couple had earlier inscribed "Mary and Douglas" in the wet concrete at the edge of their newly completed dam. When Douglas came down to Ranch Zorro with his new bride, "there was a race before she got here to erase Mary and Douglas from the cement," recalled Jean. Lady Sylvia disliked the seclusion of the country and did not take kindly to her role as a Rancher's wife. When Douglas Fairbanks died of a heart attack at age fifty-six, in 1939, of a heart attack, Lady Sylvia married the legendary film actor Clark Gable and, within five years, she sold off a thousand acres of the ranch for $50,000 to George Sawday and Oliver V. Sexton, cattle ranchers.

The property was later purchased by Watt Development and became Fairbanks Ranch in the 1980s, a community development of affluent estate homes behind guarded gates, not unlike Rancho Santa Fe and with similar homeowner restrictions. A *Los Angeles Times* article noted

Douglas Fairbanks Sr. in a classic shot being caught in full action swinging from a tree on his estate, Rancho Zorro, in Rancho Santa Fe, CA, circa 1928. *Author's collection*

that the only house in Fairbanks Ranch built by Ray Watt—founder of Watt Industries—was a 9,000-square-foot version of the home designed, but never built, by Wallace Neff for Douglas Fairbanks and Mary Pickford. Ray Watt never lived there having sold it the day after its opening party. It's now known as Casa Zorro. The manager's house where the Smart family lived was renovated and sold to former president Richard M. Nixon's chief-of-staff, H. R. Haldeman, who has also since sold it. And Lilian's elegantly designed pump house has been converted into a community library, a transformation that no doubt would have had her complete approval.

19.

Don Bing

The pump house conversion into a library seemed to me to be a very practical repurposing of Lilian's building and it reminded me of how in my native England many structures from antiquity have been saved from demolitions by transforming them into something more usable, without destroying their historic integrity. When I traveled to England in the summer of 2008, I reconnected with my immediate family and we arranged to meet with my uncle and his wife in an old-world pub, a fine example of this repurposing. The rooms were cramped, the ceilings low, and the walls thick, but the atmosphere was priceless, and if the walls could talk, what a tale they would tell. This was an early seventeenth-century building, remarkably still standing, completely intact with its thick beamed ceiling and original Tudor timbers. Our conversation ebbed and flowed as I spoke with my uncle about my own family here in America. Just like my father, my uncle was attracted to the culture of the USA. Despite being the older brother, Ron looked ten years younger than my father. This slim, attractive man, dressed immaculately in a traditional blue blazer with brass buttons, with a full head of white hair that accentuated his blue eyes, was a gentleman, in the truest sense of the word.

"What are you working on these days?" he asked of my writing projects. I told him that I was doing research for a book on an obscure lady architect.

"You won't know her," I remarked. But surprisingly Ron did recognize Lilian's name.

"Didn't she do some work for Bing Crosby on his estate in California?"

As my jaw dropped, Ron explained that he was the photograph archivist for the International Bing Crosby Club, and recalled seeing photos of Bing at his Rancho Santa Fe Ranch. There was a magazine article written about its remodel, which he offered to send to me. How little I knew my uncle, it seemed.

As promised, Ron, who despite his eighty-four years, was up to speed with e-mail, sent an attached copy of the published magazine article that he referenced that afternoon at the pub, along with several high-resolution photographs of Bing Crosby, posing at his hacienda in Rancho Santa Fe.

The race was promoted as "One of the Greatest Match Races of All Times." The date was set for August 12, 1938. The Del Mar Racetrack had been opened a year and Bing Crosby had literally put his life on the line when he used his life insurance as collateral to fund what started out as a WPA project, but when the funding stream was axed, ended up as a major financial risk for Crosby. A year earlier, he had poured $600,000 of his own money into ensuring the completion of the construction of the fairgrounds that housed the racetrack in the coastal community of Del Mar, 100 miles south of Los Angeles and forty miles north of the Mexican border. He desperately needed the support of his Hollywood chums to beef up attendance during what was still a time of national financial uncertainty. Its daily attendance averaged only 6,000 in 1938, which wasn't enough to keep the track's finances in the black. The match race promised to put Del Mar on the map, and with an agreed winner-take-all purse of $25,000, the contest would be fierce, not only pitting horse against horse, but father against son. Through radio, the world would witness one of the most exciting horse races ever run: Charles Howard's Seabiscuit against Lin Howard's and Bing Crosby's Ligaroti. A twenty-foot banner emblazoned with "I'm for Ligaroti" marked the Crosby fan's section at the racetrack, which included Clark Gable, Carole Lambard, and Spencer Tracy, and scores of other Hollywood celebrities. Seated in the midst of the stars was Eleanor Dean, a local writer from Rancho Santa Fe, and daughter of Lewis A.

Bing Crosby, singer and movie star, purchased the former Juan Maria
Osuna hacienda and ranch in 1934. *Courtesy Ron Bosley*

McGowan, a prominent attorney who had gained international recognition when he served as one of the prosecutors in the Nuremberg Trials. Social and effervescent Eleanor was happy to serve as the hostess for the Del Mar Thoroughbred Club, where the most expensive seats allowed the elite few private premium views of the track.

"I remember the big build up," said Eleanor when I interviewed her in 2007. In her nineties, she still had a vivid recollection of that historic event. "There were posters plastered all over Del Mar and Solana Beach advertising the race and naturally Bing brought in some of the biggest stars of the day to the track."

The day of the race, the train brought people down from Orange County and Los Angeles and crowds from around the county arrived by bus. An estimated 20,000 people packed the facility beyond its capacity. "It was madness," said Eleanor in her posh East Coast accent. "People at trackside were very boisterous and the noise was deafening as the race began, and of course we all know how it ended."

With Seabiscuit winning by a nose and Charles Howard accepting the winning trophy from Bing Crosby's wife, Dixie-Lee, the race was forever cemented into horse racing lore, and despite Crosby's displeasure at Ligaroti's loss, it put Del Mar on the map. While Eleanor Dean was caught up in the intensity of what the *San Diego Sun* dubbed, "The most 'dingbustingest' contest you ever clapped an eye on," Lilian was working on the completion of one of her most high profile commissions of the 1930s, when she once again found herself the personal architect to a high-profile celebrity, the most famous entertainer in the nation, Bing Crosby, who had purchased the Osuna adobe and its expansive acreage in Rancho Santa Fe in 1934. The sale came with a rich history, as Bing and his family were also inhabiting the former royal seat of Juan Maria Osuna. For Crosby, who in the mid-1930s was considered Hollywood royalty, it was perhaps a fitting abode, and newspapers referred to him as "Don Bing."

After the land company had bought the final vestiges of the Osuna family's holdings, Rancho San Dieguito, and Ojuna's former hacienda, became the first administrative center for the land company management. In its former days, through the 1800s, the land had been a thriving ranch.

Bing Crosby, some seventy-five years later, purchased the very heart of this once-thriving cattle ranch with its hacienda that was said to have once sheltered General Pico's Mexican Rangers during the war between Mexico and the United States. Bing's path would align with Lilian's, and history would be revisited when her services were used, to not only transform the hacienda to modern standards, but to also build an authentic adjoining adobe home for Bing's brother and manager Everett, in addition to a race track, and stables for his thoroughbreds, tennis courts, and a swimming pool that local kids would be welcome to use.

Curious to find out more about Bing, I perused the news accounts from his early years in radio in 1929 over a twenty-year period. The most obvious aspect of these archives is that Bing is in the paper every day, sometimes twice a day, which in itself is telling of his widespread celebrity status. Bing's fame began in radio, his signature velvet voice airing from

Los Angeles KFRC. Movie shorts led to full-length feature films and, by the mid 1930s, Bing Crosby was a household name.

In the post year's of the stock market crash of 1929, the entire country struggled to survive and the radio brought much-needed light entertainment into people's living rooms. Along with the new technology of the movies, entertainers enjoyed a reach to their fans that was unprecedented and they took on royal status. The media clamored to provide the fans with any tidbits of information about their idols. But "celebrity" came with a price. A panic gripped the rich and famous as aviator Charles Lindbergh grieved for his young son who was kidnapped and subsequently murdered in the early 1930s. On March 22, 1934, the *San Diego Evening Tribune* reported that Bing and his wife Dixie-Lee had received kidnapping and extortion threats for their son Gary, then only nine months old. Armed guards were placed at the Crosby's home in Toluca Lake, in the San Fernando Valley. Bing also became an official sheriff's deputy and was licensed to carry a firearm. When twins Phillip and Dennis were born on Friday, July 13,1934, the Crosbys had already closed escrow on their purchase of the forty-four acre estate in the remote community of Rancho Santa Fe in San Diego county.

Lilian brought in native Mexican experts to supervise and manufacture the adobe bricks that would go into the construction of an extended wing to the existing one-story hacienda, with its white-posted, wraparound veranda. Earlier work had been completed on the hacienda when part of the main residence had been expanded and converted into temporary SFLIC offices as Lilian and Leone Sinnard worked out the plans for Rancho Santa Fe in situ. Original stables on the grounds were converted into servants quarters and new stables were constructed as part of a racetrack complex where Bing would exercise and train his thoroughbreds, the most famed being Ligarotti. By the time Lindsay was born in 1938 and the Crosby family was complete, Lilian had also added a nursery, that accommodated all four of the boys, and a nanny's quarters. She brought the main residence up to modern standards, enlarging the family room and creating a studio for Bing, but retained the original Spanish ambiance with her signature open-beamed ceiling, built-in bookshelves and niches, deep-set windows, varied floor-levels, and three-foot thick adobe walls.

None of the exchanges between the Crosbys and Lilian have survived and any conversations or written documentation about this major remodel are lost forever. But the plans for the nursery were rescued and kept by one of Lilian's female associate architects and were subsequently donated to the International Archive of Women in Architecture (IAWA). While there is little information on Lilian, there is a vast wellspring of data on Bing Crosby due to his enduring fame, which keeps him relevant today.

By the 1940s, he was voted the number-one box office attraction five years in a row. Bing had the most number-one hits; at thirty eight, he well outperformed the Beatles record of twenty-four. His rendition of "White Christmas" remains the all-time most popular record and Bing made more studio recordings than any other singer. Bing also witnessed major historic shifts in popular culture: those of the recording industry, the rise of radio, the broad distribution of sound movies, and then survived the Depression, was a major morale lifter for troops during World War II, and enjoyed a second career in the postwar era.

By the mid 1930s, Bing Crosby was the most popular entertainer in the world. As well as being a movie and recording star, he co-owned Binglin Stables. Crosby also placed the nearby coastal city of Del Mar on the world map when he loaned money in 1937 to complete the construction of the Del Mar Race Track. *Courtesy Ron Bosley*

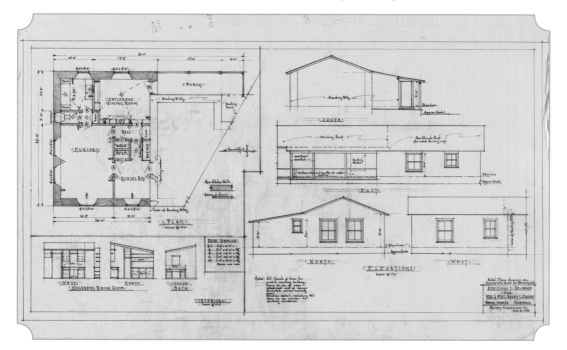

Floor plans that show Lilian's nursery addition to the Crosby ranch house. Dated 1938, this was one of the last projects on her books and would have been completed under the supervision of Olive Chadeayne, who took over her firm following Lilian's death. *Author's collection*

Jerry Ward, a Solana Beach resident, shown with Lindsay Crosby, at the Crosby estate in Rancho Santa Fe. Circa 1940. *Author's collection*

A handsome and charming young man, Jerry Ward, who lived in nearby Solana Beach, was employed by Bing and Dixie-Lee to watch over their four boys, to teach them to swim, and ride horses. I was fortunate to meet Jerry when he was ninety-four and still very active, and had a clear memory of the Crosby family.

Jerry was orphaned at an early age and was taken in by the St. Johns of Solana Beach, a religious family who adopted him from the San Diego Boys and Girls Aid Orphanage in the 1920s. Part of the relationship was that Jerry helped with raising their own four boys. With the onset of the Depression in 1929, Jerry, then a teenager, had no choice but to find work when the St. Johns could no longer support him and asked him to leave. Fortunately, he got a job with nearby Conley Dairy and milked fifteen cows twice a day, for the meager sum of $30 a month.

His respite came at the beach, which was both source of recreation and sport for Jerry, who was a strong surfer and swimmer. Life changed when actor Bing Crosby sent one of his PR men to make inquiries about hiring a local boy to supervise his four sons. Judge Cochran, who had his office in the Solana Beach Hotel, recommended Jerry for the job. An interview was set up and Jerry was hired by Bing and paid $6 a day, plus food, to teach swimming and horseback riding to the Crosby boys. Jerry told me how he remembers well those years with the Crosby family. The boys were rambunctious with high energy and Jerry had his hands full, "but they were never any trouble; I just played with them," he said. The later accounts by Gary Crosby of his father did not ring true for Jerry. "Mr. Crosby was strict because he didn't want his sons to be spoiled, but I never once saw him abusing them," Jerry said. "I personally never did see a mean-spirited side of him."

Bing helped Jerry start a newspaper delivery business. "He loaned me $500 so that I could buy a car and purchase the route," said Jerry, who drove about a hundred miles daily delivering the *Los Angeles Examiner* in North County San Diego. When he entered the Navy during World War II, Jerry still owed Crosby $350. Hoping that perhaps the loan would be forgiven, Jerry nevertheless sent his final payment to Bing, who subsequently cashed the check, "which supports the reputation of him being a notorious tightwad," said Jerry.

During his time in Rancho Santa Fe, which spanned about ten years, Bing Crosby was a welcome addition to the Ranch's roster of rich and famous. He brought new life into the foundering golf course that had been designed and created by Max Behr in 1927. The years of the Depression resulted in the golf club's low membership, so Bing, an avid golfer, agreed to organize highly publicized celebrity golf tournaments to bolster it. Known as clambakes, these lighthearted competitions provided media moments and brought Rancho Santa Fe much-needed press. When the Del Mar Race Track opened in 1937, Jerry attended the opening day. "I remember well that Bing was there greeting people at the gate," he said. The opening of the fairgrounds, in 1936, and the racetrack a year later, brought a new sense of hope to San Diego County and offered a welcome escape from the pessimism of the depressed 1930s. Surprisingly, it had ushered in a period of industry for Lilian's architectural office.

William Krisel

Lilian's colored pencil and water color rendering of the front elevation of the Krisel ranch house in Rancho Santa Fe, CA, circa 1935, not built. *Courtesy William Krisel*

The 1930s for Lilian proved to be a decade that now represents a high point in her career. President Franklin D. Roosevelt's New Deal meant that local architects had opportunity and Lilian was one of them. She gained commissions for public projects during this era of economic uncertainty, but she also landed several residential commissions, too. One of these projects, that was never realized, however, was the Krisel residence in Rancho Santa Fe. I have in my collection of Lilian Rice materials a manila envelope that contains precious papers, that would be meaningless to most, but for me it has great value. Inside an ivory cardboard folder, yellowed and tattered through over eighty years of existence, are several letters of great historic value. These papers arrived in a priority mail envelope on the morning of May 14, 2012, and when I received them, I felt like all my birthdays from the past decades had been rolled into one, I was that excited. I didn't know what exactly what was inside but I knew it was special as the person who had sent the package was Bill Krisel, the son of Alexander and Cecilia Krisel who had commissioned Lilian to design their Rancho Santa Fe home in 1935. Bill had e-mailed me a few days earlier mentioning that he had been clearing out some old papers and that these may be of interest to me. They were more than interesting, they were treasure.

Meeting Bill Krisel was one of life's happy events born from fortunate timing. Andrew Wright, an architect in Rancho Santa Fe and a member of the Rancho Santa Fe Association's art jury (in that role, he is the modern counterpart to Lilian) called me. He advised me that Bill was clearing out his papers and architectural effects from his former office on Paseo Delicias in Rancho Santa Fe and that if I was quick I could meet him and share with him about my work on Lilian Rice. If I hurried, I could possibly interview him. It was a kind gesture, Andrew knew of my interest in architecture and at the time, 2009, my first book on Lilian Rice was in progress and still in the research phase. But I said I was free to take a break from my work and asked Andrew to let Bill know that I was going to drop by, and so to expect me.

Within twenty minutes I was knocking on the door of Bill's former office and he was gracious enough to stop what he was doing and sit down to chat with me. I recorded his interview and it is now part of my digital audio archives. The interview is dated March 23, 2009, just two days after my fifty-first birthday. On meeting him, I observed that Bill was casually dressed in a comfortable cardigan, his hair was thick and white, and he sported his signature moustache. He looked kind and very approachable, and that's exactly what he was. He reminded me very much of Charlie Chaplin in his later years, which proved coincidental because Bill's father, being connected with the movie industry in the 1920s and '30s had been very closely associated with Chaplin. We talked mostly about Bill's family connection to Lilian Rice, who designed a home for his parents in Rancho Santa Fe and how her advice would spark in Bill a lifelong love for architecture. He told me:

> My dad had met with Lilian before he came back to China. When they came home on the ship, I remember meeting them and they had this box that they were handling very carefully. Inside was a clay model of the house that Lilian had made to represent the actual building and they'd brought it back to China along with all the preliminary plans.

At the time the Krisel family—parents Alexander and Cecilia, and three boys, Henry, Lionel, and William—lived in Shanghai. Alexander was a copyright attorney, but also the distributor for films produced by several major motion picture companies. He represented them in China, Japan, the Philippines, and India. Bill said:

> He was in the Diplomatic Corps after he graduated from law school. He went to China where he spent eight years in the State Department until he resigned. But rather than return to the US he stayed in Shanghai where he opened a law practice. In those days there was a lot of problem with the pirating of films so my dad proposed to United Artists Corporation that he would go after them, which he did, and he was successful. That's how dad first got in business with Douglas Fairbanks and Mary Pickford.

Alexander proposed that United Artists Corporation could retain him as the distributor for its films in the Pacific Rim, which it agreed to; then he contacted all the other major industry studios and represented them—during a ten-year period from about 1927 through 1937. Bill was born in Shanghai on November 14, 1924. He lived there for the first twelve years of his life, and naturally it would have had a lasting impression on him. The Krisels returned to the US every two years and, with Alexander being close friends with Douglas Fairbanks, the family would stay at Pickfair in Beverly Hills. On one of these visits Alexander mentioned that he was thinking of retirement and Douglas recommended California, "You should go down to Rancho Santa Fe. I'll take you down there," he suggested. Alexander visited Rancho Zorro but stayed at La Morada. "My dad and mom liked Rancho Santa Fe very much, so they bought a lot on Via de Fortuna, twenty-three acres," said Bill. The property was purchased through the land company real estate agent, Mr. A. R. Bishop whose junior partner then was Reg Clotfelter.

The Krisels also bought a piece of property by the golf course, which was devoted to a ten-acre grove of Sunkist oranges. Ray Badger, the orchard contractor, planted and maintained the crop. But this was 1934 and still the height of the Great Depression. "So every year we lost money," chuckled Bill. "My dad had a great idea that he proposed to Sunkist for making frozen orange juice—there was no such thing then; they thought it would save the growers from throwing away their oranges, but they couldn't figure out how to do it. So we ended up throwing a lot away."

The restrictions in Rancho Santa Fe meant that the Krisels had to plant their acreage to agriculture or build a house within a year of purchasing the property. They commissioned Lilian Rice in 1934 to design the house on Via de Fortuna, but there was competition. Word soon got out about the Krisel's land purchase and, as times were hard and architects were struggling to find new projects, Alexander was contacted by Welton Becket, a partner in the firm Plummer, Wurdeman and Becket. Without consulting Alexander, he had swiftly drawn up preliminary plans for a proposed residence, drove down to Rancho Santa Fe from their office in Beverly Hills, and presented them to the Krisels. Bill said:

> My dad was quite impressed [with the design] but he came to the conclusion that since he was going back to China he had better use a local architect and everybody liked Lilian Rice.

While in Rancho Santa Fe Alexander stayed at La Morada and Lilian conveniently lived just behind it in her little cottage and her offices were down the street. He also wanted the home to blend in with all the rest, and as the design restrictions mandated that homes should conform to a Mediterranean type, Lilian was the best architect for the project. Due to the distance between client and architect, as the Krisel family returned to China, there was much correspondence back and forth between Lilian and the Krisels over this two-year period from 1934 to 1936.

A letter typed on the day of Lilian's forty-fifth birthday, June 12, 1934, confirmed the oral agreement between Lilian and Alexander Krisel. In an attempt to cut costs, reducing Lilian's fee from seven percent to six percent, Alexander suggested that Mr. A. R. Bishop—Rudy—then on site manager of Rancho Santa Fe, should act as supervisor of the project. By September 4, 1934, an agreement was put in writing that satisfied all parties and the work proceeded.

Lilian's offices drew up the preliminary plans by the fall of 1934 and created a three-dimensional model in clay that was very carefully carried by hand the 7,500 miles to China. As Bill observed his parents studying Lilian's plans back in Shanghai, the conversation naturally turned toward fine-tuning them and the changes that Alexander and Cecilia agreed on would be relayed by Western Union telegram and through letters to Lilian. Alexander dictated this correspondence to his secretary, who typed it up and sent it off to Lilian's Rancho Santa Fe office. Bill would sit and listen carefully to this dictation, then he would go to his room, take a piece of paper, and sketch out how he visualized those changes might look. Then he would ask his father, "Is this what you meant?" and Alexander would answer, "Yes, that's it exactly!" The sketches were included in a return letter to Lilian who wrote back to Alexander conveying advice that would help shape Bill's future career, "Your son shows talent; he should become an architect."

The project moved along and, by September 1935, it was at the point of breaking ground for construction. Lilian had completed the drawings and produced front and rear presentation renderings. The ranch house was single-story, and, like the Cord home, lay as a horizontal structure on the terrain with views of Black Mountain. Alexander had seen the home of a friend, Mr. Meyer, who had recently built a residence in the Ranch, and Alexander used it as design reference for his home, which was rustic in its exterior but luxurious inside. The proposed interior walls of a spacious living room and dining room were wood paneled, floors were laid with oak, there were five fireplaces finished in natural toned Batchelder tiles topped with solid wood mantels. Windows were fixed sash, several with wooden grilles for privacy. There was an exterior patio fireplace with built-in seats, a flower room, laundry room, children's bedrooms and playroom with built-in box couches, maids' quarters, a garage, a tool room, several bathrooms, and separate powder room, master bedroom with private patio and walk-in cedar lined closets, and a stately library with knotty pine walls, modeled on the oval room in the White House.

The landscaping, by resident landscape architect Paul Avery, complemented the home and included horse bridal paths, decorative plantings, succulents, sycamores, oak, and eucalyptus, with the majority of the lot dedicated to acres of citrus and avocado groves. There were also stables and a horse corral, designed by Lilian, a swimming pool, and tennis courts. With all the custom features, the project grew with an anticipated cost of about $5 a square foot for a house that was over 4,000 square feet, which would prove to be a sticking point for the budget of the project.

As it was the month of September, it was also the time of year when local students were heading back to classes. Cecilia naturally had a keen interest in looking at nearby high schools. In the fall of 1935, a brand new school district had literally just been created—the San Dieguito Union High School District. Because it was so new, the school's location had not yet been chosen and the school had not been designed. The first graduating class of San Dieguito Union High School attended classes in temporary classrooms using tents on the site of Pacific View Elementary School in Encinitas. This is what Cecilia observed as the closest high school for her sons. As a result, she felt that the school was wholly unsuitable for them and that in the cold light of day Rancho Santa Fe was not suitable to raise her teenagers.

Before they had approached Lilian to design their home, they had considered buying a house already built in the Ranch and, at the time, the

Osuna hacienda was on the market, Alexander had made a tentative offer and the property was in escrow. "My mom was walking around there one day and someone said that they'd just killed a rattlesnake," Bill told me. The comment spooked Cecilia, who refused to even look at the property, let alone live there; consequently, escrow did not close. But another buyer soon came along, who thought the property was perfect. Bing Crosby was that buyer.

Another idea was to purchase La Morada, which, in 1934, was in bankruptcy. "My dad negotiated tentatively to buy it," said Bill. He thought it would be a nice place to live while we built the house. We were moving from a large house in Shanghai where my mother didn't have to do anything as we had about twelve servants. La Morada had on site staff, so she still would have everything done for her." But Cecilia said again, "no," that she didn't want her sons to grow up there. After two years of planning, the house in Rancho Santa Fe was not built and the Krisels moved into a home they already owned in Beverly Hills on Summit Drive. While the family had been in Shanghai, MGM movie director King Vidor rented that house while he was building his own further up the street. The timing was perfect for the family to move in, as King Vidor's home was completed. Their neighbors were Charlie Chaplin, Douglas Fairbanks and Mary Pickford, and Fred Astaire, who each owned sprawling estates in the chic Beverly Hills zip code that was known locally as Rolls Royce Row.

When he was a twelve-year-old, Bill was wise beyond his years and had written a letter to the editor that was published in *Time Magazine*. His letter was in response to a story that the magazine had published about Franklin Roosevelt, who at the time was running for president. Roosevelt had a place in Warm Springs, Georgia, with a modest home, his "Little White House," that he had designed for himself, his houseman, and his dog. Included with the story was Roosevelt's floor plan. Bill told me:

> I sent a letter to the editor stating that the plan was not good. I explained what was wrong with it and made suggestions about how he should change it, and they published

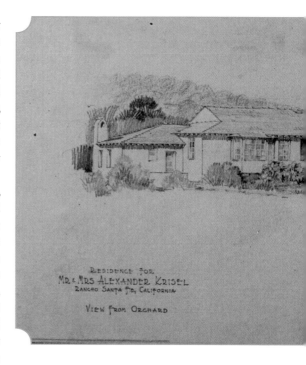

RESIDENCE FOR
MR. & MRS. ALEXANDER KRISEL
RANCHO SANTA FE, CALIFORNIA

VIEW FROM ORCHARD

my letter, along with the editor's comment: "*Time Magazine* applauds, *architect* Krisel's attempts but prefers *architect* Roosevelt's own version."

Bill Krisel graduated from Beverly Hills High School in 1941 at age sixteen, then was accepted into the University of Southern California's (USC) architectural program. But world events transpired that interrupted those studies: Pearl Harbor was bombed on December 7, 1941. Bill wanted to immediately enlist and quit school, but the Army, and his parents, advised him to complete his freshman year at university, which he did. So at age seventeen, Bill went into the Army for four years of service. Because he spoke Chinese fluently, he was sent to China where he served as General Joseph Stilwell's interpreter, traveling the country and meeting famous Chinese leaders, including Mao Tse-tung and Chiang Kai-shek. After the bombs were dropped on Nagasaki, Bill was the first American in Shanghai to witness the official surrender of the Japanese forces, August of 1945. Because he had enough points due to the extensive overseas deployment, Bill was allowed to go home, his release was signed and he arrived home as a civilian in California on Christmas Day.

Lilian's colored pencil and water color rendering of the rear elevation of the Krisel ranch house in Rancho Santa Fe, CA, circa 1935, not built. *Courtesy William Krisel*

LILIAN J. RICE, ARCHITECT

By January 1946, Bill had made arrangements to go back to school, then by February was able to return to his architectural program at USC, graduating in the summer of 1949 with a double degree in architecture and landscape architecture. During his studies, he had interned at Paul Laszlo's firm in Beverly Hills, as well as Victor Gruen's firm. A year after graduation, he received his license in architecture and started his own firm with Dan Saxon Palmer, whom he had met and worked alongside in Victor Gruen's office. They got along very well and subsequently formed their partnership, Palmer and Krisel. The two completed a significant body of work in Palm Desert and Palm Springs. Bill received a lifetime achievement award from the AIA and, in typical Hollywood style, has a star embedded in the sidewalk on the "Walk of Fame" in Palm Springs where the local historic organizations have done an excellent job in the preservation of many of the city's mid-century modernism homes, including the much sought after Palmer/Krisel homes.

After our meeting in March 2009, Bill kept in close contact with me. A documentary on his life and work was created and made into a DVD by Jake Gorst. I was in the audience when the film made its debut in 2010 in Palm Springs on Valentine's Day. Over the span of his thirty-year career, from 1949 to 1979, Bill completed 40,000 housing units. And to think it all started with a seed planted eighty years ago by Lilian Rice.

I thumbed through the delicate papers that had arrived in my mailbox from Bill, and I was immediately sent back in time almost eighty years. As I carefully read each paper, an historic time line was presented to me, one that documented, through correspondence, a building project between a prominent attorney in Shanghai, and a talented lady architect in California. Each letter from Lilian was on her company stationery, those from Alexander were on golden yellow tissue carbon copies, with the letterhead, Krisel and Krisel, and the address, 152 Museum Road, Shanghai, China. The letters back and forth discussed the design of the home to be built on Via de Fortuna and the terms of the arrangement. They spanned from June 12, 1934 to September 26, 1935, which is evidently the last letter between the parties. As the months progressed and more changes were made to the preliminary design, the costs naturally climbed. Alexander compared his home to that of a local neighbor and family friend Mr. Charles

The author with William Krisel
in Rancho Santa Fe, 2008.
Author's collection

F. Meyer (which had a completed cost of $20,250) and wondered why there was a noted difference with Lilian's projections reaching costs that added $7,820 for the construction of the house, plus an additional $2,800 for the stables and corral, for a grand total of over $30,000. Lilian carefully listed the comparisons between the Krisel house and the Meyer House, known as "La Canoncito" in a letter to Alexander that pinpointed where the differences lay; she took the time to consult with Meyer's contractor, Mr. Randall, to get exact numbers. In September 1935, lumber had increased by $11 per unit; the Krisel house was 800 square feet bigger than Meyer's and had an additional 1,200 square feet devoted to paved terracing; it required extra reinforcement and concrete, gutters at all eaves, five fireplaces, special treatment on the oval library walls, and extensive tile throughout each of the three bathrooms. Lilian congenially suggested minor changes that would reduce some of the costs and "to take care of it without any extra charge."

The value of this back and forth correspondence is priceless, as there are no other records for an entire year (letters and related papers), that are extant, from Lilian's office. In addition to the business letters, there is one of Bill's sketches rendered on thin, light-pink stock, a leaf of United Artists Corporation Rushgram paper. The sketch represents the servants' quarters, carefully drawn out with a ruler, and neatly labeled by Bill in steady capital letters. There were two bedrooms, a shared bathroom, a kitchen, a laundry room, a closet, a living area, and a garage. Clearly the plan was to have the maids living comfortably and self-contained from the rest of the house affording them privacy and independence. Also in the stack of papers were scratch notes of calculations of sizes for each room, written in sepia ink by Alexander, which is telling of his fastidious nature in the budgeting of the project. Some of the sums were hastily calculated in pencil on the stationary of S.S. *President Coolidge* of the Dollar Steamships Line, which would have been one of the ships traveled on by Alexander during his many crossings from Shanghai to California. Of greater interest though is a typed booklet of thirty-five pages that contains all the specifications for the Krisel's residence and garage. Dated June 22, 1935, it is a thorough and historic written record of the painstaking detail that was essential for a residential building project during that time. The first eight pages are devoted to the legal position of various parties connected with the project and includes an explanation of the contractor's and sub-contractors' roles and that of the architect, which Lilian interestingly refers to as "he":

> As the architect is the interpreter of the conditions of the contract and the judge of its performance, he shall side neither with the owner nor with the contractor but shall use his powers under the contract to enforce its faithful performance by both.

Paragraphs include the provisions for the creation and use of drawings and plans, a payment schedule, insurances, guarantees, surveying, plumbing and water, meters, and even the promise to install temporary toilets for the use of the work crew. Then from page nine to page thirty-five, Lilian painstakingly itemizes every detail of the construction of the house, from its foundation, to the landscaping, mason work, carpentry, fenestration, floor treatments, interior wall finishes, built-ins, tile work, metal work, electrical, plumbing, telephone wiring, bathroom fixtures, heating and more. When reading through this booklet, typed up flawlessly on letter-sized paper, I can imagine Lilian seated at her desk, likely with a Royal typewriter in front of her, tapping away well into the late evening hours, on its clumsy, stiff keys. And in the final analysis, it was all for nothing, as the home was never built.

21.
Paul Ecke Ranch

Fortunately for Lilian, most of her commissions in the 1930s did come to fruition. One of the most high-profile projects, in 1935, was for Paul and Magdelena Ecke. Paul Ecke Sr. was famed for his introduction of the poinsettia into North County, San Diego, which ultimately sealed its fate as a quintessential Christmas plant. The Paul Ecke Ranch in Encinitas, California, was the center of operations for the growth and creative development of the humble poinsettia. Its widespread plantings in North County put the small coastal Southern California enclave of Encinitas on the world map.

There was a momentary feeling of being overwhelmed as I rolled up my sleeves and began the important task of gathering the Paul Ecke Ranch and Ecke family historic collections into some semblance of order. Temporarily stored in various places in the Ranch complex, the archives were vast. The sheer volume of the business and personal papers of Paul Ecke Sr. alone would have given even the most seasoned archivist that "deer in the headlights" feeling. I recall it well as I turned the key in the rusted padlock that secured a treasure trove, and opened the creaking, slightly misaligned door, the entry into what was once the meager quarters for ranch hands. No creature comforts here, I thought. Long abandoned, the cramped space on the upper-level of Barn Two on the Paul Ecke Ranch was filled from floor to ceiling, wall-to-wall, with boxes of papers, bills, and business documents, and decades-worth of floricultural trade magazines. Many of theses papers were tied in brown paper with fragile, brittle string, meticulously saved for future benefit by Paul Sr., who had an unusually astute regard for posterity. My trepidation soon changed to excitement

as I quickly assessed the treasures before me and started to unravel the string to reveal the contents of this collection, which I discovered after spending about six months to sort, rebox, and label, what would ultimately represent more than a hundred years of Ecke history. The family's storied past began in Baden-Baden, Germany, where they owned a health spa business. The family then migrated to Hollywood as Albert and Henrietta, with their children, Hans, Margaret, Paul, and Frieda, left Germany permanently, sailing for California in 1906, crossing the country by train when they learned of the San Francisco earthquake. Relocating 100 miles south to Encinitas in 1923, Ecke's revolutionary breeding, shipping, and marketing methods transformed the poinsettia into the world's most popular household plant, synonymous with Christmas, surpassing even the ubiquitous Christmas tree. The historical content of the Ecke family business collection, that also included personal letters and photographs, was immense. Not only did these archives tell the story of the rise of the poinsettia into *the* Christmas plant, but they also told a local story about Encinitas, a national story about the business as it grew and the customer base swelled from coast to coast, and an international story, as Ecke Ranch farming operations moved off shore to survive in a competitive global market.

The contents of a particular box in the collection revealed past accolades, trophies for service in the industry and community, perhaps the most prideful being the award held in a blue-velvet folder, still pristine, beautifully preserved, that represented Paul Sr.'s induction into the Floricultural Hall of Fame of the Society of American Florists in 1970. But tucked in between the proclamations and plaques was a simply-framed award certificate—wrinkled from decades of ambient moisture and heat—

Framing of the Ecke ranch house, 1935. *Courtesy the Ecke family*

presented to Paul Sr. by the Women's Guild of Temple Emanu-El, San Diego. Paul was being honored as a "Gentleman of Distinction" for his "years of service of loving kindness and the betterment of the San Diego Community and of humanity in the area of horticulture," as printed on the certificate, dated January 24, 1970. The framed award had been handed to him as a rolled scroll, much like a high school diploma, on that date. Attached to the back of the frame there was a newspaper clipping from the *San Diego Union* headlined: "Emanu-El Women Honor 21," which had been published the following day after the award banquet that had gathered 650 people in downtown San Diego's El Cortez hotel to recognize and to celebrate these remarkable men of distinction.

The formal affair was organized and presented by several of the ladies from the guild and those being feted that evening included men of note in science, sports, medicine, education, and more. Architect Sam W. Hamill was one of the twenty-one men being honored (although he was unable to attend) for his personal contributions to city of San Diego's beautification. The accolade must have resonated deeply with Paul Sr. as the opening paragraph of his biography, "Poinsettia King," written by Vera Dutter in 1975, described the pride that Paul Sr. felt as he attended the banquet with his wife Magdalena and his three adult children, Paul Jr., Barbara, and Crix, and their respective spouses. This opening scene served as a flashback as Paul Sr., then in his mid-seventies, reflected on his life, captured and retold in his historic biography.

My work on the Ecke family and Paul Ecke Ranch business archives followed years of recording the biography of Paul Ecke III (Paul Sr., and Magdalena's grandson). I met him in March 2007 after he e-mailed me to inquire if I would have an interest in the documentation of his biography and his contributions to the Ecke Ranch business, which went through three definitive stages as first Paul Sr., then Paul Jr. and Paul III took the reins of the family-owned floriculture business. "I would be honored," I wrote in my e-mail back to Paul III. I didn't know it then, but the endeavor would span almost seven years. Each month Paul would meet with me and we would capture on a digital audio recorder that month's news. I then transcribed each month's updates on the Ranch business, Paul's philanthropic work, his family, and his outside interests with Rancheros Visitadores. I considered my role privileged and I did not take it lightly or for granted, as I had an acute sense of the future history that was being played out and documented in real time during this unique and special collaboration.

The Ecke family has been associated with Encinitas since 1923, when Paul Sr. moved operations there from Hollywood, as rapid subdivision and subsequent housing and commercial development squeezed out the farmers who worked the farmlands in close proximity to the burgeoning movie studios. Over the decades since then the Ranch in Encinitas became part of a vast acreage of farmland and Paul Sr. astutely recognized the future value of the coastal land itself and had the wisdom to purchase many lots in North County San Diego for future development. The coastal town, located about a hundred miles south of Hollywood, began calling itself the Flower Capital of the World due to the Ecke's poinsettia operations and the floriculture crops of other growers who were attracted to the area. It was Paul Jr. who further developed the business into an international force, as shipment by air replaced railroad freight cars, coinciding with the movement of Ecke farming operations from the fields into the greenhouse in the 1960s. His larger-than-life personality, his boundless energy and charisma, and his knowledge of marketing cemented the poinsettia as a global symbol of Christmas. Through product placement on broadcast news sets, on popular television shows like the *Late Night Show with Jay Leno*, and *The Dinah Shore Show*, and as a decorative holiday focal point in the White House, at its height of market share, Ecke Ranch collected royalties on ninety percent of the poinsettia cuttings worldwide.

As the marketplace rapidly changed, Paul III—who purchased the family business in 1990—placed an emphasis on the breeding and development of poinsettia rooted and unrooted cuttings and

The Ecke ranch house built by Lilian in 1935.
Courtesy the Ecke family

moved farming operations offshore to Guatemala to remain competitive in a global market, leaving the Ranch in Encinitas to focus on plant research and breeding. In 2012, Paul III sold the operational side of the business to the Dutch-based Agribio Group. Always the family-man, like his father and his grandfather before him, the need to spend more time with his family and focus on his philanthropic endeavors, overrode the necessity to head up a global business concern.

While having a keen interest in the four generations of the Ecke family, whose twentieth-century story began as a family of immigrants from Magdeburg, Germany. I was also excited to spend time in the Paul Ecke Ranch house, which was designed and built by Lilian in 1935. I asked Paul III what he knew about the history of his home; he had spent his childhood in that house, along with his sisters, Lizbeth and Sara, and his parents Jinx and Paul Jr. He suggested I talk to his mom about it, "She'll likely know," he said.

The petite lady with a strong presence, a keen mind, and a sparkle in her eyes, greeted me warmly at her home in La Jolla. Jinx had been the matriarch of the Ecke Ranch for several decades, as she followed in the footsteps of her mother-in-law, Magdalena. Both women not only took care of their own families but saw to the domestic and culinary needs of the Ranch workers. Jinx was happy to retell the history of the Ecke Ranch and shared my interest in the Ranch house, constructed during the Depression when building contracts were few and far between. Unlike other businesses, the Ecke Ranch was faring better than most, despite the economic downturn. The poinsettia plant was an inexpensive luxury for households to afford during Christmastime and the demand for the crimson, leafy shrub named for Joel Poinsett, American consul to Mexico, meant that the Ecke business survived when many businesses collapsed.

I asked Jinx how it transpired that Lilian was chosen as architect for the Ranch home, which replaced a much smaller dwelling built by Paul Sr. and Magdelana when the couple initially purchased the acreage in Encinitas in 1923, and she knew instantly that it was through the influence of two women. Magdalena had mentioned casually to her close friend Mildred that they were planning to build a larger home to accommodate their family said Jinx. "It was Mildred who suggested to Magdalena that she should hire Lilian Rice," Jinx added. At that time Lilian was being considered for the commission to design and build a high school for the soon-to-be-formed school district in the area: the San Dieguito Union High School. Mildred was a teacher in Encinitas and had advance knowledge of the plans for the new school and its lady architect who was bidding against many local male architects. And so with that solid reputation Lilian Rice was hired to build a splendid new Ranch home for Paul and Magdalena that would overlook a sea of brilliant red poinsettias.

Organizing the family archives gave me an opportunity to attempt to seek out more concrete details about Lilian's Ranch house project, as I focused on files from the 1930s, but frustratingly there was a dire lack of actual documentation of its construction. However, salvaged from the construction project, and thoughtfully kept by Paul Sr., were several high-quality monochrome photographs that show the home in varying stages of completion. It was clear that it was an important improvement to the working ranch, and would be a home that was more fitting for the stature of the Ecke Ranch business. The structure, which utilized natural materials like cedar, pine, and oak in its construction, with its ivory siding and multi-pane windows and a brick chimney that sided the full height of its north side, was sited to take full advantage of coastal breezes and a spectacular view of the poinsettia fields and the Pacific Ocean beyond. Perhaps due to the depressed economy it was modestly built using a board and batten construction and wood siding. But the interior was tastefully designed and Lilian made full use of built-in features, storage cupboards and even a central vacuum system and laundry chute. An interior rustic fireplace made from locally quarried stone served as the focal point of the living room and became the gathering spot for many family photographs, especially around Christmastime when the wood mantel was festooned with sprays of fur and poinsettias.

As I delved into Paul Sr.'s archived files, I was hoping to find some written documentation of Lilian's architectural project. There were several snapshots of the framing of the house, one which showed the family standing inside the wood-frame skeleton that would soon become their home—holding hands as if in celebration. There were images of the completed house in the family album, and some professionally shot photographs of the house just prior to the addition of its hardscape and landscape. Disappointingly, there were no plans, blueprints, or

Three generations of Paul Eckes: back left, Paul Ecke III; back right, Paul Ecke Jr.; front, Paul Ecke Sr. 1978. *Courtesy the Ecke family*

presentation drawings to be found. Jinx explained to me that Magdalena would have an occasional purge and throw out items that she considered clutter, that she felt were not important, although we have no way of knowing if this was the case here. However, I did locate two letters from Lilian, typed on her business stationery, and two check stubs of monies made out to Lilian that confirmed her association with the project. This is a rarity and, as far as my research is concerned, there are no other extant check stubs for payment to Lilian from her clients or any of her personal or business letters that have survived. Consequently, I had discovered a unique treasure.

The first letter, May 16, 1935, laid out the changes that had evidently been made to the original specifications that required Magdalena and Paul Sr.'s approval. Its contents indicated that August Anderson, of Encinitas, was the general contractor who collaborated on the project. Paul Sr. had a hand in the building, too, and perhaps this was another reason why Lilian was chosen, with her agreement to accept her client's involvement. Several questions were asked in the letter:

- Will you see if it is possible to run a flue in the same chimney with the fireplace instead of providing for a an extra chimney?
- What have you decided to do about heating water for bath and kitchen? Where is the water heater to be located?
- Do you prefer to use wood shingles or composition shingle?
- Will the stairs be carpeted or shall we specify a full oak stairway?

The answers to these questions have been lost to time, but period photographs show clearly that composition shingle was used on the roof, there is just one brick chimney, the stairway was full oak (but carpeted later), and the water heater was located in the basement.

The second letter, dated June 6, 1935, inquired of Paul Sr. whether he had made a decision on the size of this basement, which would be equipped with several cash registers and serve as a point of purchase. As he had opted to take over this aspect of the construction project himself, Lilian needed to know the basement's exact measurements in order to determine the size of the lower floor joists, and if the decisions for the dimensions were final, so that if Paul wished to "push ahead with the building" she could "practically complete the drawings before they go out for bids." Lilian added, not hesitating to point out that these changes did not come free of charge, "I am sure you realize that you have added considerably to the cost of the building."

The Ranch house was at the heart of Ecke family life for about sixty years; it ceased to be used as a residence in the mid-1990s. It then served as a venue for Paul Ecke Ranch corporate meetings and seasonal horticultural shows. Today, the house plays a role in the outreach of the Leichtag Foundation, a nonprofit organization that purchased the sixty-seven acres of Ecke Ranch lands on Saxony Road in Encinitas, along with the Ranch house, barns, and ancillary buildings, in December 2013. In spring the following year, Leichtag began a cosmetic renovation of the house, which over many decades had been through several modifications to increase the living space, which added an upper deck, expanded the master bedroom and bathroom, and included a kitchen remodel. With Solana Beach-based general contractor David Kramer leading Leichtag's renovation, the upper-deck was removed and the silhouette of the structure restored to be more reflective of Lilian's original design. David said:

> The idea was not to change the character of the house, that was our guideline. Areas used more frequently—like the dining room, living room, and kitchen—were refurbished. The infrastructure was updated and original materials, like the oak floors, were sanded and burnished. We also refurbished the front door and cleaned up and replaced hardware, so nothing has really changed except for the kitchen which we upgraded with new cabinet doors, counter tops, appliances and plumbing fixtures but not a new layout.

Jim Farley, Leichtag Foundation president, expects that many community groups will use the space of the Ranch house in future years. Specifically, it will serve as a community gathering place for the Jewish Food Justice Fellows, organizations in the North County Jewish Hub—Leichtag's Jewish

How the Ecke ranch house looks today. *Photo by Diane Y. Welch*

nonprofit partners—and other community organizations, especially Leichtag Foundation grantees. The foundation has innovative plans for the former Ecke Ranch acreage to be transformed into a working agricultural farm, cultivating produce, crops, and orchards for community benefit. Like history repeating itself, this was how the Paul Ecke Ranch aided the war effort in the 1940s with the flower business taking a back seat for the duration of the conflict. By returning the Ranch to agriculture, it also echoes the early twentieth-century origins of Ecke farming in California when Paul Ecke Sr.'s parents, Albert and Henrietta Ecke, purchased their first farm in Eagle Rock, which was planted to tomatoes, vegetables, and berries, and acres of citrus and apricot orchards that sustained the local communities.

22.
Schools

*M*y journey on Interstate 805, which took me twenty-five miles from Solana Beach to south Chula Vista, ended as I coursed off the ramp at the exit L Street and headed down the side streets toward my destination: the slightly neglected elementary school that stood at the corner of L Street and Fourth Avenue. On this occasion I was surprised, pleasantly so, to see that the school was undergoing a cosmetic exterior facelift, with fresh stucco and paint. The school looked modern and newly constructed, I thought. The colorful marquis broadcast in large black letters: Lilian J. Rice Elementary School. The school started life as the South Chula Vista School and then was renamed in honor of Lilian, the building's designer and architect, shortly after her death in 1938. I had visited the school in 2012, the year that Chula Vista celebrated its 100th anniversary of cityhood. The school's principal gave me a guided tour of the school and pointed out parts of the school as Lilian had originally designed them; these few classrooms were of a modest size and light-flooded with large multi-pane windows practically filling the exterior walls. To serve a growth in the local population after World War II, the school was expanded considerably and the local paper reported regularly of these changes and, over time, the little school, that will reach an eighty-year milestone in 2018, continued to evolve.

The day of my visit, some of the students interviewed me on video to learn more about Lilian and my work on her biography, as part of a media lesson. They were interested to discover that Lilian was also involved in teaching, an endeavor that she continued to pursue even when she worked full-time as an architect. It was also common for Lilian to lecture to women's groups and non-profit organizations, and she encouraged her staff to attend courses to improve their professional skills or learn new ones. And even as Lilian directed a busy office in 1935, she still found the time, on January 31, to give a lecture for those signed up for the adult education program at the Sweetwater High School in National City. The *San Diego Union* reported that Lilian's course in home improvement, in cooperation with the national housing act, taught her students the skills of "architectural drawing, planning additional rooms and making improvements in general."

With parents who met as students in the teaching program at the Normal School in Randolph Vermont, it comes as no surprise that Lilian would inherit, either genetically or environmentally, the same propensity to teach. Julius Rice would spend a great deal of his adult working life in education besides real estate.

As mentioned, a connection to education did not cease when Lilian became a full-time architect. And throughout her career, Lilian was contracted to design and build several schools, her first one in Rancho Sante Fe, located in the civic center on Paseo Delicias. With its simple pueblo-influenced design with rustic log vigas as roof joists, deep-set windows and a thick stucco cubed-shaped tan exterior with the ubiquitous red-tiled roof, it did not give a hint of a traditional educational setting, as Ruth Nelson wrote in a 1925 article in the *San Diego Union* paper about a guided walking tour of the civic center making mention of its "patio and parlors."

The school catered to all grades and opened in 1924 with only fourteen students and, at the end of its first academic year, just one student graduated: Ivy Fidora. Lilian was one of three trustees for the school that was then in the Aliso School District. She presented to Ivy a special plaque painted with a pleasant landscape design, at the graduation celebration, which was still held for the sole graduate. As word of the exclusivity and beauty of Rancho Santa Fe spread via the national marketing campaign, more families were attracted to the area. Initially, the families there were of support staff who came to work in the community as its development took shape. But then the numbers increased sharply in the 1930s as families moved to the area because of

The San Dieguito Union High School, now San Dieguito Academy.
Photo by DarrenEdwards.com

its many qualities and opportunities, especially its investment potential through the bounty of orchard estates. The small school could not accommodate this influx of children and soon plans were underway for another school, which was built on Avenida de Acacias in 1931 by Lilian in partnership with architect Hammond Whitsett. When the size of that school also became inadequate, it was reused as offices for the Rancho Santa Fe Association, and a third school was later constructed on La Granada, now known as the R. Roger Rowe School for Dr. Roger Rowe, the highly regarded educator, principal, and district superintendent whose often-repeated axiom was: "learning to study is studying to learn."

As building starts struggled to gain momentum through the years following the Wall Street Crash of 1929, President Roosevelt introduced his New Deal, which brought about the passage of the National Recovery Act. Additionally, the Works Progress Administration was founded, which helped to put to work some of the nation's millions of unemployed people. In coincidence with this national political climate, the coastal towns of North County, San Diego, were fighting a local drive to form a new school district. One of the community's most respected civic leaders, Herschell Larrick Sr., spearheaded this movement in 1934. A businessman, who formerly owned the Solana Beach Lumber Company that

supplied much of the lumber for the homes built by Lilian in Rancho Santa Fe, Larrick was a civic powerhouse who got things done; he had also become a trustee of the Oceanside School District when Eugene Batchelder, Del Mar realtor and brother-in-law of Ed Fletcher, abruptly resigned when the heated debate over the need for a high school in the San Dieguito area was broached. An election was held by the Oceanside school board to determine if the promotion of a new school district was feasible, and through the determination of trustees Annie Cozens and Herschell Larrick, and other voting members from the Vista school board, the debate for the standalone San Dieguito Union High School District was allowed to go to a local vote in a general election held in January 1936. Local residents supported keeping tax dollars in the local communities and so the measure passed 524 to 8. The school was partly funded by local bonds that raised $160,000, combined with a Public Works Administration grant, which financed the design and construction of the campus that cost in total $358,828.70 as reported in the *San Dieguito Citizen* newspaper. By March, school board trustees were elected, among them Larrick, who served as president and Dr. Carl Bertschinger of Rancho Santa Fe, one of five trustees. Various sites were suggested for the school's location, but ultimately a forty-acre site in Cardiff-by-the-Sea,

Reproduction of Lilian's colored pencil and water color rendering of the San Dieguito Union High School. *Recreated by Sara Motamedi*

with an ocean view, was selected by the board. Harry Muns was singled out as the building contractor and local architects were invited to bid for the project. One of these architects was Lilian.

That ocean view became a winning-feature of the school campus that also included a middle school, and which was lauded as a "model school" by the *Los Angeles Times* in an October 1937 article. Lilian had been successful in her bid to win the project and lost no time in the reorganization of her staff to accommodate the increased workload. She hired Leonard Neal, a graduate from the Royal Institute of British Architecture; George C. Hatch, who was trained at the Massachusetts Institute of Technology; John R. Dodd, who had worked as a draftsman with Lilian in Rancho Santa Fe since 1926; and Olive Chadeayne who, like Lilian, was a graduate of Cal. It took several years for the building to commence after the school district was made official, likely due to the way the funding was pieced together. However, the local papers reported often on its progress although little was said about the architect and her team who were the talent behind the project. In the fall of 1937, those living within the bounds of the school district pitched in as volunteers and donors supplied hauling equipment and material; this school belonged to the community and many were invested in its success. The grading was started by summer of 1937, then the infrastructure and finally the framing was well-underway by September as the campus began to take shape. Lilian's design was considered state-of-the-art at the time of construction. The *Rancho Santa Fe News* reported that it was, "one of the most modern and progressive plans of any rural district in America." Her innovative design resembled a modern college campus with its single-story structure and clean, unadorned mass. A unique approach was that many of the classrooms had a southern exposure that improved lighting and heating

conditions, a design feature that was way ahead of its time and is still used today to make buildings more environmentally efficient.

The article continued, "Miss Lillian [*sic*] Rice used her former experience as a teacher to incorporate into her designs all that makes up present day educational standards." The campus was intended to create a university-style setting with its grassy quadrangle, surrounded by detached classrooms—several of which had an ocean view—a gymnasium, a library, and separate administrative offices. At the time of its construction, in the fall of 1937, half of the forty acres were devoted to agriculture, and included animal pens and a vegetable garden. The school's academic curriculum was rounded out with subjects that represented the needs of society at that time with an emphasis on agriculture, horticulture, mechanics, woodcraft, art, home economics, and commercial business. As the social climate changed with modernization and development dominated the coastal towns, the communities moved away from their farming traditions. Over the decades since the school was completed, additional buildings were constructed, creating an unfortunate mismatch of architectural styles. Buildings in Senior Court—which are slated for demolition—had large rooms with metal and concrete walls with disproportionately small windows, which were constructed in response to Cold War fears. Protection from possible nuclear attack became a priority for public buildings during the 1960s and architects strove to minimize nuclear fall-out partly through the use of small windows, which today of course, seems ludicrous. However, more recently in 2005, a design competition sought out a more aesthetic, harmonious approach when a media center was added to the campus. John Sergio Fisher was awarded the project due in large part for his use of covered walkways, open space, and simple elegant lines, which mirrored that of Lilian's original design.

Building Around San Diego County

The rock entryway of the former Robinson House in La Jolla, once owned and lived in by Audrey Geisel and her then-husband Grey Diamond and their two daughters. *Photo by PaulBodyPhoto.com*

$\mathcal{A}$s the land company divested itself of its obligations to the Rancho Santa Fe project in 1927, Lilian turned her hand to creating homes with styles that veered away from the Mediterranean type mandated by the covenant restrictions in Rancho Santa Fe. She was able to spread her professional wings and undertake projects throughout the county. As there was a building boom in San Diego, during this period of the mid- to late-1920s, several opportunities presented themselves. A development in the nearby coastal town of La Jolla—about eight miles south of Rancho Santa Fe—opened up. A residence for Christine Arnberg was designed and built by Lilian in the La Jolla Hermosa tract. It was completed in 1927 for the unmarried daughter of a local shipping magnate. The home is an eclectic style and defies categorization. The exterior has English country elements with its red-brick facade and brick chimney, combined with Spanish design elements with a vaulted, heavy-beamed ceiling in the living room. The project won Lilian an Honor

Award for design from the San Diego Chapter of the AIA. The north elevation of the Arnberg residence shows how Lilian stepped the structure down the slope of the site's natural grade. There was originally a wooden bedroom balcony located on this side of the structure that added visual interest and afforded views to the west, but it was removed during a remodel in the 1980s.

Mrs. Marguerite Robinson, a widow, commissioned Lilian to design her home on the west side of Soledad Mountain in La Jolla. Completed in 1929, it had a rustic appearance with its wood and rock construction and intersecting gabled roofs. The floor plan is a basic "L" shape, but the floor levels vary inside; steps up and down flow into different interior spaces. Interior walls are heavily wood paneled with built in shelves and niches throughout; an impressive living room affords unobstructed views to the Pacific Ocean. The rock chimney on the north side of the house and the heavy shake roof, reflected the ideals set down by the Bay Region architects who created homes for members of the Hillside

The Robinson House interior living room.
Photo by PaulBodyPhoto.com

Club, who affirmed that a home should use indigenous materials and nestle unobtrusively into its surroundings. Dr. Grey E. Dimond and his wife of twelve years, Audrey Stone Dimond, purchased the home in 1960 for $63,000. The couple spent eight years there with their daughters, Lark and Lea, selling the home in spring 1968 to Mr. and Mrs. Norman Holter.

The year after Marguerite Robinson's home was completed Lilian built a residence in the Country Heights subdivision of coastal La Jolla for William and Anna Bradley. Designed in the English Tudor style, characterized by its half-timbered front elevation, this was a radical departure from Lilian's preceding projects and likely a welcomed reprieve from the scores of Mediterranean-type homes that she was bound to design in Rancho Santa Fe. A prominent, sweeping south-facing gable added a storybook design element to the building's facade. The home is known historically as the William S. and Anna R. Bradley/Lilian Rice/E. W. Dewhurst House. Anna had strong family ties to Britain and requested

that Lilian design a house that reflected her English background, ignoring the trend for Spanish-style architecture, "She would have been the last person to build a house that anyone else thought was popular," wrote her daughter, in a note to Mary and Rod Alexander, family relatives who still live in San Diego County. This was the first house built in La Jolla by Ernest Dewhurst, the project building contractor who was specifically selected for his English heritage. The fine work completed on this project helped springboard Ernest toward a prolific career as a general contractor with the Dewhurst family-run business continuing his legacy today.

The house was built on a sloping irregular lot, so Lilian raised the foundation to keep the floor level, rather than flatten the lot. Mary and Rod shared a family photo album with me that tracked, week by week, the progress of the building project. One early shot captured Anna breaking ground at the beginning of the construction phase; the rest of the photographs show the wood framing and the progression of the shell of a house through

Lilian's graphite sketch of the Bradley House in La Jolla, 1930. *Courtesy the Alexander family*

Period photo of the Bradley House just after completion in 1930. *Courtesy the Alexander family*

to the completed project. The front elevation faces south, but upper-story windows and dormers have views west to the ocean. When the home was built, there were no others in close proximity affording the owners privacy and a great deal of open space, quite different from the area today, which is now densely populated. The road was then named Romero Drive, but in a show of affection, the couple renamed the road Remley Place, a coinage of their last names, Remington, which was Anna's maiden name, and Bradley.

Other La Jolla homes would soon be added to Lilian's roster: a beach home in the Barber Tract for Mrs. Charles E. Sterns, now owned by Mitt and Anne Romney; the Martha Kinsey residence, built in the La Jolla Park development of the Villa Tract subdivision, now listed on the National Register of Historic Places; the Dr. Francis Smith residence, on Virginia Way; the Rubin H. and Elizabeth Fleet residence on Pepita Way; and many more homes, some of them built as speculative projects. Lilian also designed a charming English country-style, two-story residence in El Cerito, and an eclectic home in La Mesa for a former seafaring client, Commander Simard.

Additionally, there were commercial projects undertaken during the 1930s, with the expansion of the mutual water company offices in Escondido and plans for a new city hall in National City. The city hall would be built around an existing fire and police department building and would be funded through the State Emergency Relief Administration, an agency formed to improve conditions in California during the Great Depression.

The *San Diego Union* published an article about the project on February 1, 1935. At the time of the publication, bids had already been sent out to local contractors. Lilian's plans called for a forty-foot addition to the building's north and a forty-two-foot addition to the east. In keeping with the popular trend, the style was Spanish with stucco finish and a red-tile roof. Typical of Lilian's design ideology, she did not grade the land, even though the existing structure was sited on a slope. Instead, she adapted the building to fit the slope with two stories in the front and three in the rear. As part of the interior make-over, Lilian created a jail on the first story, with eight cells for men and, interestingly, two for women, with the rest of the building devoted to administrative offices for the police and fire department.

In the column next to this article, the editors included notice that Lilian would be teaching evening classes for adults in response to the US government's National Housing Act. Offered through the Sweetwater High School, the classes included instruction in architectural drawing, planning room additions, and general home improvements, which is telling of Lilian's desire to continue to pass on her knowledge as an educator.

In 1930, Burnet C. Wohlford and his wife Mildred hired Lilian to build their ranch home on E. Valley Parkway in Escondido, on land they had purchased in the fall of 1929. Like many ranchers in Southern California, the Wohlfords owned vast acreage devoted to citrus. The *San Diego Union* published notice of their sale on November 3, 1929, with the headline: "Escondido

Shows Spirited Growth in Construction." The article went on to report:

Tentative plans [are] being drawn by Lilian Rice, official architect for Rancho Santa Fe, to be used in the construction of a home of artistic appearance and utility...on what is known as Eureka Ranch in the north part of Escondido Valley. The house will be of early California type. Work will start this winter and will be completed in spring.

Almost sixty years after those plans were drawn up, Cora Jane Jenkins, a volunteer for the San Diego Historical Society (now the San Diego History Center), had the opportunity to interview and record Mildred Finley Wohlford, in 1987. The transcription of their conversation is archived in the San Diego History Center. Copies were openly available for research and I read them with keen interest, as this oral history is a very rare account that includes Mildred's firsthand recollections of one of Lilian's building projects that took inspiration from the mission-era haciendas.

Mildred told Cora that she was introduced to Lilian at the time of their land purchase through Harriet Wimmer, a local landscape designer. Mildred commented as a side note that Harriet, like Lilian, was a former teacher who had developed a keen interest in remedial reading and had a close friendship with Theodor Geisel. Beside being an expert in reading, Harriet worked in partnership with her husband in their landscape architecture firm. Harriet carried out the work, while her husband drafted the plans. "She knew more about flowers and had a genius for flower arranging; she was a natural. She became probably the most esoteric, elegant...landscape gardener in San Diego," said Mildred. Harriet was very familiar with Lilian's work as she had subcontracted with her firm to design the landscaping for several Rancho Santa Fe estate homes. She told Mildred, that if she wanted an adobe, then Lilian Rice was the best person to do it.

Mildred wasted no time in contacting Lilian. The two arranged to meet with Mildred bringing her son Wully, along for the adventure. The three of them scoured the countryside looking at old, half-decayed adobes for inspiration while enjoying picnic

lunches together. Lilian was able to translate these antiquated designs into a modern home and the house was completed in 1930. Cora asked Mildred if it was made of adobe. Mildred answered:

No it isn't. We tried to make it adobe, but we couldn't because adobe could not be made in the winter...Everybody thinks it's adobe but it isn't.

The home was actually made of cement block that created very thick walls and, at the time, the house was a novelty, being the only ranch house in Escondido. "Everybody came out [to see it] and said, 'this looks like a jail,'" laughed Mildred.

When Ranch houses were being originally built by the owners of the Mexican land grants, a main structural beam spanned the full length of the building, creating a lengthy horizontal aspect to its mass. Lilian and Mildred looked at the Osuna adobe in Rancho Santa Fe, but settled on the Trujillo Adobe as a model for the final design, which echoed this approach. Lilian heightened the ceilings, added extra windows for light, and included extra rooms, but the house was authentic in that it matched the irregular quality of an original Mexican adobe, including the crooked aspects of the construction, "That's copied exactly," said Mildred.

Cora asked Mildred if she still had the house plans, Mildred said that she did. Cora stated:

You know those are historical documents because Lilian Rice was quite famous. "Well, do I know it!" stressed Mildred.

Mildred and Mrs. Bakewell, at the time the secretary for the Rancho Santa Fe Association, were close friends and had a common bond in that they were the only two Lilian Rice homeowners who had actually worked closely with Lilian; Mildred especially was very proud of that fact. The house cost $12,000 to complete with the Wohlfords cutting costs where they could by using their own ranch labor. The building contractor was a man named W. A. Simmons, who had worked with Lilian on several homes in Rancho Santa Fe and La Jolla. Lilian was very fastidious, Mildred recalled. The Escondido subcontractors were not used to precisely following the architect's specifications, and Lilian had requested that the beams should be old and weathered. The laborers took blow torches to the beams and chipped them to give an impression of hand-hewn lumber. One contractor said:

> Miss Rice came over and was quite interested. She was a young woman, about thirty-nine I think and her eyes—she was kinda pretty, sweet looking—they were just like steel. She said, "You will have to build a huge bonfire, big enough for these beams, and burn them and watch them until they're charred, and then you'll have to take wire brushes and brush them down. That's the only way you'll get that weathered look like they've been washed around in the sea or just laid out on Palomar Mountain somewhere." So that's what they did.

In the *Escondido Times Advocate,* notice was given on Wednesday, December 16, 1931, that the Wohlford home had been given honorary mention in a contest conducted by the national publication *House and Garden Magazine.* The contest was for artistic homes at moderate costs. The accolade was especially meaningful as several thousands of entries were received. The home was also featured in *House Beautiful Magazine* in July 1932. Three full pages were dedicated to large photographic images, taken by Padilla Studios, of various aspects of the home. The spread also included a copy of Lilian's floor plan and some explanation about the design aspects. It was evident from Cora's interview with Mildred, that took place inside this home, that it was held very dearly by Mildred, who at the time was eighty-four years old and had lived within its walls for over fifty years. It was a sad day when I received notice that the house had been demolished by its new owner in 2007, who deemed it non-historic, to make way for a new, modern housing development.

Thankfully, there is a fine example of a Lilian Rice Ranch home that has survived the decades. It was built for George and Caro Hillebrecht's avocado ranch in Escondido and it stands today just as it did when Lilian designed it almost eighty years ago. I visited Ben and Edie Hillebrecht, who now own the home. Ben is still in the family business of farming avocados, and his son works with him on the ranch passing the family traditions down to the next generation. His daughters manage the selling side of the business by providing produce throughout the county to agricultural stands and farmers markets.

During my visit, we talked about the Ranch history. Ben's parents moved to Escondido in 1924, first building their own home on fifteen acres of land that they'd cleared and transformed into citrus groves that overlooked their ranch, which over time expanded to 200 acres mostly planted to avocados. As their family grew, a larger home was needed. Ben said:

> "People ask me how long I've lived here and I tell them, always! I can remember going down to Lilian's office once, in Rancho Santa Fe, with my parents, but I was very young so don't recall the details. But I do recall well that Lilian only lived a short while after this house was completed. And in 1937 there weren't very many lady architects in San Diego, and there still aren't that many."

Ben also recalled that his mother Caro had some specific things that she wanted in the home because it was a ranch house. He continued:

> The window sills, she didn't want any, and no mantle over the fireplace because you have to dust it all the time and she didn't want to do that.

It was a modern low-maintenance home with double doors, oak floors, three bedrooms including deep, cedar-lined closets, with built-in shoe racks, and a screened sleeping porch that could accommodate the whole family.

The home was designed with unusual features: an electric hot water heater on the roof, solar panels, and a water softener system, hi-tech luxuries for the 1930s, especially when the house was of a traditional type manufactured out of adobe bricks. The home was carefully sited with a massive boulder left in place where nature had planted it, which remained in the backyard of the house. The structure was positioned with a westerly aspect so that when the entry-door and rear door were open, a through breeze

Front elevation of the Hillebrecht ranch house in Escondido. Lilian built the house from adobe brick in 1935 for George and Caro Hillebrecht. Their son Ben now lives there with his wife Edith. *Courtesy the Hillebrecht family*

cooled the interior during the summer. A family tale that brings a chuckle is the fact that George Hillebrecht was not willing to add an extra few cents to the unit cost of the building to have bitumen added to the adobe clay, making it more durable. Consequently, the interior and exterior walls need to be regularly maintained by a coating of paint to seal the bricks. But despite that oversight, the home has not changed since it was built, and is a very rare surviving example of a Lilian Rice designed Ranch house made of adobe. When Ben took over the upkeep of the house from his parents, a friend asked when he was going to demolish it and build a new, modern home. Fortunately, the Hillebrchts had the vision to understand the historical significance of their home and it remains a local treasure that is valued. "It was a showplace for 1937," said Ben, "and it's still a pretty comfortable home."

 Grace Morin created this charming water color of
Lilian, age 20, energetically working at her drafting
table, 1919. *Author's collection*

24.
1938: Lilian's Death

As Ben knew, Lilian only lived a short time after she had designed his parents' home in Escondido. In fact, she passed away December 22, 1938, just over a year after the Hillbrecht's adobe had been built. As a way to pay my silent respects to the architect who I felt I was getting to know and love so well, I visited the grounds of La Vista Memorial Park Cemetery in National City where I knew I would find her headstone. Walking into the park, I followed a gentle rise of the land to a small hill just a few steps from the cemetery offices. That's where I found the Steele and Rice family plots in close proximity to those of the founders of National City, the Kimballs. The Steele headstones were grand, made of marble and granite and doubtless marked graves that contained the actual mortal remains of the Steele family. As all four of the Rice family members—Julius, Laura, Lilian and Jack—had been cremated, their headstones were different, more modest, and had a simple uniformity to them. The small ivory-colored stone plaques were elevated slightly off the grass on plinths. I was very puzzled when I noticed an obvious discrepancy in the dates on Lilian's headstone, it was clearly etched with a birth year of 1888.

During my research it was evident that most written accounts in recent books and in magazine articles, even in listings of Lilian Rice homes on the National Register of Historic Places, her birth year is given as 1888, and Withey had listed in his directory of deceased American architects that 1888 was Lilian's birth year. I was starting to doubt if *I* was the one who had her birth year incorrect. I knew I had to visit the county recorder's office in downtown San Diego to get the correct information. So I headed down there soon realizing that this was the County Building that architect Sam Hamill was credited with as chief designer; I inwardly hoped that this historic structure with its classic art deco design and

colorful tiling would not be demolished anytime soon. I waited patiently at the window to request my copy of Lilian's birth certificate, along with the vital documents of other Rice family members. The clerk took my note, disappeared for a few minutes, then came back with word that there was no birth certificate for Lilian, but there was a death certificate. How could that be? She assured me that she had looked everywhere and could not find this important record. Nevertheless, I accepted a copy of her death certificate as a good substitute and reminded myself that in Lilian's case, a death certificate was probably just as valid as a birth certificate as it included her date of birth. However, when I examined the color copy closely, I was confused by its content, though likely not as confused as the witness who signed the document to verify Lilian's death, apparently guessing her age as fifty-two and adding a question mark as proof of her lack of facts. On the death certificate the coroner had also guessed Lilian's birth year, which he noted was 1886, falsifying it to make it fit her age. To state that this was sloppy work is a gross understatement, but as it was then just two days before Christmas Eve, perhaps it's not surprising.

Lilian's attending physician, Dr. Paull of La Jolla, noted the following cause of death on the certificate: *epithelioma of the left ovary and intestinal obstruction*. It is quite possible that the blockage in the intestines resulted in a burst appendix, and while this may have sent Lilian to the hospital late that winter night in December, it was not the cause of her death. The date of onset of the cancer was given on the certificate as July 15, 1938. Lilian was at the zenith of her career when this diagnosis was made, her firm had weathered the worst years of the Great Depression, and her business was thriving with several residential projects still on the books. She naturally looked toward her staff to continue with her work, while she scaled back her daily work routine. Olive Elizabeth Shattuck, *Liz* , a talented young architect in her office was asked if she would like to take over her business, but she declined. However, Olive Chadeayne, also a licensed architect in the firm, accepted the role, and together with her colleague Elinor Frazer, the work in progress for Lilian's firm was completed.

On the evening of Lilian's passing I could imagine vividly the large Christmas tree standing in front of La Morada, illuminated and festive, with the Ranch children being trundled though the few short blocks of the civic center by Dave Willoughby guiding a saddle horse that pulled a hay-laden wagon. The children would have been singing carols and the night would have been crisp, starry, and bright, and Lilian would have been reeling in pain. Her female staff no doubt called for the ambulance and tried to make her comfortable. In the past weeks the tumor had spread from her ovaries, metastasized into her colon, and created an agonizing, deadly blockage. Her appendix burst from this pressure, and the myth soon spread that Lilian did not have cancer, but had appendicitis. If treated promptly Lilian's life would have been saved, her colleagues surmised. But this was only a myth and as Lilian had been regularly visiting Dr. Paull, she would have known that she was given a death sentence and that it was only a matter of time until she had to make good on his dire prognosis. On reflection, it's possible that Lilian created a strategy of secrecy, and that she hid her actual terminal diagnosis from her staff, not wanting to alarm them or cause disruption in the smooth running of her firm. For years they must have felt a deep sadness that perhaps Lilian's condition, if treated in a timely way, could have prevented her passing so suddenly.

The certificate of death noted that Lilian was a white, single female and her profession was given as *architect*, for a period of fifteen years, the same length of time that she had been living in Rancho Santa Fe, which takes us back to 1923. It is noted that she last worked in her profession during the month of November 1938. Lilian kept active until the end. It must have been a very sorrowful group of women, who considered themselves friends rather than employees, who watched late on a Wednesday night as Lilian was rushed the ten miles to Scripps Hospital on Prospect Street in La Jolla. Not knowing what the outcome would

Lilian Rice's headstone after a correction was made to the birth year by Tara Tarrant of La Jolla Stone Etching in December 2012. *Photo by Diane Y. Welch*

be, and helpless to quell Lilian's pain, their grief must have been inconsolable and intense. Lilian died the next morning at 10:10 a.m. on December 22, 1938; she was forty-nine years old.

While Lilian's death certificate held valuable information, more digging was required to find her birth certificate, but eventually I did locate a copy in the Harriet Rochlin archives in University of California Los Angeles (UCLA) where I had spent many hours delving into her archived collections on women in architecture. The collections' archivist was generous enough to e-mail me a digital copy of that birth certificate that proved clearly that Lilian was born on June 12, 1889, as I had insisted. The missing document in the county recorder's office may have occurred when Harriet requested a copy of this certificate back in 1974, and as the clerk had evidently not followed procedures, this vital document was subsequently misplaced. However, with this digital copy another mystery was solved.

The mystery of Lilian's headstone though, perplexed me more. Both Laura and Jack passed away after Lilian, and naturally they both knew her year of birth, so a mistake being made by her mother or brother seemed highly unlikely. If an error was made at the time of Lilian's interment, they would have sent it back to the masons and had it corrected. So what happened?

I called La Vista Memorial Park offices to see if anyone could shed some light on this puzzle. After being passed from person to person, finally someone

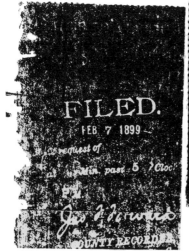

I hereby certify that if impressed with the seal of
the San Diego County Recorder, this is a true copy
of the permanent record filed and/or recorded in
this office.

Harley F. Bloom

Date

Harley F. Bloom, Recorder
County of San Diego, California

MAR 1 1 1976

A certified copy of Lilian Rice's birth certificate that
shows she was born June 12, 1889.

had the answer: the Rice family headstones had been vandalized several years ago and well-meaning volunteers had restored each of them at that time. That's why the headstones were so uniform and that's when the error was made in Lilian's year of birth. It was a plausible explanation as family members would not have made that error. Without a birth certificate on file at the county offices, it would have been difficult for the volunteers to cross check the accuracy of the year and so the obliterated year of 1889 became 1888, which has caused no end of confusion for local historians and writers.

While searching the newspaper archives to discover Lilian's obituary, I was troubled that all I could find was a poorly written notice of funeral, about three brief sentences, printed in the San Diego Union on Christmas Eve:

Rice: Dec. 22, Miss Lillian [*sic*] J. Rice of Rancho Santa Fe, daughter of Mrs. Laura S. Rice and sister [*sic*] of J. A. Rice, National City. Services, Tuesday, Dec 27, at 2 p.m. in the Bradley-Woolman chapel. Rev. C. Rankin Barnes officiating. Interment National City cemetery.

This same brief clinical statement was regurgitated with the same errors in the *San Diego Union* Newspaper on Christmas Day. There was no carefully penned obituary that retold of the many accomplishments of this pioneer lady architect whose homes had touched so many lives, no clues as to how she had filled her days, how she had influenced others to better themselves and push through barriers, how she had stood her ground and succeeded when others had failed during the dimmest days of the Great Depression, how she was the chosen architect for Hollywood movie stars.

I've been unable to find documentation of who attended Lilian's funeral services just two days after Christmas Day, so there is no way of knowing how her passing impacted her friends, family, and peers. But as she was loved by so many, they must have been devastated by the sad, sudden news, and for many, Christmas celebrations would never be the same again.

Architect Louis J. Gill, the then secretary for the San Diego Chapter of the American Institute of Architects, sent a public note to the executive secretary of the AIA Headquarters in Washington, DC. In part the note reads:

I (also) have the sad duty to inform the Institute of the death on December 22, 1938, of Miss Lillian [*sic*] J. Rice. Miss Rice was the only woman member of the San Diego Chapter and was much respected by her fellow architects in San Diego. Sincerely yours, Louis J. Gill.

Lilian's fellow AIA chapter members evidently did respect her and honored her memory with the establishment of a fund in January of 1939 that would provide scholarships for students of architecture. The San Diego Chapter of the AIA gave an initial donation of $500 of seed money to create the fund. A 1940 *Oakland Tribune* newspaper included mention of monies donated by this fund in an article titled: "University Directors Announce Benefactions in Los Angeles Meet":

Friends of the late Lilian J. Rice, class of 1910, $1382.89 contributed under sponsorship of the San Diego Chapter of the American Institute of Architects for establishment of the Lilian J. Rice Memorial Fund, to be used for loans to junior, senior and graduate students in the School of Architecture.

This amount is worth about $23,000 in today's current value. There is no mention of the fund after 1940, so it likely petered out due to the onset of World War II, which would have caused an understandable inability to continue with the fund's management and disbursement.

There is very little that has been salvaged from Lilian's effects; many of her hand-rendered presentation drawings are archived in the Richard Requa collection in the San Diego History Center and there is a fine collection of photographs of some of her work in the Rancho Santa Fe Historical Society. But, sadly, there are no diaries or journals, and a only a few business documents. However, there is a copy of her will that I discovered in the Harriet

Rochlin Collection, which gave me some clues to Lilian's financial standing at the time of her death. Interestingly, the will was dated October 14, 1927. It was perhaps drawn up at this time to satisfy the stipulations of real property purchased in Rancho Santa Fe. The will details that Lilian owned a twenty-acre lot in National City, in the Copland's subdivision, which she requested be converted to cash and installments paid to her father at $50 a month; as he died before she did, this was never realized. She also owned portions of lot 1, 2, and 3 of block 32 in Rancho Santa Fe, almost four acres. This real estate is now part of The Inn at Rancho Santa Fe. It is of interest that she bequeathed this real property to L. G. Sinnard. The legal description of the property is followed by the statement:

The above land having been hereafter conveyed to me by said L. G. Sinnard.

It appears then that there was a prior arrangement between Leone and Lilian, perhaps as a condition of her contractual position as resident supervisory architect for the Santa Fe Land Improvement Company. On the basis of this bequeathal, it has been suggested that perhaps Lilian and Leone had a romantic connection, but given his acerbic temperament, his three failed marriages, and Lilian's independent nature, this is hard to imagine. More likely, this was a predetermined business arrangement. It, however, became a moot point as Leone died six years before Lilian, in 1932, at age sixty-three. The will showed the inventory and appraisement of Lilian's assets, which totaled $10,183.26 and included a value of $550 for her 1937 Plymouth Coupe. Today, her assets have a relative economic status value of over $165,0000. In 1927, Lilian was quite well-off, and who knows what her actual worth was when she died in 1938.

It wasn't bad enough that Lilian died and left her grieving mother—no doubt still reeling from the death of Julius five years before—to serve as executrix for the estate, but a character enters the picture that spreads venom like a snake. Lilian's will was contested in court by a local resident, Frank J. Gilloon, and as a result it went to probate. A realtor and president of the Home Owners Loan Corporation, Gilloon filed suit against Lilian's estate for non-

payment of six monthly mortgage installments following her death. My friend, Chuck Larrick had some stories to share with me about Gilloon.

The type of guy he was, well he was a show-off. He was physically athletic and he could do surprising things, he walked on his hands out to the water at the beach. He could turn somersaults and liked to demonstrate his abilities to the ladies, and show what a handsome guy he was.

Gilloon's wife was associated with the Whitney family, prominent wealthy New Yorkers. He continued:

The couple were sent out here to get Gilloon out of New York and away from her family. They pensioned him off to stay out here. When Gilloon's wife died, her family told him that they would support him financially if he stayed out here, providing that he had no contact with them.

He did not endear himself to Chuck when Gilloon became an unwelcome guest, making a nuisance of himself to Chuck's mother.

He came sneaking around to see my mother, he would cry on her shoulders, and divulge his financial situation about his wife's family.

The Whitneys held large acreage between Solana Beach and Rancho Santa Fe, but in the Depression they stopped paying taxes on their property. The land was available first to the Santa Fe Irrigation District just by paying the back taxes, said Chuck. Gilloon decided that he personally wanted to control this development, so he publicly attacked the board. Gilloon wrote letters to the *San Dieguito Citizen* and *Coast Dispatch* saying that the board were crooks and targeted Herschell, who was chairman at the time.

These attacks were so scurrilous and so dishonest and so personal that a big law firm took up the case on behalf of the directors and sued Gilloon for slander; they won the suit along with a significant money award.

So this was the kind of upstanding citizen that Frank Gilloon was, a man who had no regard for the Rice family's situation and didn't give them a chance to catch up on Lilian's mortgage payments that went delinquent due to her death. This property was appraised at $4,800 and Gilloon filed his suit in the Superior Court in San Diego County. It was settled on June 9, 1939, almost six months after Lilian's death and just three days before what would have been her fiftieth birthday, had she lived. Laura must have struggled not only with the grief of losing her beloved and talented daughter, but also with the aggravation and stress brought on by Gilloon's vicious lawsuit. Within two months of the settlement, Laura Rice died from heart disease; some say she died of a broken heart. The following year, Lilian Rice's sister-in-law, Miriam, who was more like the sister that Lilian never had, also died. Jack Rice lost the three women in his life—that he undoubtedly loved the most—within a consecutive three-year period. It must have been a devastating blow and a life-changing event. With the passing of Jack Rice in 1960, and with no children on which to carry the blood line, this branch of the Rice family ended.

On Thursday, December 27, 2012, a date which coincided with the seventy-fourth anniversary of Lilian's interment in La Vista Memorial Park, *UT South County* newspaper, published a story headlined: "Important Correction is Set in Stone." On the front page of the paper, the reporter, Caroline Dipping, wrote about that "quiet and cloudy morning" as Tara Tarrant, owner of La Jolla Stone Etching installed a porcelain plaque that precisely covered the surface of Lilian's headstone. The photographer, Nel Cepeda, clicked his shutter, the camera artfully aimed as Tara crouched down in the wet grass and spread a thick epoxy film, "like she was frosting a cake" on the back surface of the plaque. Tara felt strongly that what she was doing was very important in making a correction to "when history veered off course." Her precision etching held the correct dates of Lilian's time on this earth, 1889–1938.

I met Tara through her mother Cindy Klong, a fine artist who specializes in plein-air oil paintings. Cindy and I became friends when I shared my collection of vintage images of the old Osuna adobe with her for a series of paintings that she was creating. When I put the word out that I was looking for outside funding to help set the historic record straight, she offered to sponsor the project and referred me to her daughter who was an expert in stone etching. Others were eager to support the project, too, and with the most generous gift from Miriam Sellgren, whose grandmother had married Lilian's brother, I was able to finally lay to rest the confusion caused by those well-intentioned volunteers who had inadvertently altered history.

I had brought a dozen pink roses with me to place at the headstone, a nod to Lilian's nickname, Pink, and Nel snapped an appropriate shot that captured me as I arranged the delicate pink blooms. The flowers would be shriveled and decayed in a few weeks, I thought, but this headstone will be here for a very long time.

25.
Samuel Wood Hamill

*I*n June 1921, a young man with aspirations to become an architect strode onto the stage in the great hall at San Diego High School and, like 220 others, received his graduation diploma. It was the largest graduating class in the school's history, "More than almost any other class ever graduated from the old Russ school the class of '21 has represented the true spirit of the Grey Castle," reported the *San Diego Union* newspaper.

Lilian had been a teacher of mechanical and architectural drawing on the San Diego High School staff until the year before Sam's graduation. I'd read about this, but wanted to satisfy my own curiosity to see if there was any tangible proof of Lilian's years there. So I visited the school where I knew there was a closet-sized room devoted to archived school papers, reports, ephemera, and annuals and I was given permission to delve into these haphazard treasures. While not well-organized, I was able to find two annuals from 1919 and 1920 that bore Lilian's name as one of the art faculty and that were signed by her, which provided important proof of her time line. After 1920, Lilian transferred to San Diego State Teacher's College, now San Diego State University, until 1922, where she taught mechanical drawing and descriptive geometry. While Lilian did not teach Sam in high school, she did know of him and had an interest in his talent shown for architecture. Sam described this in an oral history in the 1970s:

> One of my teachers in San Diego High School (there were two teachers who were actually graduate architects)...was Lionel C. Sherwood and he became a teacher strictly because he had to make a living as all the architects in San Diego were starving to death. The other was Lilian Rice. The people that knew her loved her. She was a

lovely darling woman. She was not an instructor of the class I had but I got to know her and lo and behold there she was also on the State College staff when I decided to take my first college year here at San Diego State.

The Hamills came to San Diego from the mining town of Globe, Arizona, when Sam was six years old. The family lived in a modest wood-framed bungalow on Fern Street, in a new San Diego neighborhood close to Balboa Park. Early in his boyhood, Sam became aware of the importance of gardens and plantings through lectures given by Kate Sessions at the Brooklyn Elementary School, which he attended. When the Panama-California Exposition of 1915 opened, Sam was a twelve year old and, mature for his age, his mother bought him a season pass. It was an experience that made a lasting impression. Sam talked about it in an interview in the 1970s:

> I knew at that moment that I wanted to learn all I could about these beautiful buildings; to be able to enjoy them to the fullest degree...I wanted to have these wonderful buildings last forever, to be appreciated by all people who came to San Diego in the future.

During his many visits to the park, Sam absorbed the buildings and gardens and developed an appreciation for the design of the Spanish colonial structures. Constant exposure to this physical beauty proved influential and as Sam, who had been doodling ever since he was a small child, was encouraged by

Sam Hamill, left, with brother, Joe Hamil, circa 1936. *Courtesy Del mar Turf Club*

his mother to choose drafting classes in high school. In response to a question posed during career day, he selected architecture as his interest and attended a lecture given at school by architect William Templeton Johnson, who later asked Sam to work for him that summer doing a survey of some of the downtown buildings that Johnson was planning to revive. It would pave the way for a future lengthy career in architecture.

While at the San Diego State College, Sam took Lilian's course in descriptive geometry. Sam said:

It's a horrible course and the reason for many young budding architects never following the career. Fortunately because of Miss Rice, I passed.

Lilian encouraged Sam to take some preparatory courses that would be necessary later to graduate as an architect from the University of California, in Berkeley.

She told me she thought that State College was certainly the wrong place for me…that I had better get busy and go north.

Sam went on to say that Lilian was a "Godsend" as it was her connection with the "despot," Bessie Sprague, the architectural department's administrator, that allowed Sam to enter the architectural degree course in the middle of its four-year program, which was a near impossibility for others.

There is some confusion as to Sam Hamill's time line as in some historic papers it has been erroneously stated that Sam graduated from Cal in May 1927 then was hired by Requa and Jackson's office, which sent him to Rancho Santa Fe. But there is some fine detail that is important to document here.

In Sam's own words:

I didn't go immediately to Berkeley because money was critical.

One of his friends, Robert Ryan, was moving with his family from San Diego to Los Angeles. He invited Sam, without his parents' approval, to stay with the family so that he could attend the University of California, Los Angeles. Sam was attracted by the fact that Paul Cret, a École de Beaux Arts graduate and architect of the Pan American Building in Washington, DC, was the head of school and this was its inaugural year. But the lack of money meant that Sam could not return to UCLA after his first year of study. Sam says:

> I decided I would stay out for a while, make some money and then go back to school.

It was during this period that Richard Requa offered Sam a job working as a draftsman. Sam said:

> When I first went to work on a Monday morning at Requa and Jackson's office, Jackson told me that he had had a call the previous Friday from Miss Rice asking if she could borrow one of the draftsmen from the office…And so they sent me out there. Actually I started my work for Requa and Jackson by going to work for Lilian Rice in 1923.

Through Lilian's influence and earlier coaching for the difficult task of descriptive geometry, Sam had been able to enter the architectural program at Berkeley in his junior year and graduate in May 1927 with his degree. By the 1930s he had made a name for himself in San Diego as the lead designer for the county administration center, as well as helping to design the Del Mar Fairgrounds and Race Track. In 1934, he was part of a team that helped restore Balboa Park's House of Hospitality, then worked on the design plan for the county courthouse and sheriff's department facilities in the 1950s. He was the architect for the Marston Co. and the Union Title & Trust Co. and, like Lilian, designed several school buildings. In the 1960s, Sam worked with five other architects in the design and construction of the Community Concourse, became a founding member of San Diegans Inc., and the Committee of 100, and helped preserve Balboa Park buildings. The AIA elected Sam a Fellow in 1957, the San Diego Floral Association made him an honorary member in 1971, and in 1980 San Diego County Board Supervisor Roger Hedgecock honored Sam in a public ceremony as architect for the County Administration Building. He retired in 1968, after forty years of practice.

In the mid-1970s Harriet Rochlin, a writer and historian, was conducting several oral histories to gather materials for an article that she was writing on California women architects for *Ms. Magazine*. Her research was extensive and in later years she donated her papers to UCLA. I spent many hours perusing these papers, which was very exciting for me. I anticipated that some of my nagging questions about the mystery of Lilian in those early days of Rancho Santa Fe would be answered, and they were. Harriet's transcribed interview with Sam Hamill was among these papers and in its pages held a firsthand account that would help exonerate Lilian's reputation.

> Miss Rice was a very sweet person and now I realize that she was almost exactly the same age as my oldest sister who was some fifteen years older than I am, in essence I was my older sister's baby brother. I was accustomed to all the special treatment that I received and I undoubtedly was being spoiled again.

Sam said that Lilian had been working part-time for Requa and Jackson's firm since 1921 and had established herself as a trusted employee and that by the time he arrived in Rancho Santa Fe in 1923, Lilian was full-time and had been working there as a representative of the firm since 1922. Because this was a new community that was being developed from scratch, engineering and planning had to be worked out on the site. There weren't any accurate maps available of the property then, so it was necessary for Lilian to be on site to discuss aspects of the project with the on site civil engineers.

Sam said:

> So it became necessary to give increasing responsibility to Lilian, to adjust things and continue with them right there and then on the site.

Lilian was a very responsible person, according to Sam:

> She didn't in any sense of the word supplant her employer. It's simply that her meshing in with the whole Santa Fe program was so direct and was so satisfactory on both sides and the ranch was sufficiently far

away…and the construction projects were not grand, and the fees were not substantial enough to support a lot of participation by the city office. I think all of those factors probably converge to suggest that the whole operation be turned over to her. She stayed there and all the houses and things…were her creation.

When Sam was sent to Rancho Santa Fe on that first day of work for Requa and Jackson, on a Monday morning in 1923, he found a village center being developed as though on a blank canvas right before him. There was no street paving; civil engineers were working throughout the civic center, and their stakes were strategically positioned, "You had to be careful not to move any stakes or they'd tell you off in no uncertain words," Sam recalled. There was a lumberyard and a materials yard with everything dumped there to start a brand-new community. There was so much activity with laborers, masons, and agriculturalists on staff telling everyone how the ground was good and the climate was conducive for orange groves. Harriet asked Sam if Lilian worked well with Leone Sinnard. Yes, she did, he recalled, which was quite an accomplishment due to Sinnard's temper and austere nature. "He was not an approachable man. He was the boss and wanted everyone to know that he was the boss," Sam commented.

While Sinnard needed to be in charge, Lilian had an unusual quality in that she became her client's advocate in getting them what they wanted for their projects. She worked hard on behalf of them and seldom tried to impose her ideas on them, and inevitably she became their trusted friend. This resulted in more time spent on each project than perhaps a more commercial firm would have done. She worked very closely with her clients and many were wealthy, but she was careful never to impose on them.

Sam says:

I recall her as a person who I never saw any negative aspects whatsoever. She was always cool, calm and collected and always very warm and thoughtful.

Harriet asked: What were her feelings about architecture, did she have a devotion to it?

It consumed her whole life…It was like a calling, it was not simply a means of economics…

Could you describe her physically? she asked.

She was a blond girl and very fair complexion. She had no blemishes of any sort. She was very restrained in her use of cosmetics…no eye shadow, artificial eye lashes and all that but she was not an old maid type.

Was she available to human exchange? asked Harriet.

Yes, she was a lovely woman, she really was.

As I listened to this interview between Harriet Rochlin and Samuel Wood Hamill, in the quiet solitude of the archive room in the library at UCLA, it seemed like it wasn't a leap of faith to state that Lilian was the architectural designer of the civic center of Rancho Santa Fe, and that she designed all of the homes there over a fifteen-year period, from 1923 though 1938, the year when she died. But the Requa supporters disagreed. And I wanted to delve deeper into its argument to ascertain who did what when, to untangle the puzzle and to solve the mystery once and for all.

26

Lilian Rice: Liar and a Cheat?

Like Hazel Waterman before her, Lilian Rice was not a licensed architect. That changed when she was allowed to take the necessary examinations, and, on passing them, received her license in February of 1929. Not unlike her mentor, Lilian was nevertheless able to freely offer her services as an architectural designer before that date and obviously accepted many commissions around San Diego County, including her very first commission by her father, the modest "grey cottage" designed in the summer before her junior year, in National City. For the early work done in the civic center of Rancho Santa Fe, it is feasible that Richard Requa instructed Lilian, by then a capable asset in his firm, to design a modified version of the downtown buildings in Ojai, built when Requa was in partnership with Frank Mead.

The idea of the original civic center plan was Leone Sinnard's, who conceived and drew it out as a draft plan. When looking at the modified plan that was finally implemented, it is in Lilian's hand. Naturally, it is customary for the architect of record to have legal claim to all the design work done in its office. Consequently, often up-and-coming architectural designers do not receive any recognition for their talent; Ayn Rand wrote so poignantly about this fact in her book, *The Fountainhead*, when Peter Keating used Howard Roark's designs so freely and claimed them for his own. It is evident that Richard Requa trusted Lilian's professionalism and gave her artistic freedom in the design of the civic center buildings, as proved by the skillfully produced presentation drawings in Lilian's distinctive hand. But as was customary, the firm of Requa and Jackson rightly would lay claim to the designs regardless of whose hand and creative acumen actually conceived those designs.

In an attempt to get a balanced view of the unanswered questions with regard to the design of early Rancho Santa Fe, I spoke to William Chandler, a San Diego-based architectural historian, to see if he was willing to tell me his side of the story, which I knew favored Requa supporters. He was happy to share what he knew about the period of time from 1922 through 1928, based on knowledge told to him by a dear friend of his, now passed away, who once owned Block F in the civic center, formerly property owned by Louise Spurr-Badger. We talked at length about what little evidence there was either to refute or prove Lilian's factual role. But Will's friend was in the possession of a memo that clearly stated that Lilian's only contribution to the design of the civic center was the interior decor and the lighting fixtures of La Morada. Further, that based on evidence from his friend's conversations with Louise Badger, proved that Lilian deliberately lied to her—and evidently to other clients—when she told them that she was the architect of the civic center, a deceitful claim as she had no such authority, according to Will.

In addition to this overstatement of her professional role, for Will it was obvious that those first buildings in the civic center, designed in hues of mustard and tan with turquoise trim, were stylistically typical of Richard Requa's work, and therefore could not have been Lilian's designs. But from my research, they typified Lilian's signature style, which was one of simplicity based on an eclectic blend of pueblo, Mexican, and Spanish colonial revival. In fact, they are exactly as she would have designed them.

By the 1990s, local historians had begun to understand the value of our local architects and to appreciate the work that they had completed in San Diego County. One person, more than any, poured his own funds and endless hours of volunteer work into culling records, plans, drawings, photographs, magazine articles, and film, into one cohesive architectural archive, now held in the San Diego

History Center in Balboa Park. That person was Parker Jackson, Richard Requa's biographer. As these archives were being organized and accessed, the question was raised, why did Richard Requa pass on the high-profile commission of Rancho Santa Fe to Lilian? When interviewed in 1993 by Ann Jarmusch, then architectural feature writer for the *San Diego Union* newspaper, Parker commented,

> Somewhere out there, there's some explanation for why Richard Requa walked away from the Rancho Santa Fe commission.

Why Requa relinquished this project to Lilian is considered one of the major mysteries in local architectural history. Apparently it seems inconceivable that Lilian Rice's local success and fame, closely associated with Rancho Santa Fe, was based mostly on this conspicuous project that Richard and Jackson let slip through their fingers. But there are a couple of likely explanations as to why Requa gave Lilian the Rancho Santa Fe commission. Heavy demands on his firm at the time were more focused on the Davis-Baker project in Kensington Heights—a plausible reason, and with a low commission of only six percent from the land company, it is understandable that Requa would be happy to pass on the project to Lilian. In effect, she got the booby prize. In 1923, his only child, Richard S. Requa Jr., tragically died, which must have caused unimaginable grief for both him and Viola; and Herbert Jackson, Richard's engineer, was hospitalized just as the development was getting underway.

But that doesn't explain away the controversy surrounding the civic center work. Both Will and Parker cite a memorandum in their possession that gives written proof that Lilian had little involvement with the design of the buildings of the civic center in Rancho Santa Fe, if any at all, and that she deliberately lied to others when she claimed that she did. But without a reference to this document, it was impossible to be objective about their claims. I knew I had to get a copy of this memo.

Thanks to an elderly, kindly gentleman named Rea Mowery, a copy would eventually find its way into my hands. Rea had worked in the bank in the

village of Rancho Santa Fe, and was long retired but, like Sam Hamill, had also been interviewed by Harriet Rochlin in the 1970s, so I knew his name and understood that he had intimate knowledge of the history of Rancho Santa Fe. Through an online search I was able to locate him and I hand-wrote a letter asking him if he was willing to share any information that, through his own research, he might be able to pass along to me. When he unexpectedly came into San Diego, in 2007, we met briefly. Rea shared his knowledge of the Ranch and shared how he inadvertently discovered an abandoned building with a cupboard filled with blueprints, documents, and photographs from the 1920s era in the Ranch. Not unlike an archeological finding this was a veritable gold mine, which would become the seeds for today's Rancho Santa Fe Historical Society's archived collections. Rea also had a copy of the mysterious memo, which he gladly gave to me along with copies of vintage photographs, old magazines, and a plat book of the covenant lots.

This is what I discovered in the copy of the memorandum. It was dated December 17, 1969, and was included as an enclosure in a letter from Earnest Marsh—then chairman of the Atchison, Topeka, Santa Fe Railway Company—to a friend of his, Curtis Barkes, who was planning to buy property in the Ranch. The document is eleven pages long and gives a detailed history of Rancho Santa Fe from its land grant days to its development by the Santa Fe Land Improvement Company as a high-class community. On page five is written:

Mr. Sinnard was a specialist in laying out, developing and marketing ranch lands and with his associates...saw the natural beauty of the lands and proposed laying out the whole area as a great landscape garden with its historic aspects, the pervading romance of Old Spain.... [He] suggested a community with a civic center with Spanish motif as a monument to the early builders of California. The plan provided for a hotel, a school group, shops, garages and other community buildings with building restrictions that would make it highly exclusive and a choice place of residence.

Then on page seven:

At the Civic Center, Richard S. Requa, an architect with intimate knowledge of the architecture of Old Spain, designed the original group of buildings true to type in all details using adobe bricks, made and laid by experienced masons, natives of old Mexico. The lighting and interior features paid tribute to the artistry and taste of Miss Lillian [*sic*] Rice."

The text goes on to describe the guest house:

La Morada (The Home), the chief building of the group, was at first probably the only hotel of its kind....the guests were usually there for a limited time and were selected because of their likeliness, financially and otherwise, to become permanent residents of the Rancho Santa Fe.

This memo naturally raised an important question for me. Why was Lilian considered the lighting and interior designer, (albeit one with artistry and taste) when it cannot be doubted that the actual design of the building, especially its exterior, was rendered in her hand?

Over the duration of my ten-year period of research the Internet's reach grew enormously, and as such, previously hidden documents came into sharp focus. It wasn't long before I stumbled upon the source document that was used to pull "facts" for the history memo that Earnest Marsh mailed to his friend Curtis Barkes. This was a breakthrough discovery for me—the smoking gun! An online search led me to an article written by the contributor known simply as "Maque" for the May 1923 edition of *Valve World*, a trade magazine published by Crane and Company, purveyors of plumbing and sanitary fixtures, who provided La Morada with wash basins, bathtubs, and toilets. The story was titled "Where Capital Bows at the Shrine of Beauty." As I carefully read the text, it became evident that chunks of Maque's article were lifted verbatim and inserted into the Marsh memo. The article is enhanced with photographs and a copy of Lilian's own artfully rendered drawing of the guest house and long shots of the civic center buildings spread across two pages. Maque writes about the hotel, his exact verbiage evidently being rewritten in the 1969 memo, however, with an important difference. Maque's version follows on from the prior quotation:

Guests for La Morada are selected because of their likeliness, financially and otherwise, to become permanent residents of the Rancho Santa Fe. Harmony in color and line reigns throughout this delightful building, and restfulness is suggested on every hand, beginning with the homelike living room—there is not a suggestion of the conventional lobby or office—and running throughout the corridors and rooms. The lighting and fixtures and many of the interior features pay tribute to the artistry and taste of Miss Lillian Rice, designer of interior finish.

So, in Maque's version, Lilian Rice is also only credited with the interior decor of La Morada and nothing more. How can this be? The article is published in May 1923, just two months after the guest house opened. I reread the article trying to find clues and then it struck me like a thunderbolt. Maque follows on the quotation with:

> Looking down the broad avenue running from the front of La Morada, palm-lined and tan colored, one has the remaining buildings of the group as a picture, the business buildings on the right and the schools on the left....

Eureka! The specter of doubt was risen. It was obvious that the writer, Maque, had never visited La Morada or Rancho Santa Fe, as the schools he described in his article were a figment of his imagination, and in fact there was no school group ever built; just one school was constructed and it was completed in 1924 by Lilian, a year after the story ran. This naturally brings into question then the factual basis of the entire article. Likely relying solely on marketing materials produced by Leone Sinnard, where no mention is made of Lilian Rice's efforts or even of Requa and Jackson's firm, the writer Maque has made up his story, which then became the basis for the Marsh document, which then became the basis for a damaging smear campaign that has tainted Lilian Rice's reputation and has sadly led to the demolition of several of her buildings, which were deemed non-historic and therefore of no value.

Archived plans, renderings, and photographs held in the San Diego History Center in Balboa Park, California, provided me with a clear record of the development of the Civic Center and Lilian's subsequent residential projects. The plans for these early projects bear the Requa and Jackson firm's name, as do homes designed and built by Rice up until 1928; descendants of these homeowners state though that Lilian designed and superintended the building of their homes, that Requa had no hand in them. As architectural designer, shouldn't Lilian rightly be given credit for her efforts? For a news article that featured the Larrick family home, completed in August 1928, the headline stated: "Lillian [sic] Rice of the rancho staff designed this interesting structure."

When the Santa Fe Land Improvement Company divested itself of the Rancho Santa Fe project in 1927, the management of the community was turned over to the newly formed Rancho Santa Fe Corporation. Close to that time, Lilian also severed her ties as the land company's supervisory resident architect and opened her own office in La Valenciana building in Rancho Santa Fe. She became licensed in San Diego in 1929, (license number 1671), and had joined the local chapter of the American Institute of Architects by 1931, some ten years after Julia Morgan was allowed entry; Lilian was the state's second lady architect to join this elite group of men. Prior to being licensed, Rice was given legal authority to sign building permits using the following: *Requa and Jackson, per LJR.* In her letter of application to join the AIA, Rice wrote on June 8, 1931, "I was a draftsman for the firm of Requa and Jackson, Architects of San Diego for about two and a half years; for five years I had charge of the architectural department for the Santa Fe Land Improvement Company at Rancho Santa Fe; and since February of 1929 have been practising [sic] as a licensed architect." Thus Rice's professional timeline is as follows:

1921-1923 in the employ of Requa and Jackson as a draftsman;
1923-1929 resident architect for SFLIC;
1929-1938 independent licensed architect.

Also of note, the roster of the California State Board of Architectural Examiners indicates that Lilian was the tenth woman in the state to receive her license at a time when there were 1,650 men.

Examining the term "architect" is relevant here. In March 1901, the state of California passed the act, "To Regulate the Practice of Architecture." In part it stated that a person may only name his or herself an architect and practice architecture who is a registered licensed architect, having passed the necessary examinations and been licensed by the California State Board of Architectural Examiners. Others were permitted to design wood-frame single-family dwellings not exceeding two stories, and wood-frame multiple-family dwellings not more than four units. In this way, many women who early on were discouraged or barred from actually taking this registration, were still able to design homes and other buildings that fit the criteria, like Hazel Waterman, who preceded Lilian but who was not motivated to make the trip up to Los Angeles to get her registration.

So is the case for Lilian? Or was she so cunning to deceive others into believing that she was a licensed architect to further her professional standing and career. Additionally, was there a conspiracy among her friends to spread the same deceit? When I spoke with Will about this issue, his opinion was that it was commonplace for architects to lie to further themselves. He said that Sam Hamill for example, "lied through his teeth" specifically when it came to his work done through Richard Requa's office, which resulted later in the two becoming rivals. History shows that Frank Lloyd Wright lied when he shaved two years off his age to impress prospective clients to hire him; Richard Requa lied bout Mrs. Fickeisen providing the winning design for the custom home in Kensington Heights; Sam Hamill lied about his work in Balboa Park in the 1935 restoration; and Frank Allen Jr. lied about his role in the original Panama-California Exposition as newspapers in January 1915 applauded him as the exposition designer, which incensed Bertram Goodhue. When I asked Ed Spurr if he thought that Lilian had deliberately misled his mother and other clients into believing that she had much more authority in the architectural design of Rancho Santa Fe than she actually did, he responded that as they were very close friends, it was highly unlikely not and that it would have been contrary to her character.

Lilian's friend Ruth Nelson wrote in a 1931 article published in the *San Diego Union*, the following statement:

> Miss Rice came to Rancho Santa Fe as the result of one of those emergencies which occur in every office. Mr. Requa was called away on urgent business and Mr. Jackson was taken ill just when building operations were beginning at the ranch, but as an inspector was required. It was the sketches made by Miss Rice for the Guest House which had been accepted and were being used. Could she not come and take charge of the work? To Rancho Santa Fe Miss Rice came and there she has been kept busy for the past seven years. For no magnetic needle could point its way to a pole more truly than Miss Rice has been pointed to the very corner of California, where she truly belongs.
>
> It has been her unfailingly artistic treatment of the Spanish motif required at Rancho Santa Fe which has influenced the entire development of this uniquely historic spot. Sixty four completed buildings at the Rancho for which she drew the plans are the unanswerable evidence of this. Evidenced also is her pleasant modesty in the way she mentions this rather astonishing number. For she failed to state that this number includes several groups which contain from three to five separable units.

In the final analysis, Lilian may have lied to garner more business in the competitive world of architectural design, and if so, it appears that she was following the lead of many of her male peers. Or on the other hand, she may have claimed what she did, because she actually did it. Perhaps it comes down to semantics then, with Lilian stating that she was the architectural designer of the civic center, as was perfectly allowed by law, with others interpreting this to mean that she was the architect.

Looking at the written record of work completed in Rancho Santa Fe, it appears that clients were not concerned whether Lilian was a licensed architect or not; they wanted their homes to be tastefully and artfully designed with all the modern conveniences and to have a close amiable relationship with their designer. Lilian provided this and much more.

In the 1920s, it was rare that a prestigious company like Requa and Jackson would have given any credit to a designer on their staff. But despite that fact, perhaps today, this book will finally bring Lilian's story out of the shadows of time into the light of the present. Lilian should at least be given her rightful place in the history books as a career woman and a trailblazer, who paved the way for other up-and-coming architects, both male and female, a professional who survived and thrived in the male world of architecture and for that we should applaud her.

27.
Luella Mordhorst

*T*wo sisters walked down East Second Street in National City, and felt a pang of sorrow. They had come from a milestone school reunion, the fortieth at the Sweetwater High School. Reconnecting with past fellow students was always uplifting, the remembering was the best part, taking a backward glance at the good times, rarely the bad. This momentary sadness stemmed from the scene before them that took their memories back to wonderful times, but brought them to a fearful present. Elyzabeth and Mary looked at the empty lot in disarray, littered with trash, cigarette butts, and beer cans, detritus from the liquor store just steps around the corner on Highland Avenue. They remembered how it once had been, during safer times, when they were young woman of twenty who could walk around the block, smell the jasmine in their grandmother's garden, check to see that the light was off in the store that their family owned, then walk back home to their parent's house without looking over their shoulders.

When Elyzabeth and Mary knew and loved this garden, their grandparents, Luella and William Mordhorst owned the property and the house located on it. The sisters were children when their own parents, Mary and John William, were building their home just a block away from their grandparents' home. Remarkably, through social media, I was able to locate Elyzabeth and Mary, and in so doing solve another mystery: how Lilian's scrapbook came to be in the National City Library archives and why Luella Mordhorst's name was hand-written in Lilian's copy of the English Society's *Occident*.

The garden of the Rice family home once stood on this sorry, dried up, dusty lot on the corner of East Second Street. I spoke to Elyzabeth and Mary by phone and their memories of the garden brought the scene into focus for me. Two star pines that the Rice family planted soared above all else in the garden. "They were used as airplane navigational aides," Elyzabeth told me. "There were two silk oak trees, a monkey puzzle tree, a stand of giant bamboo, and eucalyptus trees. There were begonias and a beautiful rose garden." There was also an aviary on the property and olive trees lined the sidewalk next to the house, which was demolished in the late 1960s and replaced with a self-serve car wash on Highland Avenue.

The original Queen Anne Revival house had been designed in 1882 by Elizur Steele for his much loved niece Laura, who was then recently married. When Lilian was a child, Laura completed an interior remodel of the house, added exterior embellishments, and changed the color to red. From that point on the landmark home on a prominent corner in National City became known as the Rice's "Red Wood House."

Luella, Elyzabeth's grandmother, was civic-minded, a former president of the local PTA, and very active in the National City Garden Club. In the 1950s, her brother-in-law John Volstorff built a large lath-house in the grounds and Luella filled it with beautiful begonias, fuschias, sweet peas, and ferns. "It was such a magical time," recalled Elyzabeth. "There were so many happy events there. My grandmother was also involved with the historical society and the canasta club and every year she had an annual garden party."

Elyzabeth and Mary "grew up in that garden," they told me. While the family waited for their parents' home to be completed, the two girls lived in their grandparents' home. Mary's room was formerly Lilian's room. Elyzabeth recalls about the haunting memory:

My room would have been Laura's studio, directly opposite Lilian's. I remember at

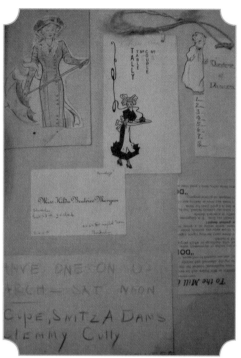

Front cover of Lilian's scrapbook, 1910. *Author's collection*

A page of Lilian's scrapbook, 1910. *Author's collection*

one of my grandmother's parties there was a woman in there reading the tarot cards. There's a book [to be written] there.

The house came into the Mordhorsts's ownership in 1939, when Jack Rice sold it lock, stock, and barrel completely furnished with all the Rice family belongings inside it. In later years, Luella donated a few of the items to the historic collections in the National City Library. Included in her donation was the Occident book, Lilian's college scrapbook, a photo album, and a small hand-sized album that was filled from cover to cover with over a hundred postcards that documented a trip to Europe that Lilian had taken before the outbreak of World War I. But most of the items were kept in the Mordhorst family, as they were considered too valuable to part with. Mary inherited from her grandmother a fine Windsor chair, two marble-topped cherry dressers, a cherry bed, fire place tools, a birds-eye maple bedroom set, three lamps, a sewing cabinet, chinaware, and a fern stand—items that were once in the Rice family and then in the Mordhorst family. These items are loved and, considered

family heirlooms, are priceless. There was one item that held a very special place in Elyzabeth's heart and would not be parted with: it was another college scrapbook made by Lilian, one that carried on from her first. This one documented Lilian's university years from 1909–1910 and was crammed with dance cards, stage show bills, calling cards, news clippings, class assignments, and graduation papers. Elyzabeth remembers:

> I would sit under the stairwell across from the music room and secretly two or three times a month, I would look through the pages. For me its memories also held those of my grandmother and the house.

She felt a kinship with Lilian: both loved this grand old house as children and while Lilian was called *Pinky* by her college friends Elyzabeth's nickname was *Pinky Posy*, which strengthened the bond in the young girl's heart.

The two little girls who found magic in the Rice home were crushed when the house was sold for $25,000 in 1968, when they were adults in their twenties. Luella was quite elderly and as the neighborhood was sinking further into disrepair, and vandalism became common, she no longer felt that the Rice's Red Wood House brought her refuge and moved into her son's house.

Mary told me:

National City didn't seem to care about preserving the home. It broke our hearts (and still does) that the home was destroyed.

Luella and her son John attempted to have the house and its grounds become a part of the historic homes registry, but at the time, city officials took no interest. When the home eventually sold, there were offers to turn it into apartments and one offer of a bed and breakfast (that offer fell through), but other than that, the offers were few and far between.

The house stood fallow for several years. John Minchin remembered that period well:

The house was surrounded by beautiful landscape gardens. After the Rice's [sic] passed away it was vacant for some time. We kids played in the yard and looked in the windows for ghosts.

While John and his friends didn't see any ghosts, the persistence of memory of its former inhabitants means that the home does live on in their imaginations. And through the furnishings and other items that were salvaged, the memories are never far away.

Elyzabeth stated:

My memory of Lilian is that her spirit and all that she contributed was melded into our family, as a spiritual presence. You can tell the kind of mind she had by her scrapbook. I know that she was with the Requa firm and did so much work in Rancho Santa Fe, then didn't get any of the credit. Lilian made many sacrifices and had to be better than any man. She was incredible.

In closing our conversation, Elyzabeth returned her thoughts to that stroll down memory lane on East Second Street, one that took her twenty years to make as the grief of the demolition of her

The Rice house in National City circa 1940. *Author's collection*

grandmother's home was too much to bear, and left me with a poignant vision.

There was a big stump from an olive tree [on the lot] and I said to Mary, 'let's take it home.' When we picked it up there was about a six-inch Asparagus Fern, which was actually the fern that was over my grandmother's cellar doorway, and I took it home with me. Believe me if you go down there, there is nothing on the sidewalks, they are dry and dirty and there was this beautiful vibrant green asparagus fern thriving in the dirt.

Elyzabeth took the cutting and transplanted it in her own yard where it grows just as healthily as it did in the Rice's garden over a hundred years ago. That tenacious little plant is a tangible link to a bygone era, both to the Mordhorst family's past and to the Rice family's past.

Before we signed off from the call, the conversation came back to Lilian's scrapbook; Elyzabeth agreed that I could borrow it and digitize it so that its contents may be saved for posterity and shared with those who have an interest. But by the time I had hung up the handset, she thought that maybe I should have it. The item was too precious to send by mail so it was agreed that as it was close to Christmas, and she would be planning a visit to her sister's anyway, Elyzabeth would take it by hand from her home in Washington to Mary's home in Bakersfield. I could pick it up in person later and give the scrapbook a new home. I had to pinch myself to check that this was not a dream.

28.

Author's Note

How The Ghost of You Clings

One hundred years after comet fever created a national sensation, my own excitement, at the official release of my initial book on Lilian Rice, stirred in me just as much emotion. It was the first book ever published that was devoted solely to Lilian Rice, and in its pages I listed a body of work that contained over 120 projects that spanned, mostly, a relatively short period of time, 1922 through 1938. By anyone's standards, that was quite an accomplishment, especially when the lion's share of the work was completed when the Great Depression was in full force. I organized an exhibition that showcased the work of several architectural photographers who worked with me to capture Lilian's buildings for this artfully designed coffee table book. A reception, that also served as the official book launch, took place on June 12, 2010. The date was chosen carefully, it would have been Lilian's 121st birthday. Dena Gillespie, a San Diego architectural designer who had restored a 1920s Lilian Rice estate home in Rancho Santa Fe, brought a birthday cake, and we celebrated with guests in the packed venue.

Despite the fact that the book had been released, a labor of love that took five years of research to complete, I felt that this was just the beginning, rather than the end of this journey. More work to be done, more mysteries to hopefully solve, more people to talk to and more presentations to make. It became clear that, when I did these presentations, the audiences were just as curious about my path of discovery as they were about Lilian's life and work. Without exception the first question was, "how did you first learn about Lilian?" and second, "why did you start to write about her?" This sparked in me the realization that this was equally an engaging story as Lilian's biography. Partly for this reason this manuscript would include part of this unfolding of a fascinating story, and I would place myself in the narrative.

Many biographies of famous people are based upon archives of that person's life that were kept by their loving and often wealthy families. In many cases, the subject is still alive. With Lilian J. Rice neither is the case. There was no one archive, no place where a majority of the information was organized and stored. The process has been more like investigative journalism: making the most of the scraps of data by comparing them to one and other, following leads (some known to be fiction), and hunkering down in libraries and historical societies.

It is because of this lack of a personal archive that my book pulls in personalities and events that bring to life the era in which Lilian lived as an adult, the 1920s and '30s. Through newspaper archives, photographs, Lilian's college scrapbooks and oral histories a clear image has come into focus. It is my goal that Lilian's long-delayed national recognition will be launched with the publication of this book. Lilian's legacy can be measured in both human and architectural terms. She was loved and respected by clients, several of them Hollywood "A" list stars, wealthy corporate retirees, and many of them women. She left behind homes rich in innovative architectural craftsmanship, both retreats for the families who lived in them and now markers of great historical significance and beloved homes to those who now own them.

From the early sparks of recognition of an interesting story, to the realization that this in fact was a huge story, Lilian Rice's life and times have gradually unfolded to me. My ten years of engagement have resulted in an extraordinary work of history and biography that pays homage to the long-forgotten lady master architect, a hidden national treasure, whose story is interwoven not only with the development of California's built environment, but

Lilian during the dedication of the ZLAC Rowing Clubhouse, in 1932. *Courtesy Helen E. Wagner*

also with its development as a young state. This story incorporates my journey of discovery as fragments of Lilian's life events became known to me. The narrative is as much about my quest, my treasure hunt to uncover information, as it is about the life and times of Lilian Rice.

This chapter's title takes its inspiration from a line in the popular 1936 song "These Foolish Things (Remind Me of You)" by lyricist Eric Maschwitz with music by Jack Strachey: "How The Ghost of You Clings." The phrase alludes to the perceived notion that buildings retain an energy in their walls, in effect the spirits of their former inhabitants, or in this case the ghost of the architect. The song's lyrics have a secondary connection to this project as they echo how fragments of information gathered during my research are treasured "reminders" of Lilian Rice and have helped to breathe life into her story.

A charismatic figure, tough enough to manage teams of male craftsmen and laborers, yet gentle enough to babysit clients' young children, Lilian was one of the most important women in twentieth-century architecture. Her sensitive artistry was respected and revered, and she stood shoulder-to-shoulder with her contemporaneous male peers. When she died, she left behind homes rich in innovative architectural craftsmanship, both retreats for the families who lived in them, and now markers of great historical significance. While many of Lilian Rice's buildings have fallen foul of the demolition wrecking ball, my sincere hope is that this project will bring Lilian's achievements to the fore and that from this point forward, her buildings will become more treasured. To help the reader further understand Lilian Rice, the times in which she lived, and those in her sphere, I have included points of interest in California, extracted from the chapters in this book, which are listed as an appendix, along with current information that was accurate going to press. If you are able to visit some of them, Lilian's story will be more tangible and I hope, appreciated.

As this project came to it's close and I was literally doing the final edit of my manuscript I was contacted by two organizations, independently. The Edmund Rice Association reached out to me as one of its members—Michael Rice—was giving a fall lecture at the association's annual gathering. Lilian J. Rice, he told me by e-mail, is a direct descendant of Edmund Rice who immigrated from England to Massachusetts Bay Colony in 1638. His presentation was on famous Rice women which included Mary Ashton Rice Livermore, a published writer and a champion of suffragette rights; Laura Ingalls Wilder, author of the Little House on the Prairie books; and her daughter Rose Wilder-Lane, an acclaimed national reporter, co-founder of the Libertarian movement, and biographer to Herbert Hoover. He also included Lilian J. Rice in his line-up of famous female Edmund Rice descendants, and I felt proud that Lilian was being considered on an equal footing with these remarkable women in history.

I then received an e-mail from a representative of the Beverly Willis Architecture Foundation—Professor Victoria Rosner—of Columbia University, New York. I was invited to prepare an extensive essay on the life and work of Lilian J. Rice as part of a project developed by the BWAF. The Foundation has received a grant from the National Endowment for the Arts to compile an online listing of pre-1940 leading American woman architects involved with the built environment. A jury selected 50 women, from a much longer list, whose profiles are being compiled for inclusion in Women of 20th Century American Architecture. The invitation sent to me noted:

"Since you have done more than anyone to bring Rice's work to public attention, it would be wonderful to have you prepare her profile for this project."

This is an unprecedented honor for Lilian J. Rice. Having her officially recognized as one of the nation's top women architects will bring her further, vital exposure that will prevent her name from slipping into the void of obscurity.

ACKNOWLEDGMENTS

Heartfelt gratitude goes to my publisher, Peter Schiffer, for continuing to be a believer and to his executive assistant, Karen Choppa, who first recognized the importance of this book, and to the Schiffer team of editors, designers, and marketers who guided my every step. Because of their continued faith and support I am able to share a deeper story into the life and times of Lilian J. Rice.

Words are not sufficient to thank Audrey Geisel for her foreword and my dream team of photographers, draftsmen, artists, and editors. Hopefully this book will be a direct reflection on their talent and that its success will be representative of my gratitude.

Over the past ten years I have accumulated many personal debts to those who willingly and selflessly lent their time, talent, and valuable family assets to make this book possible. I would like to repay these debts and record them here as a sincere *"thank you."*

Thanks go to Tom Clotfelter (deceased), my time lord, for his unwavering support; to Duncan Hadden, for information on his family history and the storied past of what was formerly La Morada; to the Rancho Santa Fe Historical Society, where I spent many hours perusing its archives; to Bob MacDonald, who shared personal stories about Lilian Rice; to Ed Spurr (deceased) for his recollections of his time spent in Lilian Rice's office as a little boy; and to his daughters, Tamara Spurr and Kim West, for sharing family photographs that captured life in the village center of the Ranch in the 1920s; to Mim Sellgren, who has been an ongoing generous supporter; to Mary Allely and Mat Nye from the Kile Morgan Local History Room in the National City Library; and to the following individuals: Laurie Barlow, Sue Barlow Loyd, Abel Silvas, Don Terwilliger, Eleanor Dean (deceased), Bill Boetigger (deceased), Phoebe Marrall, Colonel Charles Nelson (deceased), Jim and Peggy Polack, Evelyn Weatherall, Ruth Eischen (deceased), Jinx Ecke, Paul Ecke III, Jim Farley, Chuck Larrick, Jim King, Peggy Millar O'Driscoll, Jean Smart Barnes (deceased), John Minchin, Mary Grandell, Helen Wagner, Liz Shattuck (deceased), Rea Mowery (deceased), Sam Gross, Katie Holcombe, Will Chandler, Parker Jackson, Rod and Mary Alexander, Harriet Rochlin, Bill Krisel, Leroy Cole of the Society of Automatize Historians, Marc Brodsky of Virginia Tech, Jeff Rankin, archivist with UCLA's Special Collections.

Gratitude goes to Alana Coons of Save Our Heritage Organisation, who was also a believer from the start; to Helen Rydell, for her research into Leone Sinnard's family history and for sharing valuable information on W. E. Hodges; to Jane Kenealy of the San Diego History Center for aiding my research of Rice's collections held there; to Carol Olten and Mike Mishler of the La Jolla Historical Society; to the folks in the California Room in the San Diego Public Library; to Ron Bosley (deceased) for photographs from the International Club Crosby.

A special mention goes to sisters Mary Hulsey and Elyzabeth Ashcraft, who have a deep connection to the Rice family and to the ghost of its once treasured, elegant home in National City. Their shared memories and the gift of Lilian's college scrapbook are priceless and can only be repaid by my efforts to keep their stories alive.

And my deepest thanks to my loving family who have watched me spend endless hours at my keyboard and supported every key stroke along the way.

PLACES TO VISIT

$\mathcal{P}$lease visit www.DianeYWelch.com to learn more about Diane's work on Lilian Rice, Diane's scheduled walking tours, and her prior award-winning book *Lilian J. Rice Master Architect of Rancho Santa Fe, California* (Schiffer, 2010).

(THE) ALHAMBRA, SPAIN
www.alhambra-patronato.es/index.php?id=1472&L=2

(CITY OF) ATASCADERO, CA
www.visitatascadero.com

BALBOA PARK, SAN DIEGO
www.balboapark.org
(619) 239-0512

(CITY OF) BERKELEY, CA
www.cityofberkeley.info/Home.aspx

(CITY OF) CHULA VISTA, CA
www.chulavistaca.gov

CHULA VISTA HERITAGE MUSEUM
360 Third Avenue (east side of Memorial Park)
Chula Vista, CA 91910-3932
(619) 427-8092

(CITY OF) DEL MAR, CA
www.delmar.ca.us

DEL MAR FAIRGROUNDS
2260 Jimmy Durante Boulevard
Del Mar, CA 92014
www.delmarfairgrounds.com
(858) 755-1161

DEL MAR THOROUGHBRED CLUB
www.dmtc.com

(CITY OF) ENCINITAS, CA
www.ci.encinitas.ca.us

ENCINITAS HISTORICAL SOCIETY
390 West F Street
Encinitas, CA 92024
http://encinitashistoricalsociety.org
(760) 942-9066

(CITY OF) ESCONDIDO, CA
www.escondido.org

ESCONDIDO HISTORY CENTER
321 N. Broadway
Escondido CA 92025
www.escondidohistory.org
(760) 743-8207

FAIRBANKS RANCH, CA
http://fairbanksranch.hoaspace.com

HISTORIC GASLAMP AREA
San Diego, CA
www.gaslamp.org

(THE) INN AT RANCHO SANTA FE
5951 Linea Del Cielo
Rancho Santa Fe, CA 92067
www.theinnatrsf.com
(858) 756-1131

(CITY OF) LA JOLLA
7966 Herschel Avenue
La Jolla, CA 92037
www.lajolla.com
(619) 236-1212

LA JOLLA HISTORICAL SOCIETY
7846 Eads Avenue
La Jolla, CA 92037
http://lajollahistory.org
(858) 459-5335

LA MESA HISTORICAL SOCIETY
8369 University Avenue
La Mesa, CA 91942
https://lamesahistory.com
(619) 466-0197

LILIAN J. RICE ELEMENTARY SCHOOL
915 4th Avenue
Chula Vista, CA 91911

(CITY OF) NATIONAL CITY, CA
www.ci.national-city.ca.us
www.ci.national-city.ca.us/index. aspx?page=100
(For information on historic sites)

(CITY OF) OJAI, CA
www.ojaivisitors.com
(888) OJAI NOW

OLD TOWN, SAN DIEGO
www.oldtownsandiegoguide.com

RANCHO SANTA FE HISTORICAL SOCIETY
6036 La Flecha
Rancho Santa Fe, CA 92067
http://ranchosantafehistoricalsociety.org
(858) 756-9291

SAN DIEGO HISTORY CENTER, BALBOA PARK
1649 El Prado #3
San Diego, CA 92101
www.sandiegohistory.org
(619) 232-6203

SAN DIEGUITO HERITAGE MUSEUM
450 Quail Gardens Drive
Encinitas, CA 92024
www.sdheritage.org
(760) 632-9711

SAN DIEGUITO ACADEMY
800 Santa Fe Drive
Encinitas, CA 92024

SAVE OUR HERITAGE ORGANIZATION
2476 San Diego Avenue
San Diego CA 92110
www.sohosandiego.org
(619) 297-9327

(CITY OF) SOLANA BEACH, CA
www.ci.solana-beach.ca.us

(THE TOWN OF) TARIFA, SPAIN
www.andalucia.com/tarifa/home.htm

UNIVERSITY OF CALIFORNIA, BERKELEY
http://berkeley.edu

(THE) U.S. GRANT HOTEL
326 Broadway
San Diego, CA 92101
www.usgrant.net
(619) 232-3121

(THE) WEDNESDAY CLUB
540 Ivy Lane
San Diego, CA 92103
(619) 295-2438

PROJECT LIST

1908

Julius A. Rice Residence, A Street, National City, CA

1910

Produced winning design for Senior Women's Hall, University of California, Berkeley, CA. Built by Julia Morgan

1922/1923

La Morada, (The Guest House), Civic Center, Rancho Santa Fe, CA 92067
Rancho Santa Fe Land and Improvement Company Office Paseo Delicias, Rancho Santa Fe, CA 92067—
    National Register of Historic Places
Santa Fe Land Improvement Company Offices, Paseo Delicias, Rancho Santa Fe, CA 92067
Louise Badger residence, Paseo Delicias, Rancho Santa Fe, CA 92067
Garage quadrangle, Paseo Delicias, Rancho Santa Fe, CA 92067
Supply Depot, street unknown, Rancho Santa Fe, CA 92067
Santa Fe Land Improvement Company House, La Flecha, Rancho Santa Fe, CA 92067—National
    Register of Historic Places
A. B. Harlan Residence, La Flecha, Rancho Santa Fe, CA 92067
Walter N. and Edna Attrill residence, Lago Lindo, Rancho Santa Fe, CA 92067
SFLI Co. Spec House/ Ralph E. Badger residence, Via de Santa Fe, Rancho Santa Fe, CA 92067
Mr. Bowly Le Huray residence, Paseo Delicias, Rancho Santa Fe, CA 92067
Pump House, Linea del Cielo, Rancho Santa Fe, CA 92067
Santa Fe Irrigation District Shops and superintendent's house

1924

Three-room school, Aliso School District, 6024 Paseo Delicias, Rancho Santa Fe, CA 92067
William A. and Agnes Turnbull Bechberger residence and guest house, Las Colinas, Rancho Santa Fe,
    CA 92067
Mr. and Mrs. Thomas L. Carothers Residence, street unknown, Rancho Santa Fe, CA 92067
Mr. G. S. Harris Residence, La Orilla, Rancho Santa Fe, CA 92067
Miss Lilian J. Rice residence, La Gracia, Rancho Santa Fe, CA 92067
Clarence Mack and Servetta Paddock residence—purchased by Mr. Ulrich L. Voris, Via de Santa Fe,
    Rancho Santa Fe, CA 92067

Lilian Jenette [*sic*] Rice House, originated as the residence of Mary Campbell, then owned by Mr. M. E. Harrison, La Gracia, Rancho Santa Fe, CA 92067—National Register of Historic Places

Thomas Bristol Residence, Via de Alba, Rancho Santa Fe, CA 92067

1925

Restoration begun on historic Silvas/Osuna adobe, Alfred H. Barlow residence, Via de Santa Fe, Rancho Santa Fe, CA 92067—Local Historic Resource

Santa Fe Irrigation District HQ, Linea del Cielo, Rancho Santa Fe, CA 92067

Dewitt M. Richards residence, Las Colinas, Rancho Santa Fe, CA 92067

Claude and Florence Terwilliger house, San Elijo, Rancho Santa Fe, CA 92067—National Register of Historic Places

Mr. Edward S. White residence, Lago Lindo, Rancho Santa Fe, CA 92067

1926

H. P. and Florence P. Johnston Residence, La Valle Plateada, Rancho Santa Fe, CA 92067

Mr. George Megrew residence, Lago Lindo, Rancho Santa Fe, CA 92067

Mr. J. B. Parker residence, street unknown, Rancho Santa Fe, CA 92067

Mr. H.L. Porter residence, La Gracia, Rancho Santa Fe, CA 92067

Spurr-Clotfelter rowhouse, Paseo Delicias, Rancho Santa Fe, CA 92067—National Register of Historic Places

Sidney R. and Ruth Nelson rowhouse, Paseo Delicias, Rancho Santa Fe, CA 92067

Mrs. Pearl Baker rowhouse, Paseo Delicias, Rancho Santa Fe, CA 92067—National Register of Historic Places

Glenn A. and Ida May Moore Rowhouse (Casa Blanca), Paseo Delicias, Rancho Santa Fe, CA 92067—Local Historic Resource

Fred W. Joers and Harold R. Ketchum store building, La Granada, Rancho Santa Fe, CA 92067

1927

Chester Howard and Cornelia Bristol residence, Via de Alba, Rancho Santa Fe, CA 92067

Mrs. Mary B. Allen/W. O. Boetigger house, La Crescenta, Rancho Santa Fe, CA 92067

George A. C. Christiancy residence, El Mirador, Rancho Santa Fe, CA 92067—National Register of Historic Places

Pauline Neff and Frank Coffyn residence, Linea del Cielo, Rancho Santa Fe, CA 92067

Mr. Charles Cushman residence, La Crescenta, Rancho Santa Fe, CA 92067

Mr. John B. and Bessie Cushman residence, La Crescenta, Rancho Santa Fe, CA 92067

Frank William Joers residence, La Flecha, Rancho Santa Fe, CA 92067

F. W. Joers and Harold R. Ketchum Apartments, Paseo Delicias, Rancho Santa Fe, CA 92067

Ranald MacDonald residence, Paseo Delicias, Rancho Santa Fe, CA 92067

Barton and Nathalie M. Millard residence, El Montevideo Drive, Rancho Santa Fe, CA 92067

Charles F. Pease residence, Las Colinas, Rancho Santa Fe, CA 92067

Charles A. Shaffer residence, La Crescenta, Rancho Santa Fe, CA 92067—National Register of Historic Places

Norman and Florence B. Carmichael residence, La Valle Plateada, Rancho Santa Fe, CA 92067—National Register of Historic Places (demolished)

Harold E. Ketchum residence, Via de la Valle and La Gracia, Rancho Santa Fe, CA

James C. Smillie residence, Lago Lindo, Rancho Santa Fe, CA

Edward Stockton residence, Folsom Drive, La Jolla, CA 92037

Christine Arnberg residence, Folsom Drive, La Jolla, CA 92037—AIA Honor Award, 1933

Extension to the garage quadrangle, increased parking and service yard space, Paseo Delicias, Rancho Santa Fe, CA

Mr. Turner residence, Country Club Drive, La Jolla, CA 92037

Mr. Elmer C. Cord residence, Los Morros Road, Rancho Santa Fe, CA 92067

1928

Mr. John A. Bazant residence, street unknown, Rancho Santa Fe, CA 92067

Mr. John L. Fleming/E.D. and Ethel E. Williams residence, Via de Santa Fe, Rancho Santa Fe, CA 92067

Mr. and Mrs. Hamilton Carpenter residence, El Mirador, Rancho Santa Fe, CA 92067

Ralph and Belle Claggett residence, Via de Santa Fe, Rancho Santa Fe, CA 92067

Mrs. Florence J. Corbus residence, Via de la Valle, Rancho Santa Fe, CA 92067

Herschell G. and Annabel Larrick residence, La Flecha, Rancho Santa Fe, CA 92067

Mr. McCulloch residence, Via de Santa Fe, Rancho Santa Fe, CA 92067

Mr. Robert McKenna residence, street unknown, Rancho Santa Fe, CA 92067(not built)

Dr. J. F. McKitrick residence, street unknown, Rancho Santa Fe, CA 92067

Mr. and Mrs. Everette Smith residence, Mimosa, Rancho Santa Fe, CA 92067

La Valenciana Apartments, Paseo Delicias, Rancho Santa Fe, CA 92067—AIA Honor Award, 1933

Misses Alice L. and Florence E. Wilson, La Valle Plateada, Rancho Santa Fe, CA 92067

Mr. Arnberg residence, Camino de la Costa, La Jolla, CA 92037

Mr. Arthur L. Loomis, stables, Via de la Valle, Rancho Santa Fe, CA 92067

Mr. Arthur L. Loomis, Spanish Well, Via de la Valle, Rancho Santa Fe, CA 92067

Mr. Elmer C. Cord, apartments, block D, lot 17, Rancho Santa Fe, CA 92067

Mr. C. Everette Smith, lot 34, block 18, Rancho Santa Fe, CA 92067

Mr. G. A. C. Christiancy, tile roof over terrace, El Mirador, CA 92067

Mr. F. W. Joers, garage addition, lot 2, block 30, Rancho Santa Fe, CA 92067

Rancho Santa Fe Country Club, service shops, block 19, Rancho Santa Fe, CA 92067

1929

Caddy House for the Ranch Santa Fe Country Club, block 19, Rancho Santa Fe, CA 92067

Sewer Pump House, block 19, Rancho Santa Fe, CA 92067

Rancho Santa Fe Country Club, caddy shed, block 26, Rancho Santa Fe, CA 92067

Mrs. Marguerite M. Robinson residence, Ludington Lane, La Jolla, CA 92037—Local Historic Resource

SFLIC, speculative residence, lot 47, block 26, Rancho Santa Fe, CA 92067

Rancho Santa Fe Corporation, Beach Club clubhouse, Solana Beach, CA 92067

1930

Mr. and Mrs. Bradley residence, Remley Place, La Jolla, CA 92037—Local Historic Resource

SFLIC speculative residence, Thomas and Mary Day McCutcheon/Angel House, Via del Alba, Rancho Santa Fe, CA 92067—Local Historic Resource

The Tomlinson/Rule residence, addition, El Mirlo, Rancho Santa Fe, CA 92067

Mr. F. L. Hammond, caretaker's cottage, lot 4, block 43, Rancho Santa Fe, CA 92067

Mr. Carmichael, caretaker's cottage, lot 1, block 16, Rancho Santa Fe, CA 92067

Mr. E. L. Walbridge Estate, stables and grooms quarters, lot 8, block 7, Rancho Santa Fe, CA 92067

Mr. R. E. Badger residence, addition, lot 4, block 27, Rancho Santa Fe, CA 92067

Mr. H. G. Larrick, service yard wall, lot 1, block 30, Rancho Santa Fe, CA 92067

Mr. Carmichael, lath house, lot 1, block 16, Rancho Santa Fe, CA 92067

1931

Elementary School for Rancho Santa Fe School District (with Hammond Whitsitt), Avenida de Acacias, Rancho Santa Fe, CA 92067

SFLIC speculative residences, two cottages, lot 1, block 31, Rancho Santa Fe, CA 92067

Mr. S. H. and Floy Bingham Residence, Rancho Santa Fe, CA 92067—National Register of Historic Places

Mr. and Mrs. Burnet C. Wohlford residence, E. Valley Parkway, Escondido, CA 92025—House Beautiful Design Award, 1932

Escondido Mutual Water Company, street unknown, Escondido, CA 92025

1932

Mr. S. H. and Floy Bingham residence, lath house, Rancho Santa Fe, CA 92067

The ZLAC Rowing Club Boathouse and Clubhouse Facility, Pacific Beach Drive, San Diego, CA 92109—AIA Honor Award, 1933

Mr. Harry L. Crosby residence, lot 14, Block 43, Rancho Santa Fe, CA 92067

Mr. H. E. Harrison, lot 4, block 32, garage and servant's quarters, Rancho Santa Fe, CA 92067

Mr. Briggs C. Keck, remodel, lot 2, block 37, Rancho Santa Fe, CA 92037

Vernon I. Bogy, street unknown, Rancho Santa Fe, CA 92067

1935

Dr. Francis Smith residence, Virginia Way, La Jolla, CA 92037

Mr. Charles F. Meyer, caretaker's cottage, Rancho Santa Fe, CA 92067

The Alexander Krisel Estate, Via de Fortuna, Rancho Santa Fe, CA 92037 (not built)

Mr. Harry L. Crosby Estate, remodel of hacienda, stables, manager's house, lot 4, block 43, Rancho Santa Fe, CA 92067

1936

Paul and Magdalena Ecke residence, Saxony Road, Encinitas, CA 92024
Mr. John Burnham, stables, lot 4, block 36, Rancho Santa Fe, CA 92067
Dr. Gordon N. Morrill residence, Las Planideras, Rancho Santa Fe, CA 92067
Mrs. Charles E. Sterns residence, Dunemere, La Jolla, CA 92037
Mr. Young residence, Eads Ave., La Jolla, CA 92037
Dr. W. M. Thompson, addition, Torrey Pines Road, La Jolla, CA 92037
Martha Kinsey House, Ludington Lane, La Jolla, CA 92037—National Register of Historic Places
F Street School, earthquake-proof remodel, F Street, Chula Vista, CA 91911

1937

Mr. Charles F. Meyer residence, lots 59 and 60, block 26, Rancho Santa Fe, CA 92067
San Dieguito Union High School (now San Dieguito Academy), Santa Fe Drive, Encinitas, CA 92024
Mr. Harry L. Crosby Estate, training tracks and paddock, lots 1 and 2, block 43, Rancho Santa Fe, CA 92067
Mr. Rubin H. and Elizabeth Fleet residence, Pepita Way, La Jolla, CA 92037—Local Historic Resource
Mr. Ranald MacDonald residence, studio, Paseo Delicias, Rancho Santa Fe, CA 92067
Mr. Frank Burnaby residence, Fremont, Rancho Santa Fe, CA 92067
Mr. and Mrs. Norman Carmichael, addition, La Valle Plateada, Rancho Santa Fe, CA 92067
Mr. Peck residence, street unknown, Rancho Santa Fe, CA 92067
Mr. and Mrs. Albin Pelko residence, Paseo Delicias, Rancho Santa Fe, CA 92067
Rancho Santa Fe Garden Club, El Tordo, Rancho Santa Fe, CA
Mr. and Mrs. Morris Townley residence, La Valle Plateada, Rancho Santa Fe, CA 92067—Local Historic Resource (owner unknown)
Monte Vista Ave, La Jolla, CA 92037
Miss Amelia Armbruster residence, Prospect Blvd, La Jolla, CA 92037
La Jolla Building and Loan Company, Mar Ave., La Jolla, CA 92037
Mr. and Mrs. Roy E. Naftzer residence, street unknown, Del Mar, CA 92014
Addition—physics and chemistry buildings (Unit D-4), art rooms and storage (Unit D-8) San Dieguito Union High School, Encinitas, CA 92024
Hillebrecht residence, Skyline Drive, Escondido, CA 92025
Tuile residence, Riverside, Riverside County, CA 92506
Mr. L. E. Knudson, Alpha, San Diego, CA, 92113
Mr. Harold R. Nichols, 3rd St. San Diego, CA (zip code unknown)
Mrs. Alice Malcolm, Alpha, San Diego, CA 92113
Mr. George W. Pardy, Monte Vista, La Jolla, CA 92037
Two speculative residences, High St., La Jolla, CA 92037
Speculative residence, Herschel, La Jolla, CA 92037
Mrs. Moreno, remodel, Kline St. La Jolla, CA 92037
Mr. and Mrs. Ackerman residence, 55th Street San Diego, CA 92115

Mrs. Frank Good residence, La Madreselva, Rancho Santa Fe, CA 92067

One room cottage, lot 1, block 32, (the Inn) Rancho Santa Fe, CA 92067

L Street School, later renamed Lilian J. Rice Elementary School, Fourth Avenue, Chula Vista, CA 91911

Commander Simard residence, Lemon Avenue, La Mesa, CA 91941—Local Historic Resource

Dr. and Mrs. N. L. LeMontree residence, San Diego, CA 92116

Mr. Charles Weikman residence, street unknown, Solana Beach, CA 92075

Mrs. Edna Burroughs residence, street unknown, La Jolla, CA 92037

Dr. and Mrs. Leon Campbell, addition to beach house, street unknown, Del Mar, CA 92014

Dr. and Mrs. Otis Spalding Residence, addition, street unknown, Del Mar, CA 92014

Wesley W. and Elsie Waite residence, street unknown, Solana Beach, CA 92075

Mr. and Mrs. Everett Johnson residence and garage, street unknown, Encinitas, CA 92024

Mr. and Mrs. Charles Davis residence, street unknown, Solana Beach, CA 92075

Mr. and Mrs. Sidney Sutherland residence, addition, street unknown, Rancho Santa Fe, CA 92067

Mr. Bert Shindledecker, Roadside Court, street unknown, Solana Beach, CA 92075

Dr. and Mrs. H. S. Savage residence, Acacia Avenue, Solana Beach, CA 92075

St. Peter's Episcopalian Church, church design, Del Mar, CA 92014 (not built)

Maud H. Piper and Helen H. Browder residence and garage, street unknown, Encinitas, CA 92024

Lunch shelter, Rancho Santa Fe Elementary School, Avenue De Acacias, Rancho Santa Fe, CA 92067

Mrs. Rosemary Schloessman residence, street unknown, Del Mar, CA 92014

Mr. and Mrs. C. W. Fletcher residence and garage, street unknown, Pacific Beach, CA 92109

Mr. R. C. Francisco store remodel, Paseo Delicias, Rancho Santa Fe, CA

Mr. and Mrs. Harry L. Crosby residence, addition of nursery, Via de la Valle, Rancho Santa Fe, CA 92067

Mr. George Megrew residence, addition, street unknown, Rancho Santa Fe, CA 92067

Mr. R. C. Francisco, garage, street unknown, Rancho Santa Fe, CA 92067

Beamer residence, Pine Street, San Diego, CA 92103 (date unknown)

Judge Hervey residence, street unknown, Point Loma, CA 92106 (date unknown)

BIBLIOGRAPHY AND COLLECTIONS

Collections

Architectural Collection, numbers AD 1014 and AD 1007, San Diego History Center, San Diego, CA

Art Jury Minutes. Offices of the Rancho Santa Fe Association. Rancho Santa Fe, CA

Ed Fletcher Papers. Collection number MSS 0081: University of California, San Diego, CA

Olive Chadeayne, Architectural Papers, 1925-56, MS1990-057: Special Collections, University Libraries, Virginia Polytechnic Institute and State University.

Rancho Santa Fe Historical Society Archives. Rancho Santa Fe, CA

The Frank Kimball Diaries. The Kile Morgan Local History Room, National City Library, National City, CA

The Harriet Rochlin Collection of Material about Women Architects in the United States,1887-1979. Number 1591: Special Collections, University of California, Los Angeles, CA

Santa Fe Irrigation District. Assessment Books. Rancho Santa Fe, CA

Select Published and Non-Published Works

Anderson, Timothy J., Eudorah M. Moore, and Robert W. Winter. eds. *California Design: 1910*. Santa Barbara: Peregrine Smith (1980).

Boal-Maddox Family Photograph Album. Unpagenated (circa 1912–1918).

Boutelle, Sara Holmes. *Julia Morgan Architect: Revised and Updated*. New York: Abbeville Press (1995): 44.

Clotfelter, Connie. *Echoes of Rancho Santa Fe*. San Diego: CONREG (1985):19.

Crosby, Bing. "Our Little Ranch in the West" *California Arts and Architecture*. (October 1935).

Darbyshire, Martha B. "Rancho Santa Fe Ranch House; the Bing Crosbys at Home in Their California Hacienda." *Arts and Decoration* (December 1935).

Dunn, Guard D. "Rancho San Dieguito." *The Southern California Rancher*. September (1944):12.

Eddy, Lucinda Liggett. *Lilian Jeannette Rice: The Lady as Architect*. Unpublished Masters Thesis in History, University of San Diego (1985): 80.

Fletcher Ed. *Memoirs of Ed Fletcher*. San Diego: Pioneer Printers (1952): 211–220.

Gebhard, David and Robert Winter. *A Guide To Architecture in Los Angeles and Southern California*. Santa Barbara: Peregrine Smith (1977): 498–503.

Hazard, Mabel Grant. *History of the ZLAC Rowing Club*. Self Published. San Diego. 1962.

Hemenway, Abby Maria. *The Vermont Historical Gazetteer: A Magazine*. Volume II. Vermont: Mrs. A. M. Hemenway. (1871): 980.

Horton, Inge S. *Early Women Architects of the San Francisco Bay Area*. North Carolina: McFarland (2010)

Jacques, Terri. *Heritage Square, National City, California*. National City: The City Of National City, Office of the Mayor (undated, unpaginated).

Jenkins, Gary C. "Almira S. Steele and the Steele Home for Needy Children." *Tennessee Historical Quarterly 48* (1989): 29–36.

Johnson, Theo F. "The Evolution of our Schools." *National City News* (June 26, 1915).

Keeler, Charles. *The Simple Home.* San Francisco: Paul Elder and Co. (1904).

Kropp, Phoebe S. *California Vieja: Culture and Memory in a Modern Place.* Berkeley and Los Angeles: University of California Press (2006): 190–193.

Larrick, Charles L. *The Larricks, an Amerian Family.* Self published, 1997.

Lord, Charles Chase. *Life and Times in Hopkinton, NH.* Concord: Republican Press Association (1890): 421.

Maque. "Where Capital Bows at the Shrine of Beauty, the Project of Rancho Santa Fe." *Valve World.* Chicago: Crane (1923):161–167.

Mattox II, Edward. *Before the Morning Star, The Almira S. Steele Story.* Eme Christian (2008)

McGrew, Clarence Alan. *The City of San Diego and San Diego County, The Birthplace of California.* San Diego: American Historical Society (1922):156.

McGroarty, John Steven. *The Endless Miracle of California.* Chula Vista, Denrich Press, n.d. [1927].

McMillian, Elizabeth. *California Colonial: The Spanish and Rancho Revival Styles.* Atglen: Schiffer (2002): 49.

National City News. 1912–1918.

National City Record. (January 24, 1889).

Nelson, Ruth R. *Rancho Santa Fe: Yesterday and Today.* Encinitas: Coast Dispatch (1947): 11-50.

_____ "Rancho Woman Architect Only One in County: Miss Lillian [sic] Rice Patronized By Many For Spanish and California Home Designs." *San Diego Union* (January 28, 1930): 4, col 1.

Newcomb, Rexford. *The Spanish House For America, It's Design, Furnishing and Garden.* Philadelphia and London: J. B. Lippincott (1927).

_____ *Mediterranean Domestic Architecture in the United States.* Introduction by Marc Appleton. New York: Acanthus Press (1999).

Oakland Tribune. 1906–1940.

Pourade, Richard F. *Gold in the Sun.* San Diego: The Union Tribune Publishing Company (1965): 204–217.

Rancho Santa Fe Progress. (January 1928): 11, 14.

Rancho Santa Fe Progress. (October 1928): 8.

Rancho Santa Fe Progress. (July 1929): 8.

Rancho Santa Fe Protective Covenant, Rancho Santa Fe, California, Adopted by Rancho Santa Fe Association, July 14th, 1927. San Diego: Frye & Smith (1937, later edition).

Rice, Lilian J. *University of California at Berkeley Scrapbook*, 1906–1908 (unpagenated) The Kile Morgan Local History Room, National City Library, National City, CA.

_____*University of California at Berkeley Scrapbook*, 1909–1910 (unpagenated) Author's collection

_____ "Architecture—a Community Asset." *Architect and Engineer 94* (July 1928): 44.

_____*Postcard album*, 1914–1919 (unpagenated). The Kile Morgan Local History Room, National City Library, National City, CA.

_____ "What Our Homes Should Mean To Us." Rancho Santa Fe News (April 1937).

Rochlin, Harriet. "Among the First and the Finest: California Architects, Julia, Hazel, Lutah, Edla." Paper prepared prior to publication of article for AIA Journal (August 1977).

_____ "A Distinguished Generation of Women Architects in California" *AIA Journal* V66, No. 9 (August 1977): 39.

San Diego City and County Directories. 1887–1930.

San Diego County Recorders Office. Deed book 399, 1412, 1447.

San Diego Union. 1887–1968.

San Diego Evening Tribune. 1920–1980.

Schaelchin, Pat. *Historical Resources Inventory: La Jolla.* La Jolla: California Office of Historic Preservation (November 1977).

Shippey, Lee. "Rancho Santa Fe: California's Perfectly Planned Community." *Architect and Engineer 76* (February 1924): 55–63.

Sinnard, L.G. *California's Community Masterpiece.* Chula Vista: Denrich Press (c. 1927).

Starke, Bruce B. "Rancho Santa Fe-Back to the Farm for Gentlemen." *San Diego Business Magazine* (February, 1927).

Taschner, Mary. *Richard Requa, Southern California Architect: 1881–1941.* Masters Thesis in History, University of San Diego (1982): 74–78.

The Nineteen Hundred and Eleven Blue and the Gold of the University of California. Berkeley: University Press (1911).

Thelan, Fannie. *The Thelan Manuscript.* (undated) Unpublished: 32. The Kile Morgan Local History Room, National City Library, National City, CA.

Thornton, Sally Bullard. *Daring to Dream: The Life of Hazel Wood Waterman.* San Diego: San Diego Historical Society (1987).

To Dragma of Alpha Omicron Pi Fraternity. 1910-1912.

Wallace, Helen Wetzell. *A History of the ZLAC Rowing Club.* San Diego: self published (1992): 49–59

Walsh, Victor A. "Una Casa del Pueblo: A Town House of Old San Diego." *Journal of San Diego History, v. 50, Winter/Spring.* San Diego: San Diego Historical Society (2004): 1–17.

Waterman, Hazel. "The Californian's Home." *Southern California Architecture* (1920).

Watson, Mark S. *The California-Panama Exposition.* San Francisco: California's Magazine, California Publisher's Association. (1915): 349–352.

Woodbridge, S. *John Galen Howard and the University of California. The Design of a Great Public University Campus.* Berkeley: UC Press (2002).

Young, J.D. *The Directory of the Grape Growers and Wine Makers of California.* Compiled by the California Board of State Viticultural Commissioners, California. State Printing (1888): 39.

INDEX

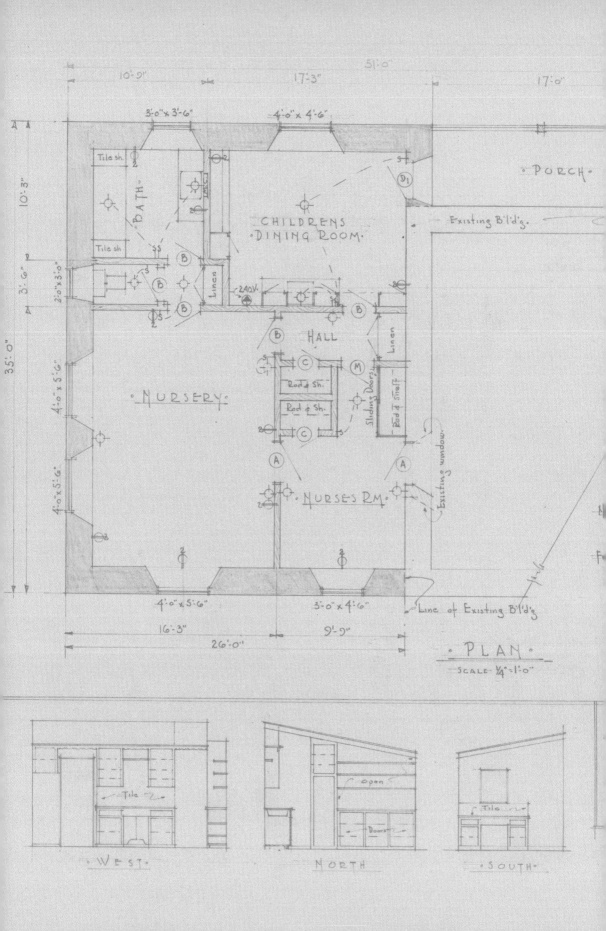

PLAN
SCALE ¼" = 1'-0"

WEST

NORTH

SOUTH